D0891753

MuzikMafia

MuzikMafia

FROM THE LOCAL NASHVILLE SCENE
TO THE NATIONAL MAINSTREAM

DAVID B. PRUETT

UNIVERSITY PRESS OF MISSISSIPPI / JACKSON

www.upress.state.ms.us

The University Press of Mississippi is a member of the
Association of American University Presses.

Photographs courtesy the author unless otherwise indicated.

Copyright © 2010 by University Press of Mississippi
All rights reserved
Manufactured in the United States of America

First printing 2010
∞
Library of Congress Cataloging-in-Publication Data

Pruett, David B.
MuzikMafia : from the local Nashville scene to the national mainstream / David B. Pruett.
p. cm. — (American made music series)
Includes bibliographical references and index.
ISBN 978-1-60473-438-6 (cloth : alk. paper) 1. MuzikMafia (Musical group)
2. Country musicians—United States. I. Title.
ML421.M88P78 2010
781.642092'273—dc22   2009040405

British Library Cataloging-in-Publication Data available

"Love Everybody . . ."

Kenny Alphin—at least once in most conversations
that we have shared since June 2004

CONTENTS

ACKNOWLEDGMENTS

There are many people whom I would like to thank for their assistance with and guidance through this project. First and foremost, I would like to express sincere thanks to my new friends and family within the Muzik-Mafia's inner circle: Cory, John, Kenny, Jon, James, Rachel, Pino, Chance, Max, Dean, Troy, Shannon, Mandy, Fred, Shanna, Damien, Adam, Brian, Ethan, SWJ, Alaska Dan, Sean, Jerry, D.D., Gretchen, Jules W., Paul, Ashley, Marc, Greg, Bill, Charlie, Jon A., Jeff, Deanna, "Mama" Alphin, Shawna P., Butter, Isaac, Virginia D., and Vicky M.

Second, I would like to acknowledge numerous scholars from the International Country Music Conference and for our annual meetings at Belmont University. Specifically James Akenson, Don Cusic, Richard "Pete" Peterson, and Erika Brady have encouraged this study of the MuzikMafia and have welcomed the frequent presentation of my findings. Travis Stimeling, fellow country music scholar and drinking buddy, has contributed much to the development of many ideas found throughout this study. In addition, I owe special thanks to Charles K. Wolfe, who passed away much too soon, for his continual support and feedback on this and earlier projects.

Several of my colleagues at Middle Tennessee State University deserve recognition. My close friend Stephen Shearon was the first person to emphasize to me the importance of this research. Steve's continual support over the years has guided me through the tough times and has inspired me to keep refining my ideas and approaches. My colleague and former director George Riordan, who asked me each week for four years how the research was going, has earned my respect, trust, friendship, and heartfelt appreciation. I also owe a special debt of gratitude to Matt Baumer who accompanied me to my first MuzikMafia show on June 15, 2004.

My editor Craig Gill is one of the best in the business. He showed genuine interest in this project years before I submitted a formal proposal to the

University Press of Mississippi, my first and only choice for a publisher for this work. Copy editor Will Rigby deserves additional thanks for a job well done.

I would also like to thank my wife Laura, who by now certainly knows more about the MuzikMafia than I do. I am indebted to her for her unconditional support, her thoughtful criticism, her meticulous copy editing, and her continual guidance throughout this research's numerous stages. Dad and Burgl also deserve acknowledgment for inspiring my love of country music and for their unconditional support over the years. Finally, I would like to recognize my son Alexander, who will one day read this book and learn about yet another facet of his southern roots.

I dedicate this book to the MuzikMafia and its Nashville fans. Tuesday nights were not just another show. They were something special, almost like family.

MuzikMafia

INTRODUCTION

The house lights go dark. In less than a second, the once ambient noise generated by the venue's approximately eight thousand fans crescendos into the immediate foreground of my attention. The sudden wall of sound sends a chill down my spine. Cowboy Troy slowly announces through a backstage microphone, "Ladies . . . and . . . Gentlemen . . ." in a style better suited to a professional wrestling match. The crowd responds with more sonic intensity. Many camera flashes appear amidst the now thunderous applause from the screaming fans. John Rich of Big & Rich is standing directly in front of me, and he gives his assistant road manager a slow "high five" in the darkness behind the stage's backdrop. Troy, who is standing to my immediate right, concludes his introduction with the words, "And now . . . Big . . . & . . . Rich," drawing out each syllable as long as possible. The fans respond with more screams, whistles, and catcalls.

The band hits and sustains a loud fermata as Big & Rich make their way from opposite ends of the sixty-foot long, elevated stage. The fireworks display of camera flashes along with the two spotlights on John and Kenny (a.k.a. Big & Rich), respectively, are enough to illuminate the entire venue. By now, the noise from the crowd has reached a deafening level, and I struggle with my video camera in an effort to cover my ears.

The venue's large size is ironic. Approximately one month earlier, the MuzikMafia had performed for free at a small Nashville club for a few hundred local fans. Tonight's MuzikMafia show (November 20, 2004) is for a sold-out crowd at the Freedom Hall Civic Center in Johnson City, Tennessee, one of thirteen stops on the Chevrolet American Revolution Tour. Most fans have paid between twenty-five and seventy-five dollars a ticket. Many had stood in line at the box office since early morning to insure getting a ticket and a good seat.

Forty-five minutes later, the MuzikMafia's saxophone player Max Abrams and I were both standing on the audience level adjacent stage left. John and Kenny had just finished their set and were headed back to the dressing rooms. The house lights went up, signaling the second of three intermissions that evening. Gretchen Wilson's crew was already setting the stage for her upcoming segment of the show. Somewhat numbed by the previous forty-five minutes of nonstop musical excitement, I turned to Max and asked him what he thought of the sold out event. "Wait 'til 2006," he replied. "In 2006 this is gonna be thirty thousand people."

I was taken aback by Max's response. The MuzikMafia had undergone considerable changes in the few short months leading up to this evening's performance—moving beyond its local Nashville roots and onto the national music scene, with platinum album successes by Gretchen and Big & Rich. MuzikMafia artists, who had once defined themselves by their common marginalization from Nashville's commercial music industry, were now part of the popular mainstream. But Max's response did not reveal the MuzikMafia's desire merely for acceptance by Music Row, where Nashville's commercial music industry is located. Instead, it hinted at further growth and change in the MuzikMafia and its popularity—what Cory Gierman, one of the MuzikMafia's founding members, had described to me earlier that year as "global domination."

I pointed out to Max the stage's backdrop that contained the single word MUZIKMAFIA in thick, white letters, each of which were approximately eight feet tall. The black background extended the entire length of the stage and was approximately twenty feet high. I asked Max if he ever thought that the MuzikMafia would reach such a level of popularity. He replied:

Oh yeah, I knew. I didn't doubt that it would come this far. I think that if you look at what James Otto and Jon Nicholson are gonna do next year [2005], Big & Rich's second record, Gretchen's second record, you'll see it all come back together in two years [2006]. It's going to be a whole different playing field. I don't think that the friendships are going to be less than they are now, but I do think that there's going to be a much broader awareness of what Mafia really is and what it really means, especially when you've got Gretchen Wilson and Big Kenny and John Rich singing on Jon Nicholson's record. Suddenly, you've got a pop audience listening to the best singer in country music on a pop single. That's when things really get interesting. That's when people are going to start to get it.

Max's statement revealed the MuzikMafia members' idea of themselves as a distinct musical community while embracing the MuzikMafia's growth and development at the national level and beyond. However, not even Max could foresee the stark changes in the MuzikMafia that would eventually comprise a complex interconnected web of MuzikMafia-derived commercial enterprises, several members' departure from the community, and the MuzikMafia's eventual downfall.

But what was MuzikMafia like before all the media hype, before national concert tours, multi-platinum album sales, and before hardly anyone had ever heard of Gretchen Wilson or Big & Rich? Probably more important is the question, "What is the MuzikMafia?" There are no simple answers, but a starting point would be the MuzikMafia's weekly Tuesday night performances in Nashville.

I remember my first MuzikMafia show on June 15, 2004, as though it were yesterday. A student of mine at Middle Tennessee State University in Murfreesboro had suggested that I take some time to go see this new "thing" in Nashville called MuzikMafia that had been performing each Tuesday night at the Mercy Lounge. About a month after spring exams were over, I decided to give it a shot. I had heard that admission was free, and Nashville was only a thirty-minute drive northwest on Interstate 24. Being a college professor alone at a nightclub seemed a bit too weird for me, so I talked my friend and School of Music colleague Matt Baumer into coming along. That Tuesday night changed my life.

The first thing I noticed was the Mercy Lounge itself, located in a supposedly renovated nineteenth-century flour mill at Cannery Row off of 8th Avenue near downtown Nashville. From the outside, the building looked like it was about to collapse. Matt and I found our way to the club which was up the stairs on the second floor. The inside of the building did not look any better. Creaky floors, thick timber support posts, and windows made nearly opaque from years of accumulated dust and dirt made us a bit apprehensive about spending our evening there.

Upon entering I expected to see an array of white rural folk, in cowboy hats, boots, and jeans suited to the club's rustic interior. Instead I found a diverse audience: blacks, whites, Asians, and Hispanics; people of varying age; some dressed in tie-dyed clothes, some with jeans and T-shirts, some with suits, some with baseball caps, some with cowboy hats. The show's start time had been advertised as 9:00 p.m.; by 9:45 p.m. I was wondering if we had come to the right place. The show finally began about 10 p.m.

I was taken aback by the variety of music that I heard that night, from artists with diverse backgrounds and musical styles. One song, "Limo Larry," was familiar to most audience members, who sang along in unison. At one point in the evening, all the musicians were on stage jamming at the same time, what I described to my colleague as some sort of organized chaos. However, everyone was having fun—musicians and audience members alike. It was apparent by the numerous group conversations and long hugs that most audience members knew each other from previous Muzik-Mafia shows.

But there was more to that evening than just diverse music. Rachel Kice stood with easel, brushes, and paints near the stage, capturing the evening's performance on canvas. Her artwork was abstract, closely resembling that of the expressionist movement during the early twentieth century. I imagined the room's vibe to be more a combination of a family reunion and Andy Warhol's artistic experiments in New York City during the 1960s than a typical show at a Nashville night club.

Big & Rich—known to most people there as John and Kenny—performed a few songs. During the middle of their set, Kenny addressed the crowd in a serious tone of voice. He announced, "Well, you know, we here at the MuzikMafia love everybody. We don't care if you're black or white. We don't care if you're big or small." Turning toward a girl in a wheelchair, Kenny continued, "We don't care if you got no legs, and we don't care if you're rich or po' [poor]." Her proud smile and slight nod acknowledged her appreciation of Kenny's straightforwardness with the handicapped teenager—in fact, Kenny had earlier asked the crowd near the stage to make some room so she could do her own kind of four-wheeled dancing. I later realized that Kenny had been describing aspects of the MuzikMafia that transcended a simple crossing of musical styles. MuzikMafia was crossing social boundaries as well and bringing people closer together. I did not feel out of place as a college professor. That evening I took pleasure in the fact that my job was of no concern at a MuzikMafia show. The only important things were having fun, relaxing, getting to know other people, and being oneself for a little while.

Following Big & Rich's set, John spent about thirty minutes in the audience hanging out with friends and talking to fans. I casually approached him and pitched my rather spontaneous idea of possibly researching the MuzikMafia. As an ethnomusicologist, I was fascinated by the MuzikMafia's shared belief in artistic diversity and social inclusivity. John enthusiastically gave me the name of music publisher and fellow MuzikMafia founding godfather Cory Gierman who, after a brief discussion a few days later, invited me to study the MuzikMafia.

The MuzikMafia graciously invited me into its inner sanctum to examine its brief history. The founders granted me direct contact with each of the MuzikMafia's artists and their entourages and families, unlimited video privileges, backstage passes to concerts, invitations to private parties, and inside access to the upper echelons of Nashville's corporate music culture. My personal archive includes over 200 hours of video footage from MuzikMafia shows, approximately fifty-five formal videotaped interviews, over 29,000 digital photographs, about 2,000 articles from newspapers or magazines, and notes from 112 MuzikMafia events. During the course of a five-year study that began in June 2004, I engaged each artist repeatedly, conducted multiple interviews, observed shows, attended private MuzikMafia events, cross-checked facts and explored the MuzikMafia's role within Nashville's ever-changing music scene. This book tells their story.

And what a story it is. One could accurately describe the MuzikMafia's history as the archetypal Greek tragedy. There is the hero (in this case, a group of heroes) who spoke for the underdogs among Nashville's music scene. Our heroes also had their rise to power: a relatively rapid climb to international commercial success in 2004 and 2005. Unfortunately, there was also the tragic flaw (here, a series of them): greed, jealousy, lack of communication, and lust for power, recognition, and money. And as with most Greek tragedies, the MuzikMafia experienced their inevitable downfall between 2006 and 2008. However, unlike most tragedies, this tale does not necessarily end in death, but rather continues, with the hint of possible rebirth in 2009.

This book is not about Gretchen Wilson or Big & Rich. It is about the MuzikMafia, which can be defined as a distinct musical community that developed from a stylistically diverse Nashville scene into both a social collective and a commercial enterprise that promoted musical excellence and artistic diversity. Since the community's beginnings in fall 2001, MuzikMafia members have frequently described themselves as a "freak show," a bunch of outcasts that have included singer-songwriters with diverse musical influences, a graphic artist, a music publisher, a juggler, a fire breather, a spoken word artist, a cowboy rapper, and a variety of auxiliary musicians. Equally important was their dedicated fanbase that included people from all walks of life: from the unemployed to corporate executives, from potheads to straight arrows, from high school dropouts to college professors—basically anybody who wanted to have a good time with friends on a Tuesday night.

This study began during the period of MuzikMafia's emergence into the popular mainstream and documents their development as it unfolded. One benefit of such an approach is an understanding of the MuzikMafia's success as comprising processes of local, sometimes illogical, decision-making rather than as evolving along a logical, linear path of development from point A to point B. Moreover, I focus on MuzikMafia artists as people rather than nationally known celebrities because of how and when I first got to know them.

When I began this study of the MuzikMafia in June 2004, the community was in a period of transition: no longer a strictly local phenomenon, but not yet part of the popular mainstream. However, the MuzikMafia's significance had changed drastically by summer's end. In August 2004 Big & Rich's *Horse of a Different Color* reached Number One on *Billboard*'s Top Country Albums chart; by January 2005 it had sold over two million copies. Co-written by John Rich, Gretchen Wilson's debut single "Redneck Woman" reached Number One on *Billboard*'s Country Singles chart in twelve weeks, and her album *Here for the Party*, having debuted at Number One on *Billboard*'s album charts in June 2004, was certified triple platinum by the Recording Industry Association of America (RIAA) by December of that year. By the time of these MuzikMafia successes, I was already a trusted affiliate of their close-knit community.

However, this book is also about Nashville, specifically the city's commercial music industry. There is a reason why Nashville is referred to as "Music City, U.S.A.," and it is not just because of commercial country. Nashville's music scene comprises a diverse community of some of the most talented songwriters and musicians in the United States with stylistic influences ranging from blues and R&B to country, rock, rap, bluegrass, Christian contemporary, grunge, pop, gospel, and drum n' bass, all within just a few square miles of each other. In fact, according to a 2006 Belmont University study, Nashville's music industry generates over six billion dollars annually—more than the music scenes of Atlanta, Austin, and Seattle combined.

A significant reason why I chose to write this book is that, despite the MuzikMafia's widespread popularity, relatively few people know what the MuzikMafia actually is. Frequently misunderstood aspects include the diverse Nashville scene where the MuzikMafia originated, what factors led to the MuzikMafia's creation in 2001, and the MuzikMafia's various periods of growth and development. The many divergent views on the MuzikMafia are owing to the community's nebulous structure, misrepresentations disseminated by the mass media, and the lack of consistent descriptions among the MuzikMafia's members regarding their own collectivity. In *MuzikMafia: From the Local Nashville Scene to the National Mainstream*, I address these inconsistencies by examining how a shared set of musical and social beliefs created a bond between several Nashville artists and how that bond, or rather its commodification, transformed the MuzikMafia into an American popular music phenomenon.

My central argument throughout *MuzikMafia* is that the MuzikMafia could not have originated elsewhere. Nashville's diverse musical history, specific geographical layout, numerous interdependent music scenes, annual multi-billion-dollar music industry, embrace of frequent change, and dedicated listening audiences each contributed uniquely to the birth, growth, and development of the MuzikMafia. I argue that the MuzikMafia is a reflection of the overall Nashville scene and that its development was mediated by the city's commercial music industry.

Finally, this book will appeal to any musician who dreams of making it big in the commercial music industry. The MuzikMafia's rise to prominence serves as a veritable how-to manual on working the system. The MuzikMafia's founding godfathers knew the music business inside and out and combined their various areas of expertise to forge a unique path to the top. However, theirs is also a story of what *not* to do: the countless mistakes that they made along the way, including those that led to the MuzikMafia's eventual if not inevitable downfall. Even as I was implementing the manuscript's final revisions in 2009, MuzikMafia artists—or more appropriately, *former* MuzikMafia artists—were rallying to try to re-establish their collectivity under the name Mafia Nation. Will they succeed? It could go either way.

Chapter One

THE NASHVILLE SCENE

I arrived at the Mercy Lounge around 9:00 p.m. Admission was free as usual. The outside noise from passing trains added to ambient sounds of conversations, cracking of billiard balls, and clinking of beer bottles. Approximately 150 people were there, only one-fourth of the club's capacity. I passed the time by talking with fans who had arrived early for the show's scheduled start at 10:00 p.m. and to a few who were there for the first time. Things did not get under way until about 10:30 p.m. One of the MuzikMafia's mottos is "You never know who's gonna show," to which I frequently add, ". . . or *when* they're going to show."

I looked around the room and saw many familiar faces. The MuzikMafia has a dedicated fanbase of approximately twenty to fifty people who regularly attend Tuesday night shows. The choice of day, time, and locale is intentional.

The Mercy Lounge is more than five blocks from the tourist area of down-town Nashville, and Tuesday is, according to the MuzikMafia's founding godfathers, "the worst night of the week" for going out to a club. Tonight, the focus is on the music rather than on dancing or meeting new people. A former student of mine is standing next to me. He had never attended a MuzikMafia event and asked what it was all about. "Just relax and listen," I told him.

Two-Foot Fred began the loosely organized show with a comedy routine based mostly on his life experiences as a dwarf. Afterwards, John Rich and James Otto slowly made their way to the small stage, where several bar-stools had been positioned behind a row of microphones. John and James sang a country-influenced duet entitled "Wild West Show." James continued with an R&B tune entitled "Good Thing Gone Bad." John then bought the audience a round of drinks—a frequent icebreaker that also feeds his ego, self-described as "enormous."

The rest of the show contained a variety of musical acts. Cowboy Troy sang several audience favorites including "I Play Chicken with the Train" and "Ain't Broke Yet." Troy frequently describes his own combination of country, blues, rap, and rock as "hick-hop." John followed with an up-tempo rock version of his and Big Kenny's song "Save a Horse (Ride a Cowboy)." Shannon Lawson, whom many fans associate with a hard-driving acoustic bluegrass style, performed an electric blues ballad entitled "She Ain't Got Nothing on You." A black artist known as Mista D continued with several pop rock-influenced selections, including "Runnin' from Love." Local singer Shanna Crooks impressed the audience with her virtuosic vocal style that included influences from soul, gospel, pop rock, and funk. Commercial country singer and songwriter John Phillips then performed a few of his latest songs, followed by a local emcee known as Timothy "Chance" Smith who combines commercial country, southern rock, and rap. At one point in the show, all the artists were on stage taking part in a group jam session—a regular component of MuzikMafia performances.

That show took place on January 31, 2006. By then, John Rich had charted as a songwriter fifteen Top Twenty hits on *Billboard*'s Country Singles charts. John and Kenny's 2004 debut album as Big & Rich, *Horse of a Different Color*, had already sold approximately three million copies. John and Kenny had made numerous network television appearances, including

The Tonight Show with Jay Leno, *The Today Show*, *Jimmy Kimmel Live*, and a cameo in the season premiere episode of NBC's *Las Vegas*. Troy's album *Loco Motive* was nearing gold certification, or 500,000 units sold. Troy was also scheduled to co-host with Wynonna the upcoming season of *Nashville Star*, the country music equivalent to *American Idol*. Rachel's paintings were selling for between $2,500 and $10,000 each. As the best-known of all Muzik-Mafia members, Gretchen Wilson had accumulated album sales in excess of five million units and had received most of the industry awards possible for a new, female solo artist in commercial country music. James Otto, Shannon Lawson, Chance, Damien Horne, and other MuzikMafia members had opened up for Hank Williams Jr. on four tour dates the previous fall. Both James and Shannon had already performed several times on the Grand Ole Opry. The entire MuzikMafia had completed a second year with the Chevrolet American Revolution Tour. The musicians on stage that evening were not marginalized by Nashville's commercial music scene as they had been in the fall of 2001 when the MuzikMafia was founded. This community of musicians was already a significant part of the commercial music industry and American popular culture.

The rise of the MuzikMafia is a story not only about a group of local artists and their shared dream of reaching the big time, but also about Nashville, otherwise known as "Music City, U.S.A." The city is a southern Mecca for recording and music publishing where stars are created on a daily basis, but is also a place where dreams come to die. For every platinum-selling artist on CMT or GAC, there are literally thousands of unknowns who perform in Nashville's dozens of live music venues. On Lower Broadway, the street that boasts the country music scene downtown, a wide variety of street musicians perform both onstage and on the sidewalk night after night, waiting to be discovered by a producer or talent scout—which happens more often than one might think. And then there are those artists who just play the same clubs week after week, hoping that word of mouth will generate some buzz around town—which is how the MuzikMafia got its break. Contrary to what the media would have us believe, the MuzikMafia did not incite a revolution in Nashville. Its founding artists merely worked the system, which is why before we discuss the MuzikMafia, we have to begin with the system itself: the Nashville scene, from both geographic and historical perspectives.

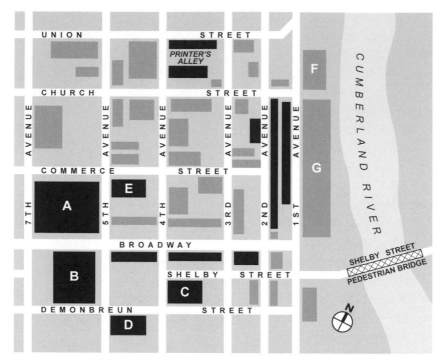

Figure 1.1 Map of downtown Nashville: The District and the northern part of SoBro. A = Nashville Convention Center, B = Gaylord Entertainment Center, C = Schermerhorn Symphony Hall, D = Country Music Hall of Fame, E = Ryman Auditorium, F = Fort Nashboro, G = Riverfront Park.

Nashville's primary area for listening to music, called The District, is located in the commercial center of downtown and contains a wide variety of music venues, tourist shops, and restaurants. The District begins on Lower Broadway at Fifth Avenue, extends down to the Cumberland River, and includes Printer's Alley and Second Avenue North up to Union Street (as shown in figures 1.1 to 1.3).

Lower Broadway is peppered with numerous country music venues. Located beside Legend's Corner at Broadway and Fifth Avenue, Tootsie's Orchid Lounge is legendary among country music fans. The locale has been frequented by Hank Cochran, Willie Nelson, Mel Tillis, Jim Reeves, Hank Williams, Patsy Cline, Ray Price, Waylon Jennings, Ernest Tubb, Merle Haggard, and many others. The club's walls commemorate its rich history with an array of signed photographs by many of country music's best-known stars. Directly behind Tootsie's is the "Mother Church" of country music,

Figure 1.2 Lower Broadway part of The District. The Cumberland River lies to the east at the bottom of the hill.

Figure 1.3 The District as seen from the east. Riverfront Park appears to the right in the photo adjacent the Cumberland River.

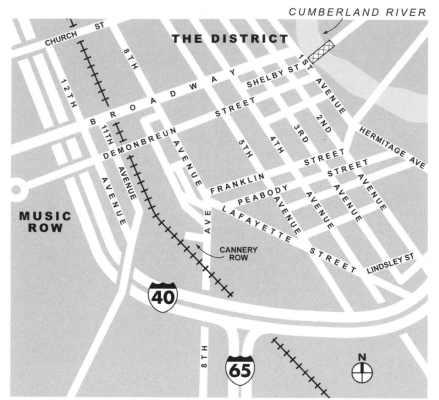

Figure 1.4 Map of SoBro.

Figure 1.5 The SoBro district of downtown Nashville.

the Ryman Auditorium, home to the Grand Ole Opry every Saturday evening from 1943 to 1974. Opry performers often exited the Ryman's back door to drink and socialize at Tootsie's between sets. Extending farther down Lower Broadway one finds other country music clubs such as Rippy's, Robert's Western World, The Second Fiddle, The Stage, Layla's Bluegrass Inn, and Nashville Crossroads.

Nashville's second primary area for listening to country music is Opryland, a country-oriented theme park that opened in 1974 approximately five miles east of downtown Nashville off of Briley Parkway. Although Opryland officially closed in 1997, the property still contributes to Nashville's country music culture through a large and extensive shopping mall called Opry Mills and the Gaylord Opryland Hotel, and through weekly performances from the Grand Ole Opry House, the Roy Acuff Theater, the Texas Troubadour Theatre, and the Gibson Bluegrass Showcase.

The MuzikMafia has frequently performed in SoBro, a formerly industrial area that extends south of Broadway to Interstate 40 and from the Cumberland River west to the railroad tracks near the Union Station Hotel (see fig. 1.4). Until recent efforts to develop the area commercially, SoBro was an unattractive addition to downtown with its trash-burning Nashville Thermal Plant and numerous run-down buildings. In the late 1990s the city began developing the area with the addition of the Gaylord Entertainment Center (now the Sommet Center) in 1997, the Hilton Nashville Downtown in 2001, and the new home for the Country Music Hall of Fame, also in 2001. SoBro's more recent projects have included the Schermerhorn Symphony Center, future plans for a baseball stadium, and Encore, a thirty-three-story condominium complex.

Music clubs in the SoBro area of downtown are stylistically more diverse than those in the nearby country-dominated scene of the District. The Station Inn, located on Twelfth Avenue South, promotes bluegrass. 3rd & Lindsley Bar and Grill features a variety of acts including progressive rock, blues, R&B, rock & roll, Americana, and soul. Bluesboro on Second Avenue South was a popular destination for blues artists and the Muzik-Mafia until the club closed in late summer 2004. The Mercy Lounge and the Cannery Row Ballroom, both located at One Cannery Row, have attracted artists such as R.E.M., Iggy Pop, Jimmy Cliff, Midnight Oil, Brett Michaels, George Clinton, Robert Cray, Yo La Tengo, Lenny Kravitz, KRS-One, and the

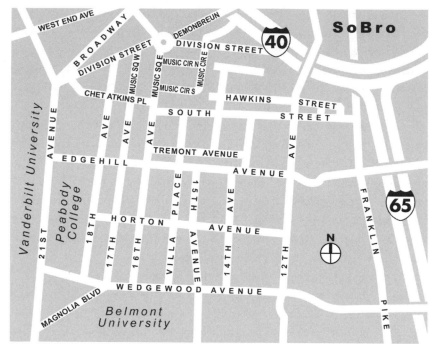

Figure 1.6 Map of Music Row.

MuzikMafia. RCKTWN on Sixth Avenue South caters to younger audiences with rock, punk, rap, and Top Forty music. One can find a variety of rock, classic jazz, blues, Americana, and singer-songwriter acts at the Basement, located on 8th Avenue South. Jazz enthusiasts flock to the Jazz 88 Bistro on 9th Avenue South. Reflections is an upscale club on 8th Avenue South that features a variety of dance music from swing to DJ-driven electronica. The Bar Car located on 10th Avenue South is the city's primary source for trance music, drum n' bass, and rap, which I will discuss later.

The bulk of Nashville's commercial music industry is located on Music Row, an area southwest of downtown between Division Street, Interstate 40, 12th Avenue South, Vanderbilt University, and Wedgewood Avenue (see Fig. 1.6). Many tourists are surprised to discover that Music Row is not a single row of music-related businesses but rather an entire square mile of city streets. The neighborhood contains most of Nashville's music publishers, recording studios, record labels, music licensing firms, management agencies, radio networks, and video production houses.

The origins of Music Row can be traced back to the late 1930s and early 1940s, when commercial country music (then frequently called "hillbilly music") was emerging onto the national scene. At the time, tensions were increasing between ASCAP and the nation's broadcasters over licensing rights. As a result, the National Association of Broadcasters established in April 1940 a rival licensing company called Broadcast Music, Inc. (BMI), which was open to all musicians and songwriters, regardless of race, genre, or economic status. Commercial country benefited from BMI's presence because of ASCAP's earlier reluctance to license indigenous American music including country, blues, and jazz.

Amid the growing popularity of hillbilly recordings and a musicians' strike, BMI attracted the attention of Roy Acuff (1903–1992) and Fred Rose (1897–1954), who in 1942, with a $2,500 grant from BMI, established the Acuff-Rose Publishing Company in Nashville. Acuff was perhaps the most popular performer and host on the Grand Ole Opry, and Rose was enjoying a successful career as a songwriter. Acuff-Rose soon became one the largest music publishers in the United States with song credits such as "The Tennessee Waltz," which Pee Wee King and Redd Stewart recorded in 1948 and that Patti Page re-recorded in 1950. By May 1951 Page's version had sold approximately 4.8 million copies. Acuff-Rose's catalog included songs written and recorded by Hank Williams, the Everly Brothers, Don Gibson, Roy Orbison, Marty Robbins, and Willie Nelson. Acuff-Rose was the first music publisher in Nashville, and its offices on 8th Avenue became the focal point of Nashville's commercial music industry, now Music Row.

In the 1950s and 1960s Music Row's emphasis gradually shifted from music publishing to commercial music recording. In 1955 Owen Bradley converted a Quonset hut attached to his house on Sixteenth Avenue into a makeshift studio. In 1957 RCA built its now-famous Studio B two blocks from Bradley's house. Artists who recorded there included Elvis, Chet Atkins, Buddy Holly, Johnny Cash, and Marty Robbins. Epic Records, which became an imprint of Columbia and then Sony, set up camp on Music Row in 1954 and later included artists such as Tammy Wynette and George Jones. Fred Foster founded Monument Records in 1954, also later bought by Columbia. Monument sparked the careers of Kris Kristofferson and Roy Orbison. In 1962 Columbia Records purchased the Bradley studio around which the corporation constructed a much larger recording facility.

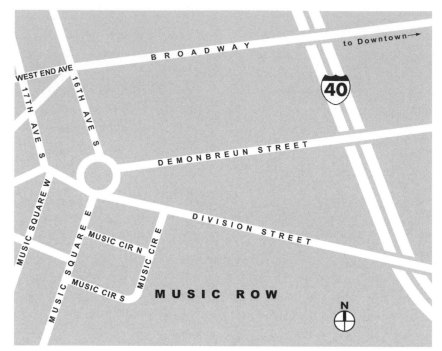

Figure 1.7 Map of the Demonbreun Street Roundabout.

Columbia's session lists during the 1960s include recordings by Bob Dylan, George Jones, and Tammy Wynette.

Today Music Row is a center for the area's commercial music industry that includes over 54,000 jobs and contributes approximately $6.38 billion annually to the city's economy, more than the combined impact of respective music industries in the entire state of Georgia as well as the cities of Seattle, Washington; Austin, Texas; and Memphis, Tennessee. Music Row's list of major record labels includes offices of Sony/BMG that includes imprints Epic, Monument, Columbia, RCA, Arista, BMG, and BNA. Other Music Row majors include Warner Bros. and Universal, which owns Mercury and MCA. Smaller record labels that have become significant forces on Music Row include Rounder, Curb, and Sugar Hill. The major music publishers on Music Row are more numerous and include EMI, Universal Music Publishing Group (UMPG), BMG Music Publishing, Sony Music Publishing, MGM Music, Sony/ATV Publishing, and Warner/Chappell.

The Demonbreun Street Roundabout is located between Music Row and Interstate 40 southwest of downtown Nashville (Figure 1.7). The

Figure 1.8 Demonbreun Street as viewed from the east near Interstate 40 toward the roundabout, which lies to the west at the top of the hill, February 2006.

Figure 1.9 Demonbreun Street as viewed from the west atop the roundabout's grass center. Nashville's downtown skyline appears to the northeast in the background.

roundabout area is a relatively recent addition to the Nashville cultural scene. Until 2000 the actual roundabout and adjacent street had been home to several kitschy shops that catered to tourists visiting the former location of the Country Music Hall of Fame nearby. However, the tourist industry along Music Row dissipated as a result of the Country Music Hall of Fame's gradual move to its current facility in SoBro in 2001. Plans to develop the

Demonbreun Street Roundabout had already begun in 1998 when Pino Squillace, a local entrepreneur and the MuzikMafia's future conga player, envisioned the roundabout's commercial and cultural potential.

By the late 1990s Pino was well-known in Nashville. He had founded in 1996 his Caffee Milano located at 174 3rd Ave. North in The District off of Lower Broadway. The restaurant/bar quickly became an integral part of the Nashville music scene, attracting well known acts such as Chet Atkins (who performed there every Monday night), Johnny Cash, June Carter Cash, Waylon Jennings, Branford Marsalis, Diana Krall, Olivia Newton-John, Alison Krauss, and Spyro Gyra. According to Pino, he organized Diana Krall's first three performances in Nashville in 1997; video footage for her electronic press kit (EPK), which included interviews with Sarah Jessica Parker and Tony Bennett, was also filmed at Caffee Milano. In June 1998 Pino and his partnership sold the establishment to the Gibson Guitar Company, who subsequently changed the name of the venue to Gibson's Caffe Milano.

In November 1998 Pino approached Nashville businessman Jim Caden with the idea of developing the roundabout area into a dining and entertainment destination. Pino suggested that Caden lease the properties to a series of diverse, consumer-based enterprises rather than to those wanting to erect office buildings, recording studios, or more tourist shops. Pino referred to his idea as the "twenty hours plan," comprising businesses that collectively operated twenty hours per day. For example, he proposed coffee shops that would serve the public beginning at 7:00 a.m., lunch cafés to cater to midday crowds, retail stores for daytime operation, restaurants that catered to evening clientele, and nightclubs that provided live entertainment until 3:00 a.m. According to Pino, he wanted to feature "numerous music venues that would showcase a variety of genres simply to reflect the history of Nashville's diverse musical community . . . really to put music back on Music Row!"

Pino and Caden modeled their plans to develop Demonbreun Street after Sixth Street in Austin, Texas, which the two had visited in late 1998. The first music venue, the Tin Roof, was home to the MuzikMafia from August 2002 to March 2003. Later music venues included the Dan McGuinness Pub that features a wide variety of music genres, including acoustic singer/songwriters, rock, country, blues, jazz, and Celtic. Two Doors Down and On the Rocks, two clubs that lie between Dan McGuinness Pub and the

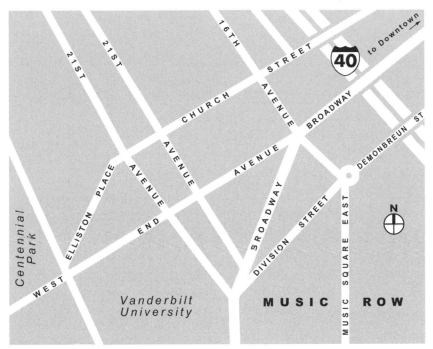

Figure 1.10 Map of West Nashville including the "Rock Block" that is located on Elliston Place.

Tin Roof, attract college audiences that favor pop and rock music. Gravity is a small club adjacent to On the Rocks and features mostly singer-songwriters. Other Demonbreun establishments include Otter's Chicken Tenders, Sushiyobi, Christopher Tennessee Pizza Company, a chic fashion store called Studio 15, Flavour Fashions, and a trendy café named Caffeine. The bulk of Demonbreun Street's clientele is industry personnel from Music Row during lunchtime and early afternoon and college students from nearby Vanderbilt and Belmont universities during the evenings.

The small Nashville area known as the Rock Block is located along Elliston Place, a five-block street between West End Avenue and Church Street near Vanderbilt University (see fig. 1.10). The Rock Block, which comprises a row of various clubs and restaurants, had its heyday in the 1970s and the 1980s, but much of Nashville's rock scene is still based along Elliston Place. One of the Rock Block's first significant musical establishments was the Exit/In, which in the 1970s catered primarily to Nashville's counterculture. Other music venues at Elliston Place include the Gold Rush, which attracts a diverse clientele and musical talent, and The End, where one can hear punk rock, ska, and reggae on a regular basis. I will discuss these and other clubs associated with Nashville's rock scene later in this chapter.

Nashville's music scene is not limited to these districts. For example, the Bluebird Café, nationally recognized for the numerous singer-songwriters who have performed there since 1985, is located four miles south of the Demonbreun Street Roundabout on Hillsboro Pike. One may hear blues or classic rock each evening at the Boardwalk Café, also on Hillsboro Pike. Another popular singer-songwriter locale is the Douglas Corner Café located on 8th Avenue South between Music Row and Interstate 65.

The numerous districts and venues that comprise Nashville's music scene reflect the city's musical diversity. On any given night, one can find a wide variety of musical genres being performed among the city's more than one hundred venues for live music. Tourists and new residents are often surprised to discover such variety in a town commonly known for its country music roots. One only needs to examine Nashville's rich musical history to understand that the city's roots are by no means limited to commercial country.

Having emerged in 2001 from the Nashville music scene, the Muzik-Mafia reflects, in many ways, Nashville's own musical diversity. The city's current population of approximately 550,000 supports a thriving music scene that has historically welcomed musics of varying styles. In addition, MuzikMafia members have confirmed to me on many occasions that they were greatly influenced by their Nashville surroundings.

The early presence and historical significance of art music, dance bands, and jazz in Nashville is little known. However, these styles have been integral components of musical life in Nashville since the first half of the twentieth century.

Between 1900 and World War II, Nashville's art music scene comprised a variety of ragtime performances, operas, a symphony orchestra, Broadway shows, dance clubs, and vaudeville. Nashville's music scene expanded dramatically during radio's Golden Age in the 1920s. The city's first significant attempt to enter the radio race was WSM (650 AM), which went on the air on October 5, 1925.

Nashville's dance bands during the first half of the twentieth century were mostly white, but the city also supported a thriving black music scene.

Educational institutions and professional schools such as Fisk University, Tennessee State University, Meharry Medical College, Walden University, Roger Williams University, and Gupton's Embalming School gave blacks the opportunity to pursue a variety of careers.

Many Nashville-based jazz bands reached the national scene by the end of the 1940s, largely because of Tennessee State University, which had one of the top jazz education programs in the country at the time. Chick Chavis founded the university's dance band the Collegians in 1946. The Collegians were voted Best College Band in America in 1949, an honor that afforded the group a performance at Carnegie Hall followed by a national concert tour.

The popularity of commercial country and rock and roll in the 1950s and 1960s eclipsed that of dance orchestras and jazz bands in Nashville. However, by this time many black musicians were already an integral part of or had decided to take part in Nashville's separately developing scenes for blues and rhythm and blues.

Nashville has supported a thriving rhythm and blues scene since the mid-1940s. Urban migration and forced segregation at that time resulted in much black entertainment being centered on 4th Avenue North and Jefferson Street. These districts housed many black theaters, nightclubs, and restaurants, the most famous of which was the Bijou Theater on 4th Avenue North.

Nashville radio contributed much to the local rhythm and blues scene. WLAC rivaled WSM for national popularity in the 1940s. During the 1950s and 1960s WLAC was reaching as many as fifteen million listeners each night, making the station one of the most listened-to nighttime rhythm and blues outlets in the country.

During the 1960s Nashville clubgoers experienced shows by many of the nation's top stars for blues and rhythm and blues. During their brief stint in the army, Jimi Hendrix and his bassist Billy Cox were both stationed at Fort Campbell located northwest of Nashville along the Kentucky border near Clarksville. The two frequently performed in downtown Nashville, including Printer's Alley and at Club Del Morocco on Jefferson Street. In 1963 Etta James recorded her live album *Etta James Rocks the House* at the New Era Club located at 1114 Charlotte Avenue in Nashville. Sam Cooke performed a concert at the Sulphur Dell baseball park in the late 1950s. Memphis-born saxophonist Hank Crawford accompanied Ray Charles during many of his concerts in Nashville in the late 1950s and early 1960s.

Nashville's popularity as a center for rhythm and blues expanded in the 1960s with two nationally syndicated television programs: *Night Train* and *The!!!Beat*. WLAC-TV debuted *Night Train* in Nashville in October 1964, five years before the show's better known Chicago counterpart *Soul Train*. *The!!!Beat* premiered in 1965, hosted by Hoss Allen, and was among the first television programs to be broadcast in color.

Nashville celebrated its R&B roots with an exhibit at the Country Music Hall of Fame from March 2004 through December 2005. Entitled *Night Train to Nashville: Music City Rhythm & Blues, 1945–1970*, the 5,000-square-foot multimedia exhibit highlighted significant milestones in the city's R&B history. In February 2004, Country Music Foundation Records released a two-disc set with the exhibit's same name that comprised era-specific, Nashville-produced R&B recordings. The compact disc set won a Grammy Award for Best Historical Album in 2004.

Nashville is little known for its rock music scene, which also includes a variety of related genres such as rockabilly, heavy metal, and punk. Yet the city has celebrated a close relationship with rock music since the rise of rock and roll in the 1950s. Significant artists from the 1950s and 1960s who either performed or recorded in Nashville include Elvis Presley, who performed on the Grand Ole Opry in 1954 and recorded over two hundred songs for RCA on Music Row; Jerry Lee Lewis; Chuck Berry; the Byrds, who performed on the Grand Ole Opry in 1968; Bob Dylan; and Jimi Hendrix.

One of Nashville's earliest locales for various forms of rock-related music was the Exit/In, which opened in 1971 at 2208 Elliston Place just off West End Avenue. Artists who performed there in the 1970s include Jimmy Buffett, Willie Nelson, John Hiatt, Linda Ronstadt, Billy Joel, Guy Clark, John Prine, and comedian Steve Martin. During the 1980s the club expanded its repertory to include Fats Domino, Dizzy Gillespie, k.d. lang, the Police, Bo Diddley, Hank Williams Jr., R.E.M., and Tom Petty and the Heartbreakers. By the 1990s the Exit/In was one of Nashville's premiere rock and pop venues, attracting artists such as Lucinda Williams, Hootie and the Blowfish, and the Red Hot Chili Peppers. Since 1998 the Exit/In has undergone a series of renovations but still continues to book mostly rock-oriented acts.

Nashville's hip-hop scene experienced a period of underground development from the mid-1980s through the mid-1990s. A former MuzikMafia rap artist named Timothy "Chance" Smith, who grew up in Nashville, remembers the Large Brothers as being the only crew of significance throughout the 1980s. By the mid-1990s Nashville's fledgling hip-hop scene included groups such as Haystack, Drop Car Full of White Boys, and Count Bass D. There were no clubs in town that supported hip-hop culture or rap music. Instead, these artists performed at a variety of venues, ranging from local house parties to campus events, especially those at Tennessee State University in Nashville or Middle Tennessee State University in nearby Murfreesboro. POW Shadows was the dominant emcee in Nashville in the mid-1990s but, at the time, the city's hip-hop culture was still considered an underground phenomenon.

The premiere venue for Nashville's hip-hop artists in the late 1990s was the Bar Car located in Cummins Station on 10th Avenue South. Turntablist United Crates organized the city's first ciphers at the Bar Car in 1998. Host Father Abraham promoted an atmosphere of friendly competition among Nashville's top emcees at the time: POW Shadows, Cash Villain, 187 Blitz, Boom Bap, and Kyhil. In 1998 the hip-hop magazine *The Source* organized an emcee battle at the Bar Car that POW Shadows won. Nashville's rap scene continued to develop after 1999 with much influence from future MuzikMafia member Chance, who organized numerous battles and ciphers between 1999 and 2004 for his and other rap crews.

Chapter Two

THE BIRTH OF THE MUZIKMAFIA

1. Respect and accept all forms of music, people,
   and forms of self expression.

2. Never speak ill will of anyone or anything.

3. Be the best at what you do.

4. Do not promote yourself before any other artist.

5. No disrespect towards women.

6. No "hard" drugs.

7. No negativity towards other MuzikMafia musicians.

8. Ask what you can give to the MuzikMafia, not what
   can you get from it.

9. Do not ask to join the MuzikMafia.

These are the rules. Since the MuzikMafia's first performance on October 23, 2001, many musicians have been
asked to join or at least to perform with the MuzikMafia.

Those who could not meet these criteria have been asked to leave. The core membership of the MuzikMafia is small—fewer than twenty individuals. Separately, they are artists, each of whom has experienced relative degrees of success and failure in their personal and professional lives. Together, they have contributed to significant change in the commercial music industry in Nashville and beyond.

But what is the MuzikMafia and where does it come from? Since June 2004, I have posed these and other questions to MuzikMafia members, tour personnel, the MuzikMafia sub-community known as the Mafia Mizfits, Nashville songwriters, publicists, agents, managers, media representatives, record company executives, MuzikMafia fans, and to myself on hundreds of occasions. The responses are as diverse as the MuzikMafia's membership. Seldom are two definitions identical, but many evoke connotations of family or a group that promotes individuality, acceptance, and musical diversity.

In order to understand the MuzikMafia, we should examine the respective backgrounds of its founding members: Kenny Alphin, Jon Nicholson, Cory Gierman, and John Rich. The MuzikMafia did not simply appear out of thin air in the fall of 2001; its "godfathers," as they liked to be called, are like-minded individuals whose lives, although diverse in background, contain similar threads of identity-building experiences. I base the following biographical sketches primarily on extended personal interviews with each artist. In order to guarantee the accuracy of information—artists, especially those in the commercial music industry, are not always forthcoming when describing their personal lives—I have corroborated most information with reliable sources such as family members, published biographical information, documents of public record, and other MuzikMafia members.

Known by friends and fans as "Big Kenny," Kenny Alphin is a significant figure in the MuzikMafia. Appropriately named, Kenny stands about 6'3" tall and weighs approximately 190 pounds. In addition to his status as godfather, Kenny contributed much to the development of one of the MuzikMafia's fundamental principles of artistic expression: Music without Prejudice.

Kenny was born November 1, 1963, the youngest of four children to Bill and Mary Alphin. Kenny's youth consisted of rural life on the family farm located approximately seven miles outside of Culpeper, Virginia. His father, a cattle farmer and insurance salesman, has been actively involved in many aspects of Culpeper life such as the Rappahannock Electric Cooperative board of directors, the Culpeper school board, the Virginia Farm Bureau board, and the Culpeper Baptist Church. Kenny's mother Mary introduced her son to music when he was approximately two years old through singing lessons in the form of gospel hymns such as "Jesus Loves the Little Children," "Give of Your Best to the Master," and "Amazing Grace" at church. She was the director for the church children's choir that she also accompanied on piano.

Kenny's parents observed his creative talent at a young age. According to Bill Alphin, "Kenneth was different than the other kids. He didn't watch much television; he was always doing something creative on his own." Mary also realized it, and did not enroll her son in kindergarten. Instead, the family invested in an encyclopedia and a craft set. Kenny and his mother spent his kindergarten year at home, exploring his curiosity through daily reading, crafts, drawing, and other outlets for creative expression. Mary remembers one Sunday morning when she noticed that Kenny had remained behind as the family was in the car preparing to leave for church. Upon entering the house to retrieve her son, Mary found Kenny on the floor reproducing a picture that an artist had been painting on a television program earlier that morning. Mary described her son to me as having "more God-given talent than any one child needed."

Kenny came from a religious family, and both parents were active in their local church. Mary believed that Kenny's religious fervor came mostly from his father, who served as deacon for the Culpeper Baptist Church. As Mary told me in 2005, "Bill is deeply religious; his faith is strong; he never gives up; he always looks on the bright side of things."

Kenny's formal musical training began in fifth grade in the school band program. Kenny's parents had purchased a saxophone, largely the result of Kenny's enthusiasm for the newly created jazz band at the local high school. Kenny and his family saw the jazz band perform weekly at high school basketball games where Kenny's older sister was a cheerleader. While in seventh grade, Kenny took additional lessons on saxophone with the high school band director, and under his supervision Kenny founded the middle school jazz band. According to Kenny's mother, "By this time, Bill was selling insurance and had to go into town every day. Ken would get up early, dress himself, and ride with his father into town without any prodding. There were a bunch of them that took group jazz lessons together. Ken loved to wear his dad's big Stetson hat that he'd [Bill] been given for purchasing [livestock] feed at a certain time. Ken often performed with that hat on."

In 1981, following his junior year of high school, Kenny attended the Virginia Summer Governor's School for the Gifted at Mary Washington College in Fredericksburg to develop his artistic interests further. He had been nominated for the Governor's School by three different high school faculty, a rare honor in the Culpeper County school system: Jane Harvey [Sisson] (art), Ashby Mitchell (mathematics), and Thomas Earles (chemistry and physics).

Kenny's parents had noticed that, in his youth, he had an insatiable desire to make money. According to Mary, "Each time I asked him to do something, he asked, 'How much you gonna pay me?' When he wanted money, he always asked me what he could do to earn five cents. That's just the way he was."

Kenny's entrepreneurial spirit became evident while he was in high school, when he employed twelve individuals in his own logging and land clearing business. After graduation Kenny opened his own contracting business, which eventually made him a short-term millionaire. As a result of a recession in the real estate business in the late 1980s, Kenny lost his business and most of his wealth. Within a year he was bankrupt. With little money, a recent divorce from his wife of five years, and few, if any, business prospects, Kenny continued to farm full-time with his father in 1992 and 1993 while supplementing his own income by making furniture.

In summer 1993 Kenny met a friend who encouraged him to start writing music. Kenny purchased an acoustic guitar and frequently sat on the family's back porch, composing as many songs as possible. According to Kenny's mother,

> I could tell exactly what he was singing about. Some of them [songs] were about his [ex-]wife; he was writing about what happened to him and his business. He wrote about how the bankers would offer him the moon and send him on these [business] trips. They were just baiting him to borrow more money. Kenny had all sorts of ideas, so why not just take the money? So he went on with his construction stuff.

The bankers didn't care about him, only their money. That's how he got through that bankruptcy and the breakup of his marriage: with music.

Kenny moved to Nashville in 1994 to try his luck as a professional musician. He had been encouraged by his modest success in songwriting and performing with local bands in Virginia. Kenny told me that he was performing at least five nights a week in Nashville, which is where he met future godfather Jon Nicholson in summer 1994. The two spent considerable time together performing at local venues, and shared an apartment in 1996 at Oakwell Farms in Hermitage, fifteen miles east of Nashville. With the help of friend Rory Lee Feek, Kenny received his first publishing contract in 1995 as a songwriter at Famous Music under Pat Finch. Six months after Kenny arrived, he met another future MuzikMafia godfather when Cory Gierman began working at Famous as a tape copyist.

In February 1998 Kenny and John Rich met. At the time, Kenny's friend Cindy Simmons knew John's girlfriend Debbie Sorenson. According to Kenny, Cindy convinced Debbie to bring John to see Kenny perform at a local Nashville bar called the Douglas Corner Café. John had just left the popular country group Lonestar in January and had embarked on a solo career. Following a brief introduction, Kenny and John arranged to meet the following month after which they became friends and songwriting partners. Although they regularly performed in each other's Nashville shows and co-wrote numerous songs together, the two did not form a commercial duo until several years later.

Kenny was making a living as a songwriter and solo artist. In 1998 Kenny's musical success led to a recording contract with Hollywood Records, which resulted in his debut album *Live a Little* the following year. In 1999 he experienced brief commercial success with the release of two singles from the album, "Candy Colored Glasses" and "Under the Sun." The video from the latter was featured on VH-1, and the song was included in the soundtrack for the film *Gun Shy* (1999), starring Sandra Bullock and Liam Neeson. *Nashville Scene* staff writer Noel Murray described *Live a Little*: "Crunchy guitars abound, and Queen-like choral harmonies, orchestral strings, dance hall piano, whizzing machinery effects, varied percussion, and filtered vocals that sound like they were intercepted from an old radio broadcast. The results are decidedly theatrical, like some weird, cacophonous cabaret."

Unfortunately, Hollywood Records did not release the entire album *Live a Little* following its completion in 1999, and subsequently dropped Big Kenny from the label. Hollywood Records did not release *Live a Little* until much later—March 2005, two months after Big & Rich's album *Horse of a Different Color* was certified double platinum by the RIAA.

As a result of his bittersweet experience as a solo artist on the national scene, Kenny decided to form a new musical group in 1999. When informed of this idea, John Rich suggested calling it luvjOi, because "that's what you [Kenny] are all about," combining Kenny's "love everybody" motto with his penchant for unique creative expression. It was during luvjOi's moderate success in Nashville when Kenny and Jon Nicholson formed the MuzikMafia in fall 2001. According to Kenny, he later went to Cory, and the three subsequently invited John Rich shortly before the MuzikMafia's first performance on October 23 that year.

However, it was not until summer 2002 that Kenny's mother suggested to Marc Oswald that Kenny and John form a duo, although Marc claims that the idea was his alone. Marc, a Nashville manager and show producer who had had considerable success in the commercial music industry with his partner Dale Morris, had managed Kenny since his solo career in 1998 with Hollywood Records. Marc had also known John since 1999, when Kenny invited John to the first of many jam sessions at Marc's house. In summer 2002, Marc observed Kenny and John performing together at a songwriter's night at the Bluebird Café, a Nashville venue well known for such occasions. Following the performance, Marc invited the two musicians to his house for brunch the next day for a "real conversation" to discuss the two as a professional duet act. According to Kenny, he and John had already been using the name Big & Rich for their Bluebird shows. Nevertheless, John described to me his own first reaction to Marc's suggestion: "Are you [Marc] out of your fucking mind? They [the country music industry] don't even get me. They think that *I* am too rock and roll for country radio; there is no way they're going to get Kenny." In a 2005 interview with me, Marc described Kenny at the time as being "a little more open to the idea, but still not particularly enthusiastic." Despite considerable hesitation, the two acquiesced and trademarked the name Big & Rich soon thereafter, with Marc as their official manager.

Jon Nicholson's diverse musical background, combined with his position as one of the four founding godfathers, makes him a significant contributor to the birth, growth, and development of the MuzikMafia. Jon describes himself as the "soul branch" of the MuzikMafia, but his musical style includes numerous additional influences, such as country, blues, gospel, funk, and rock and roll. His music is the most challenging to categorize among all MuzikMafia musicians.

Jon was born on August 4, 1973, in Madison, Wisconsin. Parents Judy and Bliss Nicholson introduced their son to diverse musics in numerous ways. Jon acquired an appreciation of commercial country stars Johnny Paycheck and Hank Williams Jr. through his father, who owned a landscaping business. Around the age of two Jon began learning how to sing from his mother and he started taking piano lessons from his grandmother. Although Jon's aunt Eileen later exposed him to "playing by the notes," Jon favored his grandmother's piano instruction that reinforced playing gospel and blues-style hymns by ear. When Jon was three years old, his parents enrolled him in Suzuki violin classes. Jon received formal piano instruction at age four, but he never dedicated himself to gaining proficiency in reading musical notation. According to Jon in an interview with me in 2004, "I would sit at the piano next to my teacher who was reading music, and I looked at the pages, pretending to read along. I did this for about a year before she figured out I was faking. After she fired me, she recommended a few other teachers who could help me develop my talents."

Among his first public appearances was the International Banjorama in Madison at age five. Jon performed two selections by Elvis Presley, "Blue Suede Shoes" and "Hound Dog," in a sequined shirt made for him by his grandmother.

Jon's musical influences span a broad range of artists and styles. Jon's first band Here and Now, founded in 1985, performed primarily hard rock, punk, and heavy metal songs by artists such as the Scorpions, Stryper, Dead Kennedys, Metallica, and Queensrÿche. As a teenager during the mid-1980s, Jon replaced his earlier interest in country music with that of the Sex Pistols and the Dead Kennedys with few exceptions: the music of Willie

Nelson, Hank Williams Jr., and Johnny Paycheck. Jon boasts that he can play most of Willie Nelson's songs by memory.

Jon's musical training further diversified during high school. He continued to develop his ear by taking the position of church pianist for Lake City Church in Madison. Although nondenominational, religious services at the Lake City Church closely resembled those of the Pentecostals and, according to Jon, exposed him to much gospel-style music. While at school he took classes in jazz improvisation and electronic music. Jon's commitments to high school wrestling and football precluded him from participating in band or chorus. Despite his outsider status among high school band and chorus members, Jon was voted Most Talented and Class Singer during his senior year, affording him the opportunity to sing a solo at his graduation in 1991.

During his late high school and early college years, Jon's listening habits became incredibly focused. He remembers purchasing one record at a time that he would then listen to intently for several months. He learned each song's melody, harmony, and text before purchasing another album. Artists who occupied much of Jon's attention in this fashion included Louis Armstrong, Lyle Lovett, George Strait, and Hank Williams Jr.

In fall 1991 Jon began his studies in biology with a minor in chemistry at the University of Wisconsin-Eau Claire. Close friend Kevin Terrell taught Jon how to play guitar using tunes by the Counting Crows and the Red Hot Chili Peppers. Jon remembers playing guitar every night, sometimes until sunrise. However, preoccupied with performing and composing music nightly, he attended class only sporadically, resulting in his eventual withdrawal from the university.

Jon left college at the end of his sophomore year and returned to Madison. He worked as bouncer in a local bar, supplementing his income with music in two ways: through solo performances and regular gigs with a local band. Jon played keyboards and sang backup vocals from winter 1993 to 1996 with Under the Gun, a country-rock group that gave Jon the frequent opportunity of performing his own material. The original members of Under the Gun included Jon on vocals and keyboards, Lane Venden on guitar, fiddle, mandolin, harp, steel, and vocals, Chris Wegner on bass and vocals, Kevin Smith on guitar and vocals, and David Maier on drums. Rehearsals with Under the Gun began in winter 1993 and performing started in early

1994. Under the Gun performed regularly from early 1994 to fall 1998, and their performances were, in most cases, sold out. The group won the title of Madison's Band of the Year in 1994, 1995, and 1996.

Jon first met Kenny in 1996, and the two ended up sharing an apartment at Oakwell Farms in Hermitage, Tennessee. The arrangement had been set up by mutual friend Mitch Ballard, a music publisher at Cupid Music. Kenny was a working as a songwriter for Famous Music where Cory Gierman was employed as a tape copyist. Jon supported himself by performing at well-known Nashville clubs such as the Courtyard Café, the Boardwalk, and the Bluebird Café. When Cory left Famous Music and began working at Broadvision as creative director, he immediately signed Jon as his first songwriter. Jon worked with Kenny on numerous projects during his first years in Nashville, including Kenny's now ill-fated solo album with Hollywood Records.

Jon first met John Rich in 2000 at Déjà Vu, a local strip club located at 1214 Demonbreun Street near downtown Nashville—a meeting that Kenny had arranged. John had just left the country group Lonestar and had been hired as a songwriter for Sony-Tree. Soon thereafter the three began musical collaborations that included songs for Broadvision and Kenny's solo album.

Cory Gierman is the only one of the four MuzikMafia godfathers who does not regularly perform on stage. A music publisher by trade, Cory oversaw many of the business-related matters of the community.

Cory was born on June 24, 1975, in Vassar, Michigan. Much of his youth was spent between Vassar, where he worked on the family's hay farm, and Pine Island, Florida, where the family spent its winters. His musical interests while growing up included popular styles on the jukebox in his family's restaurant—country music, heavy metal, rock, and rap. He studied agriculture for two years as an undergraduate at Edison Community College in Fort Myers, Florida, before deciding on a career in the music industry.

Following a move to Nashville and ultimately his graduation from Belmont University in spring 1998 with a B.A. in music business, Cory worked for several music publishing companies on Music Row, such as Famous Music, Broadvision, and Universal Music Publishing Group (UMPG). His job duties ranged from tape copyist and song "plugger" to creative director in charge of artists and repertoire (A&R). As song plugger, Cory took songs written by someone else and pitched them to major labels or song publishers for inclusion on other artists' albums.

Cory's collaboration with MuzikMafia musicians began long before the community's first performance together in October 2001. The first artist Cory signed at Broadvision was fellow future godfather Jon Nicholson. Cory and Kenny knew each other from Famous Music, where Kenny was working as a songwriter when Cory arrived in 1997. Kenny who introduced Cory to Jon when Cory became creative director at Famous Music.

John Rich's role in the MuzikMafia is multifaceted. As an established insider in Nashville's commercial music industry, John was a significant force behind the MuzikMafia's inception and its early popularity, and he was responsible for the addition of many of its members. Having achieved considerable commercial success with the popular country group Lonestar, John's familiarity with Nashville's corporate music culture opened many doors for MuzikMafia artists that might have remained closed to less well-known musicians. As a singer and songwriter, he directly contributed to the growth and development of the community by expanding its membership to include artists such as Gretchen Wilson, Cowboy Troy, and Two-Foot Fred. John played a significant role in creating MuzikMafia-owned Raybaw Records and produced albums by several MuzikMafia artists.

The oldest of four children, John was born January 7, 1974, in Amarillo, Texas. His childhood included a stern religious upbringing as well as rigorous guitar lessons. John's father was a devout Baptist preacher and a guitar instructor at a local music store. John began taking guitar lessons from his father at age five. John accompanied his father on guitar behind the pulpit during Sunday services but soon moved to bass guitar at his father's request. Although young John performed mostly gospel music, his primary listening preference was bluegrass. However, he admitted to me that his musical palate later included interest in artists as diverse as Frank Sinatra, Bob Wills, Ricky Skaggs, Steve Wariner, Vince Gill, Johnny Horton, Roger Miller, Johnny Cash, Ralph Stanley, Jim and Jesse, and Aerosmith.

John was greatly influenced by his father during his formative years in Amarillo. John's dynamic stage presence and overt charisma can be traced to his father's charismatic preaching style that John described to me as "somewhere between Baptist and Pentecostal." John acknowledges that his father's preaching is better suited for out in the street with Bible in hand than behind the pulpit. In a 2004 interview, John described an incident that exemplified his father's religious fervor:

> I was rooming with Nikki Sixx from Mötley Crüe at a songwriters' camp in California. I told him about my dad's experience when Mötley Crüe performed in Amarillo in the mid-1980s. My dad was out in the parking lot in a flatbed truck for three hours dragging a huge cross around to protest the devil's music, specifically the [Mötley Crüe] song "Shout at the Devil." He [Jim Rich] didn't want that music in *his* town, and he wanted people to know that he had a problem with it. Nikki looked at me [John] and said, "That was *your* dad?" He [Nikki] had remembered seeing from his tour bus some religious guy in a beard out in the parking lot before the show, and he [Nikki] thought about that [Jim Rich episode] the rest of the night.

The songwriting camp that John mentioned took place in summer 2002. John and Nikki were two of several songwriters from music publisher Warner-Chappell who spent time at Lake Arrowhead in southern California.

In August 1989 the Rich family moved to Chapmansboro, Tennessee, approximately thirty miles northwest of Nashville. John's mother Judy was from Tennessee, and she had suggested the move. At fifteen years of age, John was not enthusiastic about relocating because of his aspirations of becoming a rodeo cowboy in Texas. John's father Jim supported the family through continued service in the local ministry and by selling cars at a dealership called the Henrietta Motor Company.

In 1990 John's life underwent significant changes. First, John's parents separated, and his mother, brother, and two sisters moved to nearby Dickson, Tennessee, where John's mother had spent her formative years. However, John remained with his father in Chapmansboro. That same year John sang in his first talent competition. At age sixteen John competed in a talent show at the Cheatham County Fair against many talented acts, including a young Tracy Lawrence.

In fall 1990, during his junior year of high school, John and his father moved to Dickson. John spent his senior year at Dickson High School, and graduated in 1992. While in Dickson he performed at local venues, including Vance Smith's Grand Old Hatchery, a local country music club that prohibited smoking and drinking.

Also in 1990, a sixteen-year-old John began making trips to Nashville to compete in local music competitions. His first Nashville appearance was at the Judy Martin Talent Contest, held at the Broken Spoke Café just north of Nashville's downtown area near Interstate 24. Because John was under the age of twenty-one—the requirement for entering a contest in that bar—he had been instructed by the hostess to remain by her side until the show was over so that she could monitor his whereabouts. The competition that evening included future well-known country music artists such as Tracy Lawrence, Rhett Atkins, Joe Diffie, Daryl Singletary, and Doug Supernaw. The experience inspired John to enter as many talent contests as he could in the Nashville area.

John pursued his singing career throughout the 1990s. While still a senior in high school, he auditioned for and received a job the following summer performing at the Opryland theme park in Nashville, where he met Dean Sams. Both from Texas, John and Dean performed regularly in the Opryland show "Country Music U.S.A." In January 1993, along with Richie McDonald, Michael Britt, and Keech Rainwater, John and Dean formed a group called Texassee, in which John played bass guitar and sang backup vocals. In 1993 and 1994 Texassee performed over five hundred shows throughout the United States, including numerous appearances in Texas, where John met Cowboy Troy at a Dallas music club called the Borrowed Money Saloon. Texassee's considerable success led to a record deal in 1995 with RCA/BNA, a subsequent name change to Lonestar, and a series of award winning albums, including *Lonestar* in 1995 and *Crazy Nights* in 1997, both of which were certified gold by the Record Industry Association of America (RIAA).

John left Lonestar in January 1998 to pursue a solo career. He later shared with me that his reason for leaving was a difference of opinion concerning the group's direction: "The band had a different musical style than I did. I left the band because my natural style was in direct contrast to the direction they were going." According to Kenny, "Lonestar had a meeting, and they decided that where John wanted to go and where the rest of the band wanted to go was too different. He was out of the band in January, and in February, he met me."

Soon after departing Lonestar, John embarked on a solo career. Although he was known throughout the commercial country music industry, John experienced substantial difficulty in acquiring a solo record deal with a major label. After considerable rejection from Music Row, he consulted friend, mentor, co-writer, and future manager Sharon Vaughn, who had already penned numerous hits with major artists. Sharon agreed to co-produce several demos that John distributed to record company executives and industry personnel.

John's new material reached Joe Galante, head of RCA/BNA Records. Pleased with what he heard, Galante offered John a recording contract in fall 1999 and supplied him with a production budget. John's debut album entitled *Underneath the Same Moon* was scheduled for release in October 2000. He had co-written a single from the album entitled "I Pray for You" with Kenny in 1998. The song was the second song that John and Kenny had written together. The song also appears on Big Kenny's 1999 album that Hollywood Records did not release until March 2004.

However, RCA/BNA canceled John's contract prior to the scheduled release of *Underneath the Same Moon*. He received the news in June 2000 via an email that had been sent by Galante's secretary to John's manager. John was on his way to a local radio station to promote the album's newly released single when he received a telephone call from Sharon informing him of RCA/BNA's decision. The radio appearance had been scheduled by John's booking agent Greg Oswald, vice president of the Nashville branch of the William Morris Agency and brother to Marc Oswald, who was managing Kenny at the time of John's record deal with RCA/BNA. Greg had been John's agent for much of his tenure with Lonestar.

According to John, he felt "disrespected" and "bent" because his professional career and life, for all intents and purposes, "had just stopped." John was disgruntled by the whole situation, especially when BNA ultimately released the album in 2006, capitalizing on John's commercial success with Big & Rich. Needless to say, I have never witnessed John mentioning *Underneath the Same Moon* in public.

In December 2000, John and Kenny performed at the Vanderbilt Children's Hospital in Nashville—an event that eventually led to John's independent album *Rescue Me*. On December 22 John, Kenny, and guitarist Adam Schoenfeld, among others, performed a Christmas show at the hospital for all patients who could attend. Following the performance, John suggested that the musicians visit children in their hospital rooms as well. While visiting the room of Katie Darnell, who had been admitted to the hospital to undergo chemotherapy for brain cancer, Katie asked John if she could sing a song entitled "Rescue Me" that she had written earlier that year. Inspired by Katie's medical history and the song's sentiment, John recorded "Rescue Me" at a local Nashville studio and included the song on a self-financed, independent album of the same title.

Katie's life story and John's recording of "Rescue Me" received considerable national attention in early 2001. In February of that year disc jockey Gerry House of WSIX in Nashville aired the song over the radio, and following an influx of caller requests, sent an MP3 file of "Rescue Me" to twenty-three stations across the country. The exposure was accompanied by considerable public feedback that subsequently led to personal appearances that year by Katie and John on NBC's *Today Show* and ABC's *The View* and performances on April 4 for George W. and Laura Bush at the White House and on September 1 at the Grand Ole Opry. John completed the album *Rescue Me* in 2001, and because he had no corporate funding, he sold the recording independently from his website, donating the proceeds to the Darnell family.

In spring 2002 Darnell's cancer went into remission, and she returned to high school in her hometown of Princeton, Kentucky. In fall 2002, only a few months after forming the duo Big & Rich and having secured a record deal from Warner Bros., John and Kenny accompanied Darnell to her senior prom. The following year Wynonna recorded "Rescue Me" and included the song on her album *What the World Needs Now Is Love* that Curb/Asylum Records released in August 2003. In April 2001 John and Kenny wrote "She's a Butterfly" based upon their experiences with Katie. The single was recorded by Martina McBride and included on her self- titled album released in September of that year.

Jon Nicholson and Kenny conceived the idea of the MuzikMafia in early 2001. Later that year the two discussed their ideas with John Rich and Cory. Jon and Kenny's conversations throughout 2001 concentrated on two themes: a) Music Row's marginalization of them because they are artists who combine genres and b) the distance that Music Row maintains from the average Nashville musician.

In October that year Jon and Kenny unofficially formed the MuzikMafia with themselves, John Rich, and Cory as "godfathers." They drew upon

popular secular connotations of the term "godfather" as depicted in television, literature, and film, for example, the *Godfather* movie trilogy based on
Mario Puzo's 1969 book by the same name. In this context, a godfather was
someone of Italian descent who oversaw a relatively secretive but socially
powerful, family-oriented, and often illegal, commercial enterprise. The
godfathers' conversations concerning the MuzikMafia name took place over
several meetings at a club called 12th and Porter located in downtown Nashville across the street from the Pub of Love. Cory later told me: "We wanted
to screw 'the man' for having all of the power. We [John, Jon, Kenny, and I]
all felt as if we had been beat down by the system. We're *gonna* keep doing
what we're doing . . . let's just do it together. Let's go play music 'cause we
want to play music and see what comes out of it. Let's do it Mafia style."

Cory also said that the Mafia reference was first used in a joking manner. The four godfathers liked the toughness that the Mafia connotation
suggested and welcomed the term's association with secrecy, illegality, and
the underground. According to Cory, "It wouldn't be just John Rich going
in to talk to a record label; it would be all four . . . we wanted to use intimi-
dation . . . you know, where we'd just walk in there [to record companies]
and demand stuff." In actuality, the godfathers probably demanded nothing
from major labels on Music Row at the time, but Cory's sentiment clearly
expresses the godfathers' wish to exchange power roles with industry
executives.

The godfathers promoted their beliefs in musical hybridity and the
interests of the common man quite casually during the MuzikMafia's
inception. The eclectic music that John, Kenny, and Jon created was the
result of a myriad of styles they had grown up listening to and those that
were abundant among Nashville musicians. The godfathers assumed that,
because their respective musical influences were diverse, most listeners
also had eclectic tastes. The godfathers did not intend for early MuzikMafia
performances to be a rule-breaking social spectacle, but rather a gathering
place for friends and fans simply to hang out, have a few beers, and to be
themselves.

Defining the MuzikMafia is no simple task. Self-definitions are similar
among the community's members, but the MuzikMafia's emphasis on individuality and diversity accounts for its members' divergent views on their
collectivity. Since June 2004 I have repeatedly asked "What is the Muzik-
Mafia?" Many of the following responses came from the MuzikMafia's core

members. Additional definitions come from people directly involved with the MuzikMafia, including musicians who regularly performed with the MuzikMafia but who were not yet viewed as full members.

According to Jon, "Everybody involved has a different idea of what it [MuzikMafia] is and what it means. [The] only ones who really know are the godfathers . . . similar to the gospels of the Bible." Jon expanded on his views about the origins of the MuzikMafia approximately one year after our first interview and amidst the MuzikMafia's considerable national popularity:

> MuzikMafia is an outbreak of a musical virus . . . Everybody has their own interpretation. It matters when you came into the MuzikMafia, what was going on at that time, what experiences were happening. In the later years here when everything is going, you know, gangbusters, we got record labels, and people selling millions of records and all that. It seems like it's this big thing where, you know, with these guys are involved in all kinds of stuff. But really what it was about was a bunch of friends hanging out and bullshittin', you know, and talking about world domination and all that stuff. [We were] talking about kicking everybody else out of Nashville, all the old-timers that were messing up the music business and manufacturing artists—all the stuff that pissed us off about the music business. And we wanted to change all that. So we got all our friends together and started playing, started networking, and created something more powerful than any of those people [industry personnel], that's more powerful than any record label or anything else. It [MuzikMafia] is the governing force in Nashville. It takes all the lines out and all the borders and everything, and makes it wide open for whatever kind of music you want to make.

In a 2005 interview, Kenny described the MuzikMafia to me as follows: "We're a family; we check each other; when one of us gets too far out of hand, everybody pulls them back. It's hard to screw up with so many people behind you. It's like a group of trees standing in the forest with their branches touching. No one tree can fall. If it does, there are trees on all sides there helping him stand tall."

Cory, the only godfather who did not regularly perform on stage with the MuzikMafia, viewed the MuzikMafia as an empowering and a somewhat visionary entity: "It [the MuzikMafia] is tough; it's our own organization to take the power away from the big companies. We want to join people up to go in as a force. It gave us something to feel bonded by and to give each other support and encouragement to follow their dreams."

John described the MuzikMafia to me in an interview in 2005 as being:

Multi-pronged: it's family, but it's also a representation of the absolute best of the best of the best that the world has to offer—at least our world here in Nashville—to music. There is nobody better in Nashville than [Muzik]Mafia. If they were, we'd already have invited them over. It's people covering your back. It's a gang; it's blood oath. "Abundance" and "alliance" both have been used from the beginning; but alliance is really it. It's not anti-establishment; it's anti–certain thought processes.

Not long after their first performance at the Pub of Love, the godfathers created an acronym to define the community further: M.A.F.I.A. (Musically Artistic Friends in Abundance). The word "abundance" was changed to "alliance" in January 2004. This revealed a change in self-perception and intent. The MuzikMafia began as an open jam session at a local club called the Pub of Love, free for anyone who wanted to attend. The initial acronym referred to the godfathers' idea that there were undoubtedly many more people who shared the same belief of "Music without Prejudice"—a populist-based motto that the MuzikMafia has used since its beginning. The "alliance" reference reflected the godfathers' more unifying intention among its membership amidst rapidly growing popularity.

In order to define the MuzikMafia further, I turned to several artists who are regular fixtures on the MuzikMafia stage. Former Mercury recording artist James Otto, who was with the MuzikMafia at its first performance, described the community to me in 2005 as "friends and a group of artists. It has become a creative cocoon to me, full of creative spirits bouncing off the walls. Everyone is supporting each other's vision for who they are and what they want to become, helping to chip away and define what's great about each artist. It's a place to take criticism from those whom you respect. It's a place where everybody is encouraged to be the best they can be."

Drummer Brian Barnett, who was also with the MuzikMafia at its first show and who toured with Big & Rich from summer 2004 through summer 2006, reinforced the familial relationship that the MuzikMafia's musicians shared with one another. In addition, Brian emphasized the humility that each musician was obligated to have. He said in 2005: "MuzikMafia is like a family of musicians. . . .You have to be able to step up to the plate as far as musically [sic] . . . and you need to be humble are far as socially [sic]. . . . In order to be a part of the [Muzik]Mafia you have to have gone through some shit, basically, because you really don't know how to be humble if you've only had success. That's what keeps everybody together."

Damien Horne (a.k.a. Mista D) is a more pop- and rock-oriented musician who began performing with the MuzikMafia in August 2002. He frequently expanded on public conceptions of the community. According to Damien:

"Musically Artistic Friends in Alliance" is just the basis. It's really more than that. It's a family. They took me under their wing and helped me in all areas of my life: musically, financially, etc. They pull each other up. They elevate everyone else in the Mafia. It's a body, but everyone is his own part. You don't necessarily get along with everyone else all the time, but they're still your family.

The MuzikMafia's membership included two artists who combined rap and commercial country. The first was Troy Coleman (a.k.a. Cowboy Troy), an African American cowboy rapper who had known John from Lonestar tours through Texas in the early 1990s. Troy described the MuzikMafia as a place where "friends get together regardless of genre of music or type of art that you perform. . . . If it's painting, playing, singing, rapping, poetry recitation, whatever, you get together to display your wares. . . . Friends give you feedback and give you support."

Timothy "Chance" Smith was the MuzikMafia's second rap artist and an official member from 2004 through 2006. During his early days with the MuzikMafia, he described the collective to me as "a breeding ground for greatness. It's a place where, if you need help, there are people to help you."

Shawna Pierce (a.k.a. Sista Soul) is a funk/soul singer who regularly performed with Chance throughout 2004 and 2005. She explained the MuzikMafia to me as "An alliance of musicians and friends who come together for the purpose of sharing music in a non-territorial and loving environment. It's a network of friends and family who help one another and encourage one another. It's just like a sanctuary. The purpose is to celebrate music of up and coming artists in a non-territorial environment. It's a tribe."

Virtuosic blues-rock guitarist Dean Hall performed with the MuzikMafia from mid-2004 through early 2006. By the time of his induction, MuzikMafia artists Gretchen Wilson and Big & Rich were growing in popularity via widespread exposure in the mass media. In a 2004 interview, Dean described the MuzikMafia to me as "Not a band; even though there is a band playing on stage. [The MuzikMafia] is a philosophy and an idea of people helping one another. It *really is* 'musically artistic friends in alliance.' It's people who are talented and who are trying to fight this town [Nashville]. You never have to look up; you only have to look back to help the next person in line. It's completely opposite of how this town operates."

The MuzikMafia's regular auxiliary musicians closely identified with the family metaphor. Hispanic bass guitarist Jerry Navarro, who started performing with the MuzikMafia in January 2004 at Jon's invitation, recognized the MuzikMafia as a family. He continued:

> They've taken care of me both monetarily and emotionally; they're great friends and great people. They help in any way they can. They have literally helped me pay my bills, including monthly rent. It has taken me a while to accept their kindness, because I'm used to being a sideman. They want to help everybody rise up; help each other out. The musicians grow to know each other on a deeper level; that creates an understanding beyond the music.

Saxophonist Max Abrams, who assumed the role of lead auxiliary musician and stage manager at performances, was with the MuzikMafia from November 2001 to January 2008. Max understood the complexity of the MuzikMafia, and he regularly reflected on both its public representation and its personal meaning to him. According to Max:

[The MuzikMafia] is a lot of things. It's kind of a closed society for the disenfranchised. It's a lot of things because you're dealing with a collection of individuals who have slightly different goals. There is a sphere of ideas and views circling around about what it is. It's a collection of individuals who have a fundamental belief in the idea that the boundaries that exist between genres [of music] are less than people perceive. The boundaries between people are less than people perceive. We are all actively interested in showing people through multiple senses how narrow those barriers really are.

Auxiliary percussionist Pino Squillace, a native of southern Italy, expanded on the Mafia metaphor and its Italian connotations in 2005:

The [Italian] Mafia started in Italy to empower the individual; it was good for the people who couldn't act against political corruption; created by families whose sole responsibility as an unpaid volunteer was to bring justice where there was injustice, because the institution was corrupt and biased. MuzikMafia doesn't realize this yet, but it is doing the exactly same thing. They're saying, 'fuck the institution; who gives a shit about radio!?' We're going to give the individual the power against the institution; we are protecting the citizen of the music world. There is a real correlation between MuzikMafia and the Italian mafia, that's its essence. The MuzikMafia comprises people who are respected in the [Nashville music] community who have a sense of justice and responsibility and who look out for the community. They [the Italian Mafia] took care of the people so that all has [sic] an equal opportunity.

Here, Pino was alluding to the empowering aspect of the Italian Mafia. He extended the metaphor to the Nashville scene because he and many other musicians felt that Music Row was, to a certain degree, corrupt in that major labels worked in concert with radio conglomerates to make money and to create genre archetypes rather than promoting artistic creativity. Pino suggested that the MuzikMafia's purpose was to empower the disenfranchised Nashville musician. I should point out that Pino claimed no ties to the Italian Mafia. However, his position as an Italian immigrant who had been a successful businessman in Florence fueled many humorous discussions among MuzikMafia members.

Talented painter and performance artist Rachel Kice was also with the MuzikMafia from fall 2001. She often appeared with the MuzikMafia on or beside the stage, capturing the atmosphere of each performance on her canvas. Rachel considered the MuzikMafia to be "a very good time; it's a love for music, a love for talent. It's a lot of different people who are outside the mainstream building a house together." Two-Foot Fred, who starred in Big & Rich's video for the song "Save a Horse (Ride a Cowboy)," defined the MuzikMafia as a "close-knit group of friends who get together for the sake of playing music."

After hearing responses from the MuzikMafia's core performing artists, I turned to those who were actively involved in the MuzikMafia but who were not official members. Marc Oswald, who managed Gretchen Wilson, Big & Rich, and Cowboy Troy, described the MuzikMafia to me as a collective group of artists accumulated by the godfathers:

> Some they [the godfathers] have brought in and kicked out. Some they've brought in and they've stayed in. Now it's basically a not-for-profit collective that operates purely for the creative benefit of the people who are in it. Record companies call it "creative process A&R." I call it R&D [research and development]. That's the way they create their music and imaging. The way that they work together, it's more like a laboratory of trying things out—no bounds.

Paul Worley, an award-winning producer and the former Warner Bros. executive who signed Big & Rich to the label in August 2002, described the MuzikMafia as "a tribe." According to Paul, "The MuzikMafia travels as a tribe, with each new successful artist pulling the others along with them."

John's brother Isaac also participated in the MuzikMafia. Isaac was present at many of the Pub of Love shows and made a cameo appearance in Gretchen's video for her hit song "When I Think About Cheatin'." In addition, Isaac co-wrote songs with Chance and other MuzikMafia artists. In regards to defining the MuzikMafia, Isaac emphasized the community's early days:

It started out among people who were tired of doing the grunt work of the music business. Instead, they decided to get together to have fun and to enjoy the music, not having to worry about microphones; to just get together to play each other's stuff. Mafia is a group of friends who are amazing artists in whatever they do who have something to offer: to build the mafia and to make it better; it's the most amazing thing in the world to see. You never know who's going to be there.

Isaac's last sentence is important. During the MuzikMafia's first few years, the godfathers seldom knew who was going to perform at shows either. Cory later told me that sometimes he would assemble a makeshift lineup of any given Tuesday evening's performance that afternoon based on who happened to be in town.

From the above responses, it is clear that the MuzikMafia's organization was ambiguous at best, with individual members having numerous interpretations of their collectivity. However, there were similarities in meaning and connotation, especially with regard to familial relationships among MuzikMafia's members. There was also a purpose involved in coming together. The MuzikMafia was a kind of self-help group that provided benefits to its members. But the membership was not limited to musicians, especially in the case of Rachel, a graphic artist, and Two-Foot Fred, an entrepreneur.

I compared these responses with those of other MuzikMafia insiders to arrive at a composite definition. I understood the MuzikMafia of 2004 to be self-defined as a *distinct musical community that developed from a stylistically diverse Nashville scene into a social collective and commercial enterprise, both of which emphasized musical excellence and promoted musical and artistic diversity*. Most MuzikMafia artists, including the community's four founding godfathers, are aware of this definition, and they agree with my analysis. Unfortunately, this creates only a partial understanding of the MuzikMafia. In order to grasp the essence of the MuzikMafia, one must examine the context of its first public performances as a musical community at the Pub of Love.

At many MuzikMafia performances from 2004 through 2008, the stages were adorned with an array of candles, incense, lava lamps, couches, chairs, and coolers of beer. I asked numerous MuzikMafia musicians the reason

Figure 2.1 The Pub of Love, July 2005.

behind the added props. Most responded with a nostalgic smile, informing me that such was the atmosphere at the Pub of Love.

The Pub of Love, where they first performed as a collective, became a metaphor signifying the heart and soul of the MuzikMafia. Located at 123 12th Avenue North in an underdeveloped area on the fringe of downtown Nashville, the club was in dire need of renovation at the time of MuzikMafia's performances there in 2001 and 2002 (see fig. 2.1). The upstairs performance area was small, barely twelve by twenty feet, and the building was in disrepair, including an upstairs ceiling that was sagging in several places. (The building was abandoned sometime in 2004 and remains a local eyesore.) There was no cover charge, and seldom did the lone bartender check identification.

The MuzikMafia's first performance at the Pub of Love was on Tuesday, October 23, 2001, and included an audience of fewer than fifteen people. The atmosphere was relaxed. The scents of marijuana and incense filled an upstairs room illuminated by lava lamps, candles, several standing lamps, and the streetlights through the windows. Isaac Rich reported to me that, at times, a thick cloud of marijuana smoke hovered above the heads of the twenty or so people at the first few shows. Isaac was present at many of his brother John's performances at the Pub of Love. The nonmatching couches in the upstairs performance area, a single mattress in the back corner, and an array of folding chairs created an ambiance of being at home. The atmosphere was intimate and spontaneous, similar to that of a small gathering of close friends. News of the weekly free jam sessions disseminated throughout the Nashville music scene, and the audiences at the Pub of Love grew considerably.

In the fall of 2001 Isaac Rich was studying agriculture at Austin Peay State University in Clarksville, Tennessee. He drove fifty miles every Tuesday to attend MuzikMafia shows. In a 2005 interview, Isaac told me about that first performance in October 2001:

> John [Rich] had asked me that afternoon to come down and check out the show. Nobody was at the door checking IDs around 9:30 p.m. when I got there. John came down to meet me. We walk upstairs. There was a tiny bar, some Goodwill couches in bad condition, and a full bed in the corner with pillows and blankets. About ten to fifteen people were there, including musicians. There were three barstools, some P.A. speakers, and the ceiling was sagging . . . it was a shithole.

By December, Isaac's regular pilgrimage had grown to several carloads of people who added to the already growing number of local Nashville regulars who attended each show.

James Otto was the only MuzikMafia member who performed at the first show and who was not a godfather. At the time James had only briefly known John who, after seeing an afternoon performance by James at the Country Music Hall of Fame four days prior, had asked him to stop by the Pub of Love the following Tuesday. According to James:

> It was a blast, man; it was crazy. We were passing around a joint around the room. There was a bed in the corner; there were lamps. It feels like you're in somebody's living room. Funny enough, we had [Nashville] Metro council members up there smoking weed, passing stuff around, and other interesting characters. . . . It was such a strange thing that it became so big so fast, because it was such a weird conglomerate of people doing all kinds of different music.

In addition to Rachel, who captured the atmosphere of many performances on canvas while dancing to the music, the "interesting characters" who attended MuzikMafia shows included a juggler named Scott Nery and a guy who promoted himself as Sideshow Benny who Troy later described to me:

He [Sideshow Benny] was the most unique. He would, like, take a nail and hammer it into his nasal cavity. Yeah, it was really weird. He'd blow fire. I mean, you couldn't blow fire in the Pub of Love, but he did at 12th and Porter across the street where there was more room. Sideshow Benny tripped me out. I'd sit there and watch him go *dink, dink, dink, dink, dink,* hammering the nail into his sinuses, and then he'd take that claw hammer and just pull it right out. When he was hammering, you'd hear this hollow sound coming from his sinuses . . . uggh, oh man!

Fans' reactions to early Pub of Love performances also provide insight. Ashley Worley began attending regularly with the third MuzikMafia show. Ashley had heard of the weekly event from a co-worker at Paul Worley Productions. Ashley was working for her father Paul at the time. In August 2002 she introduced John and Kenny to her well-known father, who immediately offered the duo a recording contract with Warner Bros. Ashley later told me about her first experience at the Pub of Love:

We were told that things would start around 10 p.m., but it didn't actually begin until 11 p.m. That was the mystique about it. . . . When I arrived you could hear bongo [actually conga] drums from the street. It was like being in somebody's attic. The second floor of this bar was not made for anything but storage, I guess. From the outside on the street there is this little bitty window, and I think they had Christmas lights hung around it. . . .and you could hear bongo drums; nobody else had started. I thought, "What am I getting ready to walk in to?" It was surreal. . . .

The downstairs was pretty empty, not a lot of people. Everybody was [upstairs] waiting for the music to start. There was about twenty people. It was real real low key. Not necessarily all young, but mostly twenty- to forty-year-olds. And they were all nonconformists. It was definitely a wear-what-you-want-to kind of thing. Everybody was drinking and having fun, and laughing. The whole dynamic was different. People were there because they loved music. John, Kenny, and Jon were performing that night, and Joanna Janét. Pino was there; James was there. I don't remember if Rachel was there. I remember walking in and everybody was talking about some circus freaks there that night, a juggler or something . . . weird.

These testimonies describe a distinct atmosphere in which MuzikMafia performances regularly took place. Kenny often described Pub of Love performances as a "freak show" or "freak parade," and phrases such as "love everybody" that he often emoted there became staples at most MuzikMafia performances thereafter.

Approximately one year after beginning my study of the MuzikMafia, I met Nashville media consultant Mathew Dyer, who had videotaped many Pub of Love performances. Mathew had been following the progress of Kenny's earlier band luvjOi and had recorded many of Kenny's appearances, including those with the MuzikMafia at the Pub of Love. Mathew allowed me to view over eight hours of footage from nine separate performances.

Of particular significance is footage of a MuzikMafia performance that took place at the Pub of Love on May 1, 2002. There is a P.A. system consisting of a speaker on a stand on each side of the musicians' area. Several candles are lit in each of the small room's three windows. The area directly in front of the musicians has two or three rows of people sitting in chairs, couches, or on the floor. Several rows of people are standing shoulder to shoulder in the back near the video camera. Forty-six minutes into the performance, John, Kenny, and Jon begin a song entitled "Limo Larry." After several verses about living and loving for the rest of one's life, Kenny shouts to the crowd, "Why, why? Do you know why I wanna smile?" Following a quick affirmation from the audience, John and Kenny sing the song's chorus which contains the line, "Limo Larry take you anywhere. Where you wanna go? Where do you want to go?" The crowd has obviously heard the song before. Many onlookers sing in unison with the musicians while swaying from side to side.

After several verses, Kenny motions for the musicians to play more quietly, vamping on the chorus. Kenny talks directly to the audience:

So most of you hopefully know Limo Larry by now. And if you don't, I'd like to ask Limo Larry to raise his hand up. There he is standing over there by the steps. The one and only, Limo Larry, six foot three inches of pure love right there. And, of course y'all all know that Limo Larry has a limousine service. We here at the MuzikMafia do not condone drinking and driving. We condone the use of Limo Larry when yo' ass is drunk. You get Limo Larry to take you home. Matter of fact, you get Limo Larry to take you anywhere you need to go.

However, Kenny's address to the crowd contained more than a brief introduction to Limo Larry and his local limousine service. Kenny continues:

'Cause you got a choice in life, by God. It's like yes and no. It's a simple answer. You can go anywhere you want. You can go to Hell, or you can go to Heaven [Kenny shouts]. And I can promise you [that] until I wake up in the gardens of Heaven, no one will *ever* convince me that I cannot get just a little bit higher . . . no one. And I can promise you one other thing, and that is, if you walk far enough in life, you will never ever have to stand in line [pauses for reflection] . . . to take a leak [Kenny laughs].

Kenny frequently delivered religious sermons like this during "Limo Larry" at the Pub of Love, in which both song and personal choice took on deeper meaning. Personal choice implies freedom to aspire to greater things—and, in the case of the MuzikMafia, freedom from stylistic categorization or social mores. According to many who were present at Pub of Love performances, "Limo Larry" was the MuzikMafia's anthem. Versions of the song would sometimes last more than fifteen minutes.

A similar occurrence takes place during John and Kenny's next song that night, "Under the Blue Sky." Following several verses and a chorus, Kenny again brings the band down low. He shares with the audience one of his many secrets to life, "You know, if you never want to have a problem with a cop, become the cop's friend. If you never want a snake to bite you, get to know the snake." This takes on new meaning when applied to the fact that John and Kenny were signed as Big & Rich to Warner Bros. three months later; the duo made friends with the snake or cop, which, in this case, represented the commercial music industry.

In January 2002 the MuzikMafia made the first of several trips to cities outside the Nashville area. On January 18 the community drove to Chicago to perform at the Hideout, a small bar obscurely located near the sanitation headquarters. The Chicago entertainment guide *Centerstage* describes the Hideout as "home to great music, cheap beer and an 'I don't care who you are or what you're wearing, come on in and have a drink' attitude." The venue's clientele resembled that of the Pub of Love. MuzikMafia artists who performed included John, Kenny, Jon, Troy, Brian Barnett, James, and Joanna Janét. The show's format was similar to that of Pub of Love performances in impromptu flow, song choice, informality, and instrumentation.

By the spring of 2002 the Pub of Love was a center of musical activity on Tuesday nights. MuzikMafia shows were attracting hundreds of people, and the venue was often standing room only. At one point, the owners of the Pub of Love removed an upstairs wall to make room for the growing number of MuzikMafia fans. Those who could still not squeeze into the upstairs area crowded onto the staircase, waited patiently downstairs, or congregated outside on the street. According to Jon, "The show started getting super active: a hundred fifty to two hundred people upstairs, downstairs, out the back—all of their [MuzikMafia's] friends."

MuzikMafia performances also attracted well-known figures in the music industry. Isaac remembered a slovenly dressed male in the audience at a show in spring 2002. "He was a homeless-looking fellow. The guy later performed; he'd written a few George Strait songs. John said that the guy was worth about $8 million." The songwriter was Anthony Smith; along with Tony Lane, he had penned the tune "Run," a *Billboard* Number One country hit for George Strait in early 2002. On a separate occasion, Isaac met an individual whom he described as "crazy-looking guy with black ratty hair"; John later told Isaac that the man was Josey Scott of the heavy metal band Saliva. Isaac specifically remembers how Josey played guitar left-handed later that night with John and Kenny. Jon Nicholson remembers seeing well-known singer/songwriter Jim Lauderdale perform at the Pub of Love on occasion. Greg Oswald, who is Senior Vice President of the William Morris Agency in Nashville, frequented shows with his younger brother Marc, who later managed Gretchen, Big & Rich, and Cowboy Troy. The appearance of well-known music industry personnel at MuzikMafia events confirmed MuzikMafia's growing significance in Nashville at the time.

By summer 2002 it was evident that the MuzikMafia was a significant part of the Nashville music scene. The Pub of Love could no longer contain the large crowds that came each Tuesday night. Isaac later recalled: "People were trying to sneak in, but the whole place was packed; people were hanging off the fence in the back; the police often came to control the crowds. . . . That's when Pub of Love starting checking IDs: when the crowds started showing up." The Pub of Love was incapable of accommodating the MuzikMafia and its rapidly growing fanbase, and for several weeks in summer 2002 they performed outside in the adjacent parking lot.

The MuzikMafia's popularity peaked in July 2002 when John and Kenny were selected to participate in the MasterCard Priceless Edge Sweepstakes. The nationwide contest received entries from over fifteen thousand college students who were interested in a career in the music business. The top fifty finalists were invited to Nashville for six weeks during June and July to work with leaders in the music industry. The program's guest speakers included recording artist Alanis Morissette, Clear Channel Entertainment CEO Brian O'Connell, Spring Communications CEO John Rubey, producer Jack Clements, and entertainment lawyer Henry Root. John and Kenny were invited to provide songwriting workshops and studio demonstrations for the finalists. Included in the students' six-week program were several excursions to Tuesday night shows at the Pub of Love. The sweepstakes generated considerable media exposure for John, Kenny, and the rest of the MuzikMafia.

The MuzikMafia's popularity resulted in considerable tension between the community's members and the owners of the Pub of Love. The godfathers insisted on not charging admission to its weekly shows but also did not receive any portion of the large profits generated from alcohol sales each Tuesday night. Cory later reported that other Nashville bars wanted "in on the action" and that they offered the MuzikMafia money to relocate. Given MuzikMafia's financial need and the fact that they had outgrown the Pub of Love, the MuzikMafia accepted an offer from Jason Sheer, who owned the Tin Roof, a small restaurant/bar near the Demonbreun Street Roundabout. The MuzikMafia performed there Tuesday nights from August 2002 to March 2003.

The Pub of Love is where the MuzikMafia created its self-described freak show that highlighted social and musical diversity, a place where artists and listeners could be themselves. No MuzikMafia member as of 2009 had acknowledged the Pub of Love's commercial significance, largely because the community's performers were not paid for performances there. However, the MuzikMafia godfathers did organize a show for public consumption at the Pub of Love. Only towards the end of the MuzikMafia's tenure there, amidst a rapidly growing Nashville fanbase, did the godfathers exploit their celebrity with a move to the Demonbreun Street Roundabout. In creating a show for public consumption, the godfathers assumed that there was a commercial market for music that crossed musical boundaries.

The early performances at the Pub of Love were significant in many ways. First, the location symbolized the supposed marginality of the MuzikMafia: physically and figuratively distant from the commercial country scene on Lower Broadway, despite the club's proximity to downtown Nashville.

Second, the time, day, and diversity of Pub of Love performances reveal the MuzikMafia's intent to attract specific audiences. MuzikMafia performances there were intentionally held late each Tuesday evening because Tuesdays were, according to the godfathers, "the worst night of the week." The godfathers wished to avoid the club crowd that frequented weekend Nashville locales, focusing instead on those individuals who were dedicated to an intensely intimate and social musical experience at an inconvenient time and day of the week. Performances were free and featured diverse musical acts, spoken-word artists, a juggler, a fire-breather, and a painter. Everything was acoustic and usually performed on guitar accompanied by a percussionist who played a set of older conga drums with drumsticks.

Third, it was at the Pub of Love where the godfathers first collectively promoted their own version of artistic diversity. The various musical genres at MuzikMafia performances, the message of inclusivity, and the interconnectedness among artists and fans resonated throughout Nashville. The MuzikMafia's numerous mottos such as "Music without Prejudice," "Love Everybody," and "Freak Parade" were all pillars of the Pub of Love experience.

Fourth, performances at the Pub of Love rapidly developed into a weekly ritual that the MuzikMafia used to expand its community of artists and fans. The atmosphere was generally consistent from week to week with slight variations, comprising similar songs by regular musicians for devoted audience members. Furthermore, MuzikMafia musicians and audience members rarely remembered dates or times of specific Pub of Love performances—probably due to drug and alcohol use—but rather described their experiences to me in broad terms of positive feelings or emotions associated with the locale.

Fifth, Pub of Love audience members engaged the musicians and each another on numerous levels. Regardless of age, ethnicity, sex, financial status, social ranking, or belief system, everyone was welcome at MuzikMafia performances. Tuesday shows were an opportunity for MuzikMafia musicians and audience members to be themselves, rather than representations of society's norms. According to Cory, the godfathers wanted to create a nonterritorial and noncompetitive environment in which people of various backgrounds could assemble to celebrate their commonality and diversity. In the process, the musicians and attendees formed a deep social bond with one another.

MuzikMafia artists and audience members repeatedly described to me their intense feelings of inter-connectedness at Tuesday performances. Audience members often sat shoulder to shoulder, swaying from side to side, not unlike musical events among 1960s counterculture groups in San Francisco or Andy Warhol's artistic experiments at the Factory in New York City. Audience members at the Pub of Love interacted with the musicians in the form of singalongs, and musicians often adapted song texts to include any given current context. The result was a Pub of Love experience that was communal and an important part of the MuzikMafia "family."

Chapter Three

AUGUST 2002 TO MARCH 2004
Growing Popularity in Nashville and Beyond

The Tin Roof was the first restaurant/bar to open along the Demonbreun Street Roundabout. Owner Jason Sheer had modeled the establishment after its counterpart the Tin Roof Cantina, which he had opened six years prior in the trendy Buckhead section of Atlanta. The Nashville Tin Roof attracted large crowds from its opening day on February 11, 2002, featuring music of varying kinds, little of which was country. The clientele who frequented the Tin Roof and later restaurants/bars on Demonbreun Street consisted of an eclectic mix of Music Row label people, interns, songwriters, artists, students from Vanderbilt and Belmont universities, and young professionals.

Figure 3.1 The Tin Roof, July 2005.

The Tin Roof is relatively small (see fig. 3.1). The restaurant/bar is about 3,300 square feet and has an indoor legal capacity of 200. During any given performance the Tin Roof can accommodate in excess of 500 people due to its sizable stage area outside the building's rear entrance.

At the time that MuzikMafia started at the Tin Roof in August 2002, the restaurant/bar was already a center of musical activity. The Tin Roof was popular among Nashville musicians because Sheer consistently paid more for musical talent than any other bar in town. The Tin Roof also became a trendy locale that attracted diverse audiences. Some patrons frequented the establishment to hear rock and pop music. Others came to be around the cultural elite of the music industry.

Sheer had heard of the MuzikMafia through his bartender Regis. Following a meeting with Kenny that Regis arranged, Sheer invited the MuzikMafia to take over the Tuesday night slot indefinitely. There was no contract other than the fact that the godfathers would receive $600 or twenty percent of the house gross for each evening.

The MuzikMafia's audience demographic changed drastically. Damien Horne, whose association with MuzikMafia began at the Tin Roof in August 2002, later remembered the large number of college students who attended weekly shows. The new popularity of John and Kenny as major label recording artists combined with the new, weekly performance venue near Music Row and Vanderbilt and Belmont universities resulted in a decidedly different audience demographic from that of the Pub of Love. According to John's brother Isaac, "The Tin Roof was a regular college crowd from Belmont and Vanderbilt; the [Muzik]Mafia show didn't translate well; some listened to the show, some met other people, drank. It was more social; Gretchen is in the picture, record deals, popularity, and so on."

Saxophonist Max Abrams hated the Tin Roof because "the sound was funky," and as a result, he did not perform there as often as he had at the Pub of Love. James and Gretchen also performed infrequently at the Tin Roof. James had signed his record deal with Mercury in early 2002. Gretchen divided her time between working as a demo singer and bartender, raising her daughter, and auditioning for various Music Row labels for a record deal of her own. As a result, the MuzikMafia's weekly performance included only John, Kenny, Jon, and Pino, with numerous but inconsistent appearances by other MuzikMafia artists.

For the first time, the MuzikMafia received payment for Tuesday performances. However, Sheer stated to me in 2006 that MuzikMafia performances were not much different from other songwriter nights at Nashville clubs: "MuzikMafia always thinks that they are on the cutting edge, like 'Hey, look at us.' But actually, people had been doing that for years in Nashville. It's all marketing. They're great marketing guys. They're great business guys, and they're very talented."

The defining feature of performances at the Tin Roof was the fact that the MuzikMafia had become a commodity in the form of a clearly defined show with a beginning, middle, and end. The godfathers had transformed a once disorganized group of Pub of Love entertainers into a structured show for public consumption, influential exposure, and economic gain.

The MuzikMafia's tenure at the Tin Roof was problematic at best. According to Sheer, the friction was with John almost from the beginning: "John Rich would take twenty-five shots of Patrón tequila and just give them to the customers. John never got the concept that people who drank for free diminished the house gross. That's when all the friction started. But he was often too drunk to discuss the matter at the end of the night. I remember having a few meetings with the guys [MuzikMafia] to discuss the problem." John's solution was to host a series of "pre-parties" at his apartment each Tuesday evening. While there, MuzikMafia friends and fans would drink together before heading over the Tin Roof. According to the bartender, the result would often be a full house of 400 patrons, many of whom ordered only glasses of water.

John's situation with the owner only worsened. Sheer reports that John was sometimes so drunk that he could not finish an evening's set. In addition, John was well known for turning tables over and throwing chairs during his breaks. John's drunkenness, extensive bar tab, and his belligerence resulted in Sheer often having to deduct as much as $200 from the MuzikMafia's payment to cover damages and profit loss. As of 2007 John maintained that Sheer still owed the MuzikMafia as much as $2,000 for disputed payment deductions.

The MuzikMafia's eventual departure from the Tin Roof was the result of months of problems, including two specific incidents that occurred in early 2003. Sheer described to me the first incident as follows:

> John was so absolutely hammered and so pissed off about something
> . . . Bobby was the manager here at one time, and Chris was a bouncer,
> a big huge dude. And John Rich threatened that he was gonna kill
> them. He was threatening to go to his truck and that he was going to
> shoot them, and kill them. He then got in his truck and drove it around
> to the front of the building. They [Bobby and Chris] locked the doors.
> They were scared and hid under a table. They thought that John was a
> freaking nutbag, and he's wasted, and he's gonna kill them. John was
> pushing with his truck up against the front of the bar's glass doors,
> pretending that he was going to bust through. Finally, he just drove off.

The second incident involved the pilot for a television reality show entitled *Under the Tin Roof* that was filmed in Sheer's restaurant/bar. MuzikMafia members appeared in the pilot's first few episodes because they frequently patronized the Tin Roof during filming. John's appearance in the pilot caused much tension. According to Sheer:

> John Rich is on there [the pilot] going nutty. . . . He always wanted to
> be the center of attention . . . He was inside one time when he pulled

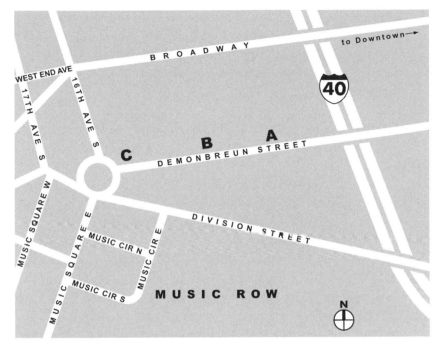

Figure 3.2 Map of Demonbreun Street Roundabout Area and club locations as of February 2006. A = The Tin Roof; B = Two Doors Down; C = Dan McGuinness Pub.

Figure 3.3 Two Doors Down, July 2005.

his pants down to his knees. A few minutes later, he went outside and was doing pretty rude things to a light pole. All of it was on tape. Marc Oswald later tried to keep the footage off the series, but I told him about all the signs and disclaimers stating that video cameras would be taping.

The above incidents contributed to Sheer's already growing dissatisfaction with the MuzikMafia and eventually led to his decision to fire them in March 2003.

The MuzikMafia performed single shows at various clubs around town in March 2003 before beginning a brief stint at Two Doors Down the following month. Located at 1524 Demonbreun Street near the Tin Roof, Two Doors Down opened in early April 2003, and the MuzikMafia was its first regular Tuesday act. The choice of venue was odd, considering the fact that Two Doors Down was a small sports bar, did not have a significant performance stage for musicians, and was smaller than the Tin Roof. Sheer described the performance atmosphere at Two Doors Down as "A total joke for musicians. The guys [MuzikMafia] had to compete with all of the television screens hanging over their heads." The MuzikMafia performed at Two Doors Down for only four weeks. Sheer reported that the manager of Two Doors Down experienced similar difficulties with the MuzikMafia's extensive bar tab.

MuzikMafia stopped its regular Tuesday performances altogether in early May 2003 due to ongoing problems with the management at the Tin Roof and Two Doors Down, respectively. In addition, John and Kenny were spending much of their time in the studio, recording songs for *Horse of a Different Color*. They had signed a contract with Warner Bros. in August 2002. By summer 2003 the two were engulfed in the album's promotional campaign as well as a video production for the album's first single, "Wild West Show," scheduled for release that December.

Gretchen Wilson realized in June 2003 her dream of securing a record deal with a major label. She had been working closely with the godfathers throughout the summer preparing numerous promotional materials. The now historic phone call from John Grady, President of Sony Music in Nashville, came on Thursday, June 12, 2003. Grady offered Gretchen her record deal over the phone while she, Cory, John, and Kenny were on location shooting her electronic press kit (EPK). Cory clearly remembered the date because Katie Darnell, the brain cancer patient that John and Kenny had befriended at Vanderbilt Children's Hospital, died in Princeton, Kentucky, the same day.

Other MuzikMafia members were advancing their careers through a variety of activities. Jon Nicholson was experiencing relative success with his band Stroller. He had written many of the songs that appeared on the group's self-titled debut album in 2002, earning him a respectable place among Nashville's singer/songwriters. Stroller's second album *Six Inches off the Ground* contained the single "Six Inches" that entered the rotation of approximately 200 college rock radio stations across the country in 2003. As a result, Jon was frequently out of town and unable to attend Muzik-Mafia shows. Stroller disbanded in fall 2003, and Jon spent several months assembling a backup group for a future solo career.

James Otto was also receiving significant exposure in and outside of Nashville. By late 2002 he had finished recording his debut album *Days of Our Lives,* which Mercury scheduled for release in early 2004. James had been invited to appear on the Grand Ole Opry several times in summer 2003. Most importantly, Mercury had arranged for James to open up for Shania Twain on every United States performance of her *Up!* 2003–2004 world tour. The first of those took place in Pittsburgh on September 29, 2003.

James's career milestones were bittersweet despite the widespread exposure that they afforded him. The album's first single "The Ball" had been released in late 2002 and went no higher than Number Forty-Five on the *Billboard* country music chart. The album's second single "Days of Our Lives" peaked at Number Thirty-Three in 2003. By summer 2005, *Days of Our Lives* had sold fewer than fifteen thousand copies, a flop by Music Row standards. As a result, James's music received little radio airplay. James's frustration was exacerbated by the fact that Mercury had not provided enough tour support to have a full band to accompany him on the Shania Twain tour. James paid for a drummer and a guitarist himself. According to James, "I think that it was Mercury's ditch effort." James was dropped by Mercury in January 2005 while he was recording his second album.

MuzikMafia's eight-month break from May through December 2003 provided members with time to develop as artists and as entertainers. John, Kenny, and Gretchen were well on their way to becoming significant

Figure 3.4 Dan McGuinness Pub, July 2005.

in the commercial country music industry. James and Jon were learning much from their respective successes and failures as recording artists on the national music scene. Also that year Max, Rachel, and Pino cultivated through Circvs Maximvs—a local Nashville entertainment phenomenon that I will discuss later—their interests in combining music, dance, poetry, and the visual arts.

The MuzikMafia returned to the Demonbreun Street Roundabout in January 2004, this time performing at Dan McGuinness Pub (see Fig. 3.4), which opened at 1538 Demonbreun Street (directly across from the Roundabout at the top of the hill) on Christmas Eve 2003. Owner Quinn O'Sullivan had experienced considerable success with an Irish pub by the same name he had founded in Memphis in 2001. The MuzikMafia performed there each Tuesday night from January 6 through March 2, 2004.

O'Sullivan had heard of the MuzikMafia through a mutual friend named Scotty, the MuzikMafia's newly hired sound engineer. According to Dan McGuinness Pub manager Brad Taylor, "They [the MuzikMafia] approached us because we were new in town and this was a hot area to play in." O'Sullivan paid the godfathers $200 total for each Tuesday performance.

MuzikMafia performances at Dan McGuinness Pub contained significant changes from the community's earlier shows at the Tin Roof and Two Doors Down. First, the growing popularity of John, Kenny, and Gretchen attracted even larger crowds than before. In addition to standing room only for the pub's legal capacity of 200 people, there was sometimes a line outside that extended almost halfway down the quarter-mile hill toward Interstate 40. Second, Jon Nicholson had returned with his new band that included D. D. Holt on drums and Jerry Navarro on bass. Mercury recording artist Shannon Lawson also started performing with the MuzikMafia during its tenure at Dan McGuinness Pub. Third, Scotty, their new sound engineer, brought a professional-grade sound system each week to MuzikMafia performances.

MuzikMafia shows began attracting more well-known entertainers. A frequent guest artist was Peter Wolf, who had fronted popular rock group the J. Geils Band from 1967 to 1982. Kid Rock also attended MuzikMafia shows at Dan McGuinness Pub on occasion. John had met Kid Rock at John's thirtieth birthday party on January 7, 2004, which Martina McBride and DMC from Run-DMC also attended. Although Kid Rock attended several MuzikMafia shows at Dan McGuinness Pub, the manager recalled him performing only once. Kid Rock favorably described the MuzikMafia in a May 2004 interview with Calvin Gilbert of CMT: "It's just so refreshing to see people who play music and write music and have a passion about it. And to want to form a clique—a Mafia, if you will—of other people who love music and love to play music. And that's the sole purpose of it. Not for anything else."

Kid Rock invited the MuzikMafia to perform with him on several tour dates in February and March. The first took place on Thursday, February 12, in Chattanooga, Tennessee. During the show Kid Rock encouraged Gretchen to join him on stage to sing a duet entitled "Picture" that he had recorded with Sheryl Crow. The rest of the MuzikMafia performed with Kid Rock after the show at a local club. Similar MuzikMafia performances with Kid Rock took place in Memphis on March 6 and in Detroit on March 20 that year.

The MuzikMafia left Dan McGuinness Pub in early March 2004 for several reasons. There was another financial dispute: The godfathers had requested that their sound engineer Scotty receive payment for his services independent of any monies that were paid to the MuzikMafia for performances. Taylor told me that the requested amount for an additional $700–800 was unreasonable when weighed against the house gross for Tuesday shows. The dispute was never resolved. Second, the performances with Kid Rock in Memphis and Detroit kept MuzikMafia from its weekly performances in Nashville. The MuzikMafia's last show at Dan McGuinness Pub took place on March 2, 2004.

The MuzikMafia's first significant access to Music Row came only a few weeks after relocating to the Tin Roof in early August 2002. It was during this time when John and Kenny, as Big & Rich, received their record deal with Warner Bros.

Having left Sony Music Publishing in July 2002 to accept a position as Chief Creative Officer at Warner Bros., Paul Worley met with John and Kenny together for the first time in early August. Paul had left Sony in 1999 to sign and produce new writers through a joint publishing venture with Sony Music Publishing. By the time he joined Warner Bros., Paul had produced such well-known Nashville artists as Martina McBride, Sara Evans, the Dixie Chicks, BR549, Cyndi Thomson, and Carolyn Dawn Johnson.

Paul had known Kenny since he arrived in Nashville in 1994, but had lost touch during Kenny's tenure with luvjOi. Paul had known John since he had first seen Lonestar perform in 1994 at Opryland. Paul had attempted to sign Lonestar to Sony, but the group eventually decided to record with RCA. The August 2002 meeting between Paul, John, and Kenny had been arranged by Paul's daughter Ashley, who had been a MuzikMafia fan from the Pub of Love. In a 2005 interview, Paul described the meeting to me:

> That Wednesday John and Kenny came dragging in—it was a Wednesday midday after a Tuesday night [Muzik]Mafia, and they sat down in their street clothes. Ashley [had] told John and Kenny that they were just going to play [pitch] some songs. Martina had already cut "[She's a] Butterfly" so they [John and Kenny] thought that it would be an opportunity to have some cuts. "Holy Water" was *the* one—the third song they played. After "Holy Water" I slammed my hand down on the desk and said, 'Guys, I want to do this.' Kenny asked 'You want to do what?' I [Paul] want to sign you guys; I want to give you a record deal.

Their eyes got as big as saucers. I asked them, 'Why are you surprised? Ain't that why you're here?' John and Kenny replied, 'No, we're just here to pitch some songs.'

John and Kenny thought that they had been invited to pitch some of their songs to Paul for other Warner Bros. artists. According to Paul, his interests at the August 2002 meeting lay solely with Big & Rich as the next big act for Warner Bros., not as staff songwriters and certainly not as members of the MuzikMafia. Paul did not attend a MuzikMafia Tuesday night show until mid-2004 at the Mercy Lounge. Warner Bros. released Big & Rich's debut album, *Horse of a Different Color*, in May 2004.

The MuzikMafia's transformation into a calculated commercial venture was evident by the time the community began performances at Dan McGuinness Pub in January 2004. The MuzikMafia had hired its own professional sound engineer, and the community had established its reputation as a distinctive musical movement around the Nashville scene and beyond. According to Dan McGuinness Pub manager Brad Taylor in a 2006 interview, "They [the MuzikMafia] pretty much ran their own show. They were doing it as showcases for promotions and stuff. They really didn't care about the money." He continued: "It became more of a packaged show. There was a production, and they kind of went through the same thing every week and tried to improve on that. You know, they're professionals. They came in and had everything planned out. It could have been Bedlam, because sometimes they had eight people playing on stage at one time. It was organized chaos."

It is doubtful that money was of no concern to the MuzikMafia, especially given the fact that money was a contributing factor for the community's departure from the Pub of Love, the Tin Roof, and Dan McGuinness Pub. On the other hand, Dan McGuinness Pub was optimal for professional exposure, especially given the club's location adjacent to Music Row.

Taylor's phrase "organized chaos" is significant. The MuzikMafia's performances at the Pub of Love could easily be described as chaotic. Sometimes during the end of the show, all musicians could be found onstage participating in a collective jam session. Despite the chaotic appearance of jam sessions at MuzikMafia shows, the community's performances at the Tin Roof, Two Doors Down, and Dan McGuinness Pub contained numerous elements of organization. Here, "organized chaos" reflects the inherent dichotomy of the MuzikMafia's calculated inroads into the commercial mainstream and the community's close ties to its earlier, free-spirited performances at the Pub of Love.

The fact that the MuzikMafia organized and staged its shows became even more evident in performances outside of Nashville. The MuzikMafia first incorporated the theme to the hit movie trilogy *The Godfather* while on stage with Kid Rock in Memphis on March 6. Max played the movie's theme song on saxophone in order to create suspense before the MuzikMafia began its show. Max told me in 2005:

> That [the playing of the movie theme song] first came across as a joke. It was part of the evolution of the staging of the MuzikMafia. I had a wireless mic. You want to build drama for that kind of entrance. There were these three godfathers on stage. How do you make these guys more *something*? How do you make it, not just three guys walking on stage and playing? So the house music came down, and this sax player starts playing *The Godfather* theme, which immediately creates contrast, suspense, and tension. It rewires people's brains a little bit. People loved it. I did that in Detroit, too.

This marks a significant milestone in how the MuzikMafia became the creature of its own image. What once had been a metaphor loosely applied to a community of disenfranchised musicians had evolved into a core component of the MuzikMafia's collective identity.

One cannot discount the significant role that Warner Bros. played in the growth and development of the MuzikMafia. Paul Worley offered John and Kenny their joint record deal with Warner Bros. in August 2002. That event marked the beginning of the MuzikMafia's successful relationship with Music Row, which eventually led to Gretchen's record deal with Sony/Epic, Troy's record deal with Raybaw, Jon's record deal with Warner Bros., and so on. However, it was no coincidence that Warner Bros. was the first major label on Music Row to take a chance on the MuzikMafia.

Paul was in charge of finding talented artists and developing them and their sound into a commercially viable product. He graduated from Vanderbilt University in 1972 with a degree in philosophy. His early experiences on Music Row had been that of a studio guitarist, and he recorded with artists such as George Jones, George Strait, Reba McEntire, Conway Twitty, and Hank Williams Jr. Paul later became a music producer and song publisher. He was involved in the development of artists and repertoire (A&R) for Sony Music Publishing, Sony Music–Nashville, and his own publishing company. He had signed and produced acts for Sony such as Montgomery Gentry, Martina McBride, Sara Evans, the Dixie Chicks, BR549, and Cyndi Thomson. He had arrived at Warner Bros. in August 2002, and Big & Rich were the first act he signed to the label.

In a 2004 interview, Paul told me that he identifies first and foremost with the artists with whom he works. His background as a studio musician has contributed much to his understanding of the music business and his success as an executive on Music Row. He described to me his enthusiasm for Big & Rich, who emerged during a transitional period for commercial country. According to Paul, "Country music was in the doldrums and dying. There was no passion anywhere for any music anywhere. Those of us who hadn't fled were really the ones who never came here [to Music Row] in the first place and had nowhere to go."

Max told me that Paul's attitude was similar to that of many MuzikMafia members:

> He understood enough about the system to change it to the way he wants it. He's a musician himself. He was bored; and he sincerely wanted to make music that was innovative and popular. And he found it in Big & Rich and the rest of the MuzikMafia. Paul really loves MuzikMafia. He shows up at stuff that's really not that important. He is genuinely appreciative and grateful which is rare for someone in his position. He is actually part of it [MuzikMafia] rather than someone trying to sell it.

As a result, the godfathers considered Paul an honorary member of the MuzikMafia.

At the time, Jules Wortman held the title of Senior Vice-President of Publicity and Artist Development at Warner Bros. She had received her B.A. in Mass Communications from East Tennessee State University in 1989. She had spent her undergraduate summers interning in Nashville for a promotion company called Sound 70, artist management firm Network Inc., and local performance venue Starwood Amphitheater. Since the early 1990s Jules had served as vice-president of publicity at several Music Row labels, including Atlantic, Sony, and MCA.

Jules arrived at Warner Bros. on the same day as Paul in August 2002. She told me in 2005 that Warner Bros. had hired her and Paul to "change the dynamic of the company." Jules's penchant for going against the mainstream was an asset for Warner Bros. She continued:

> I love to think outside the lines. I'm a total out-of-bounds thinker. That's my personality. I have always been an active, involved person. I've always been a free spirit. I have never really followed the rules, but I was a rule-maker. I was always a gregarious person. I was the one in school that would make up a lot of outfits and wear funky clothes. I always told it like it was. I had my own way of thinking. If you sit there in a box and try to follow the world's rules, you're never going to see what the world's all about.

Jules was immediately attracted to Big & Rich's potential, primarily because the duo's music contrasted greatly with material being produced at the time by the commercial music industry. She describes the responses from more conservative labels on Music Row: "Other arenas on Music Row were trying to kill it [Big & Rich's music], because they were jealous, and wondering 'How can we make that happen for our label?' But then there were people saying, 'Go, go go! This is awesome! Wow! Outside the box is working again.' And this is *way* outside the box."

Paul and Jules were partially responsible for Big & Rich's initial success within the commercial mainstream. It is unlikely that the duo would have attracted the attention of the more conservative labels on Music Row such as Mercury, Sony, or Atlantic. Paul and Jules allowed Big & Rich to be themselves, for the most part, while marketing the duo's uniqueness to the general public as a breath of fresh air for commercial country music.

Chapter Four

APRIL THROUGH DECEMBER 2004

The MuzikMafia Takes the National Stage

Country Music Television (CMT) declared on December 18 during its show *20 Biggest Hits of 2004* that the MuzikMafia was the Number One hit of the year. The rapid growth in popularity of the MuzikMafia was the result of its two breakout acts, Big & Rich and Gretchen Wilson, who celebrated combined record sales of approximately five million units from May through December 2004. Big & Rich and Gretchen toured throughout the summer, respectively, with some of commercial country's best known acts. By year's end Big & Rich and Gretchen were co-headlining their own national tour sponsored by Chevrolet.

By March 2004 the MuzikMafia's fanbase had grown considerably as a result of the community's ties to Kid

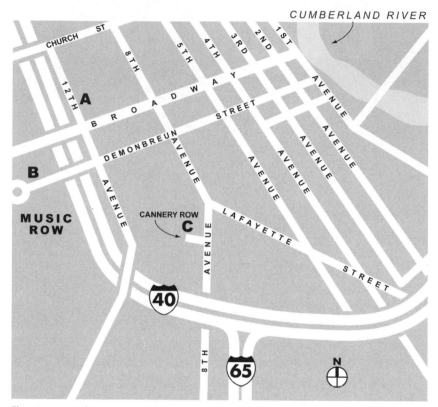

Figure 4.1 Map of MuzikMafia locales in Nashville. A = Pub of Love; B = Demonbreun Street Roundabout; C = Mercy Lounge/Cannery Row Ballroom; D = Bluesboro.

Rock and Music Row. Eager to capitalize on their growing fame, the godfathers looked around Nashville for a venue that was large enough to accommodate audiences in excess of five hundred people but small enough to re-create the intimacy of the Pub of Love, and that had sufficient sound equipment for the MuzikMafia's audio needs. The community found the Mercy Lounge located at One Cannery Row in the SoBro area of downtown Nashville.

Historic Cannery Row (see fig. 4.2) in downtown Nashville is surrounded by dimly lit streets, aging buildings in need of repair, and a few locally owned businesses. The building itself was erected as a flour mill in 1863. Cannery Row earned its name when the Dale Food Company bought the property in 1957 and began processing food, eventually opening a restaurant called the

Figure 4.2 Cannery Row, downtown Nashville, July 2005.

Figure 4.3 The Mercy Lounge at Cannery Row, July 2005.

Cannery in the early 1970s. During the 1970s the building housed a country music theater that eventually included other genres of music in the 1980s. As of 2009, Cannery Row housed the Mercy Lounge (see fig. 4.3), where the MuzikMafia regularly performed for approximately four months in 2004, in addition to the larger Cannery Row Ballroom.

By 2004 the Mercy Lounge had not been considered a country bar for almost two decades. In fact, it is more than five blocks removed from Nashville's country music scene in the District. The Mercy Lounge's musical history includes performances by numerous well-known acts such as R.E.M., Iggy Pop, Jimmy Cliff, Midnight Oil, Bret Michaels, George Clinton, Robert Cray, Yo La Tengo, and Lenny Kravitz.

The MuzikMafia's Tuesday performances at the Mercy Lounge began the evening of April 6, 2004. That afternoon Cory contacted the co-owner of the Mercy Lounge, Chark Kinsolving, who immediately invited the MuzikMafia to play. Tuesday was the least patronized day of the week for the Mercy Lounge. Kinsolving's business partner Todd Ohlhauser, who was unfamiliar with the MuzikMafia, admitted to me that he was surprised by how many people came, the size of the crowd, and how late the audience stayed, especially on a weeknight.

The Mercy Lounge was an optimal location for the MuzikMafia for several reasons. First and foremost, the bar was separate from the commercial country scene along lower Broadway. It is also distant from the Demonbreun Street Roundabout area, resulting in fewer college students and industry personnel at shows.

The sound system was adequate for the MuzikMafia's needs. According to Todd Ohlhauser, the Mercy Lounge's owners had been renting a "fine but somewhat outdated" professional sound system from the Exit/In, a well-known club in the Rock Block area of Nashville near Vanderbilt University, but in midsummer purchased a new, professional-grade system that included an Allen & Heath ML3000 console and a 2 Drive Rack 260 processor. And the venue had its own sound engineer who did not have to be paid separately by the MuzikMafia.

Ohlhauser and Kinsolving offered the MuzikMafia payment comparable to what they had received at the Tin Roof and Dan McGuinness Pub. Also, the Mercy Lounge could accommodate over 550 people and, should the MuzikMafia decide to expand, in the same building was the much larger Cannery Row Ballroom with a maximum capacity of 1,100 people.

The MuzikMafia's popularity grew significantly during its tenure at the Mercy Lounge. In early summer Warner Bros. and Sony released debut albums by Big & Rich and Gretchen; John, Kenny, and Gretchen's national recognition trickled down to the MuzikMafia. By July of that year, Tuesday night shows at the Mercy Lounge were regularly attracting the national media, including camera crews from CMT. However, their success kept Big & Rich and Gretchen from performing regularly at Tuesday shows. Godfather Jon Nicholson served as emcee for most MuzikMafia shows that summer. Faced with the realization that other MuzikMafia members would probably pursue solo careers as Big & Rich and Gretchen had, the MuzikMafia sanctioned the creation of a sub-community known as the Mafia Mizfits intended to resupply the MuzikMafia with local talent.

The Mafia Mizfits were the brainchild of Daniel Bird, known as Alaska Dan by most of his friends. Dan created the Mafia Mizfits to help develop local artists who were talented but perhaps not yet on the level of regular MuzikMafia members.

Dan received his nickname from Kenny, whom he first met in January 2004. Dan told me that he had flown to Nashville from Alaska to visit a girlfriend. The two bumped into Kenny at Dan McGuinness Pub on a Thursday evening and struck up a conversation. Dan was unaware of the MuzikMafia but intrigued with Kenny, who invited Dan back to the pub the next day to meet John, Cory, and Jon. Following an informal conversation about each other's respective life philosophies, Dan asked the godfathers if he and his girlfriend could perform at MuzikMafia the following Tuesday. Kenny's response was, "Come Tuesday night and be ready to play . . . and hey, Alaska, just don't suck." Dan and his girlfriend performed the following Tuesday as expected, and Dan returned to Alaska the following Wednesday. Inspired by his experience with the MuzikMafia, he sold all his possessions within a few weeks and returned to Nashville to set up permanent residence.

Kenny allowed Dan to set up a tent on his property just north of Nashville in Whites Creek for a few weeks. Dan did various odd jobs to assist Kenny and the MuzikMafia such as loading equipment, hanging the title banner at performances, hauling drums, and driving to gigs. According to Dan, "The [Muzik]Mafia put up with me because I wasn't going away." Dan eventually moved off of Kenny's property into his own house near the Fontanel estate in Whites Creek and began working for Big & Rich's manager Marc Oswald.

Dan envisioned the Mafia Mizfits while driving away from the CMT 2004 Flame Worthy Video Music Awards on April 21, 2004. He and Christiev Carothers, Kenny's future wife, were out purchasing beer for John and Kenny, who had attended the live broadcast. Dan started brainstorming with Christiev about the possibility of starting a community of amateur musicians that would grow and develop under the MuzikMafia's guidance. Dan wanted to provide a creative outlet for talented artists from diverse styles who might eventually become regular members of the MuzikMafia. Christiev suggested the name Mafia Mizfits. Dan shared his idea with the godfathers, who subsequently agreed to oversee the new venture.

The Mafia Mizfits first performed on April 30, 2004, at the Star Café, a local general store in Whites Creek. Dan modeled each show after those of the MuzikMafia from its Pub of Love days. Dan began each performance with a set of songs either on his guitar or harmonica, followed by a series of sets featuring Mafia Mizfits artists. Each evening featured diverse artistic performances in an informal atmosphere.

The Mizfits attracted artists of varying backgrounds but eventually settled into a core membership of what Dan referred to as the "Grape Eight." Dan identified mostly with rock music. Jennifer Bain, commonly known as SWJ, an acronym for Spoken Word Jen, performed spoken word. Damien Horne, known as Mista D., specialized in rock and pop. Bridget Tatum was a singer/songwriter of commercial country music. John Philips was also a singer/songwriter, best-known for his song "Saved" that appeared on Big & Rich's album *Horse of a Different Color*. Other core members of the Mafia Mizfits included Rick Daniel, Chad Biggs, and Keaton Allen.

The Mafia Mizfits were significant because of their close ties to the MuzikMafia and its earlier performances at the Pub of Love. Max, who frequently attended Mafia Mizfits shows, told me in 2004 that Mafia Mizfits jam sessions were similar to those of the MuzikMafia that he remembered from the Pub of Love.

The Mafia Mizfits often performed twice a week: Friday evenings at the Star Café in Whites Creek and Sundays at a club called the Sutler, on 8th Avenue South about a mile south of Cannery Row. In September 2004 the community moved its Sunday shows to Bluesboro on Second Avenue downtown, where the MuzikMafia was then performing on Tuesday nights.

Unfortunately, the Mafia Mizfits experienced only marginal success in the shadow of the MuzikMafia, and ceased regular performances in October 2004. Several Mafia Mizfits members, namely Dan, John, and Damien, received publishing deals. The godfathers invited Damien to become a core member of the MuzikMafia in January 2005. SWJ became Cory Gierman's personal assistant, a position that regularly kept her out of town on tours with Big & Rich and Gretchen; she too later became a full-fledged Muzik-Mafia member. In addition, SWJ was director of the Mafia Soldiers, a web-based MuzikMafia fan club. Dan accepted a job as one of Marc Oswald's personal assistants; his duties included driving Marc's tour bus and coordinating entertainment for tour participants.

Gretchen's performance of "Redneck Woman" at the Country Radio Seminar (CRS) in early March 2004 in Nashville marked the beginning of her national success. The response from radio programmers at the conference was overwhelmingly positive, prompting Sony to release the single "Redneck Woman" to radio on March 5. The single reached Number One on *Billboard*'s Country Singles chart in late May, approximately twelve weeks after its release, faster than any song since Billy Ray Cyrus's 1992 hit "Achy Breaky Heart." "Redneck Woman" also became the first Number One hit for any female country artist in two years. The song remained at Number One for six weeks, longer than any other debut female country artist in forty years.

Gretchen's album *Here for the Party* was likewise a hit. Gretchen's debut at the Country Radio Seminar in March prompted Sony to move the album's scheduled release date from mid-July to June 11. The album debuted at Number One on *Billboard*'s Country Album charts and Number Two on the Top 200 album charts. *Here for the Party* sold about 227,000 units during its first week, more than any other country artist in history. The RIAA certified *Here for the Party* as gold and platinum simultaneously on June 21 and as double platinum on July 19. The Recording Industry Association of America (RIAA) reported that, by November 4, the album had sold over three million copies. Gretchen even surpassed pop sensation Ashlee Simpson as the best-selling new female artist of any genre in 2004.

Big & Rich's success in 2004 was also substantial, even though their diverse musical style drew heavily upon rock, blues, soul, funk, Latin, and commercial country. Jules Wortman, then at Warner Bros., told me in 2005 about the first time she heard Big & Rich's music:

> When I listened to their demo, I thought, "This is gonna be fun, great, but oh my word, what are we going to do?" Because it [the album] was just so out there. Was it going to get played on country radio? Where were we going to take it? After listening to the whole record I thought, I cannot pitch this any other way than a body of work to the media. I wrote my pitch letter and I was able to send the record out because they had been working on it, and everything was beginning to happen.

Jules was in charge of Big & Rich's publicity—not an easy task according to her. She remembered her efforts in pitching the album to a variety of "taste-makers":

> I really threw this record out there. I really thought it through. I wrote pitch letter after pitch letter. . . . I couldn't pitch it one song at a time. I couldn't send the single out and then try to follow up. [Instead] I wrote, "It's a body of work. You need to get a cocktail, and crank it loud in your house. . . . But just don't listen to it one track at a time and put it away. You have to listen to it and dial in, and it will tell you who these people are." So I had to make that the focus in order to get people to figure out what Big & Rich was all about. And oh my word, did they get it.

Jules sent her pitch letter to such influential critics and editors as Gavin Edwards at the *Wall Street Journal*, Joe Levy at *Rolling Stone*, Craig Marks at *Blender*, and Brian Mansfield at *USA Today* in addition to the *Los Angeles Times* and the *New York Times*.

Warner Bros. released Big & Rich's first single "Wild West Show" in December 2003; the song peaked at Number Twenty-One on *Billboard*'s Country Singles chart four months later. Big & Rich's widespread popularity did not come until after the release of "Save a Horse (Ride a Cowboy)" in April 2004. The song reached Number Eleven on *Billboard*'s Hot Country Singles chart despite the fact that it received relatively little radio airplay that year.

Luckily, "Save a Horse (Ride a Cowboy)" attracted significant national attention through other media. The song received widespread exposure as the theme to ESPN's 2004 *World Series of Poker*. In addition, the song's video entered regular rotation on CMT and Great American Country (GAC), largely because of its visual spectacle—horses, the Pearl-Cohn High School marching band, a dominatrix color guard, Two-Foot Fred, a convertible, Gretchen on a John Deere tractor, the Atlanta Falcons cheerleaders, John wearing a hip hop–style fur coat and an assortment of bling, and Cowboy Troy as drum major—all filmed on the Shelby Street Pedestrian Bridge in downtown Nashville. The filming was not without incident: Big & Rich were fined approximately $23,000 by the city of Nashville. The city alleged that damage had been done to the bridge by hoof marks from the numerous horses used in the video. However, the increase in album sales generated by the incident's media coverage was probably enough to cover the fines.

Horse of a Different Color experienced considerable sales despite the relatively sparse radio airplay of its singles. The album debuted at Number Fourteen on *Billboard*'s Country Album chart in early May and peaked at Number Six on the Top 200 Albums chart on July 24. *Horse of a Different Color* replaced Gretchen's *Here for the Party* at Number One on *Billboard*'s Country Album chart in late August. The RIAA certified *Horse of a Different Color* as gold on July 7 and platinum on August 18 that year. The Country Music Association identified Big & Rich's *Horse of a Different Color* as the seventh best-selling country album of 2004, with sales in excess of 1,775,000 units.

Gretchen and Big & Rich's popularity resulted in an invitation to perform at the 39th Academy of Country Music (ACM) Awards on May 26, 2004, in Las Vegas. Marc Oswald, who secured the booking for both acts, told me in our 2005 interview, "Gretchen was a shoe-in, but John and Kenny were a big sell." He elaborated: "Dick Clark's son produced the ACMs and he wanted to bring something entirely new to the show. The ACM board members were really forward thinking. Rod [Rod Essig, the ACM President] really embraced the whole idea. They were blown away after the performance."

Marc negotiated a five-and-a-half-minute, self-produced segment—the longest in the show—for John, Kenny, and Gretchen. Marc's background as a television producer contributed to the success of negotiations with the ACM. Marc described the performance as a "watershed" for both acts.

Big & Rich's arrival at the ACM Awards was a media spectacle. Jules Wortman wanted John and Kenny to make a grand entrance and rented two horses that the duo rode down the red carpet. According to Jules in our 2005 interview: "I got it cleared through the ACMs. They thought I was crazy. They tried to kill it. Then they said, 'No, you're right, we need to allow you to do this.' So we arrived on the red carpet with these horses, with a limo, the girls from the video, and several Mafia members. The fans went completely nuts. The fans were singing 'Save a Horse (Ride a Cowboy).'"

The stunt generated considerable press coverage during and after the event. Jules asserted that Big & Rich received more press in the weeks following the ACM Awards than many of the nominees or award winners. Backstage after the show John emphasized to CMT's Calvin Gilbert the evening's significance:

> The [ACM] awards show appearance was a major moment for the MuzikMafia. It felt rather galactic, actually. We got to stand there and watch Gretchen Wilson, a girl [who] Kenny and I saw in March of 1999 singing as a bartender getting up with the house band at a little bar in Nashville. She got up and just blew the speakers out at this bar. That was five years ago. To watch her finally get up there and get her shot was just awesome.

Following the ACM broadcast, the MuzikMafia performed a late-night show that lasted until 3:00 a.m. at the nearby House of Blues in Las Vegas. Guest artists included Toby Keith, Kenny Chesney, Kid Rock, Terri Clark, and Sherrie Austin.

Big & Rich and Gretchen reached millions of fans in summer 2004 by touring with major acts. In midsummer Gretchen joined Kenny Chesney's Tiki Bars and a Whole Lotta Love Tour that had begun in March with opening acts Keith Urban and Dierks Bentley. The tour ended mid-September, having sold more than 1.1 million tickets and grossing over fifty million dollars. In June Big & Rich began their stint with Tim McGraw on his Out Loud tour that included thirty-three performances across the United States. Cowboy Troy accompanied Big & Rich, often singing a duet with McGraw entitled "My Kind of Rain." McGraw's tour sold over 750,000 tickets and grossed over forty million dollars.

Chesney's tour ranked second in attendance for all concert tours in 2004, regardless of genre, just behind Prince, who sold 1,432,454 tickets.

Figure 4.4 Bluesboro, Nashville, July 2005.

McGraw's tour ranked sixth with 764,100 tickets sold. Among tours specifically by country music artists, Chesney was tops and McGraw third. This widespread exposure fueled Gretchen and Big & Rich's own popularity and resulted in increased album sales and numerous television appearances.

The MuzikMafia decided in late July to move its weekly Tuesday night shows from the Mercy Lounge to Bluesboro, a blues club located in the SoBro area of Nashville at 217 2nd Avenue South (see Fig. 4.4). Cory told me in 2006 how MuzikMafia musicians were growing weary of weekly shows at the Mercy Lounge: "Our folks were looking to go somewhere else, too, just to do something different. Every week [at the Mercy Lounge] got old quickly. You need to do something to freshen it up in some ways. Sometimes a venue change is necessary."

Having opened in early June 2004, Bluesboro was a new addition to the Nashville music scene. MuzikMafia affiliate Mark Fortney, known among friends and fans as Butter, was a cousin to Rob Fortney, the club's owner. Mark approached Rob and Cory about the possibility of changing venues. Rob negotiated a deal with the MuzikMafia that was more generous than what Ohlhauser was willing to match. After examining the venue and agreeing to an undisclosed amount of money for weekly shows, the godfathers agreed to change venues. MuzikMafia performances at Bluesboro began on July 27.

The MuzikMafia experienced several changes as a result of its move to Bluesboro. First, their audience demographic changed dramatically. In addition to the MuzikMafia's regular following of working-class fans and industry personnel, Bluesboro audiences attracted many well-dressed young professionals. I attribute this to the club's upscale interior: glossy hardwood floors; a wood-paneled, ellipse-shaped bar with nice overhead lighting and brass fittings; a large projection screen adjacent to the stage; an upstairs balcony with a small bar; a lower-level dance/eating area with a third bar; a full kitchen and food menu; a large stage area; a sizable outdoor patio with tables and chairs; and a maximum capacity of approximately 800 people.

Second, the presence of the media became increasingly apparent with each Tuesday performance. On August 17 a crew from the television news show 60 *Minutes* arrived to film for an upcoming segment on Gretchen. On September 28 a film crew from CMT set up several stationary cameras; they were shooting footage for *MuzikMafia TV,* a new program scheduled to air in January and February 2005. The CMT film crew returned on October 6 to film a Warner Bros. showcase for *MuzikMafia TV.*

Third, the MuzikMafia's list of guest artists grew in both number and popularity. George Clinton and his P-Funk crew performed with the MuzikMafia on September 28 at Bluesboro. The MuzikMafia featured recording artists Shannon Brown and Angie Aparo in addition to James Otto and Jon Nicholson during a Warner Bros. showcase on August 3. *Nashville Star* 2003 finalist Jamey Garner performed on several occasions at Bluesboro with the MuzikMafia and the Mafia Mizfits. Producer and publisher Jerry Phillips, the son of Sam Phillips (who owned and operated legendary Sun Records in Memphis), attended James's solo show at Bluesboro on September 14. Martina McBride attended a show at John's request on October 6. The presence of such well-known personalities generated much press coverage for the MuzikMafia among the Nashville media. The result was a substantial number of people who attended each week to meet and hear popular artists.

The MuzikMafia's last performance at Bluesboro took place on October 6. The club had been experiencing financial difficulties due to low profits on weekends, and closed its doors for good in January 2005. In addition, MuzikMafia members had little time for weekly performances: preparations for the Chevrolet American Revolution Tour, beginning on November 5, were well under way; John, Kenny, and Gretchen were preparing for their appearances on the CMA Awards show November 9. Finally, the media frenzy surrounding Big & Rich and Gretchen had generated larger audiences than Bluesboro could comfortably accommodate at weekly shows. The godfathers decided that it was time for a break. The MuzikMafia ceased regular weekly shows altogether on October 6, 2004, and did not resume them until January 2006.

Big & Rich and Gretchen outdid their earlier performance at the ACM Awards with an appearance at the 38th Annual Country Music Association Awards on November 9, broadcast live on CBS from the Grand Ole Opry House in Nashville. Marc Oswald had negotiated the deal with Robert Deaton and Larry Fitzgerald who were in charge of the television committee for the Country Music Association. Marc had expected the CMA to request Big & Rich's song "Holy Water," the duo's current single at the time. Much to Marc's surprise, Deaton and Fitzgerald asked for "Rollin' (The Ballad of Big & Rich)," featuring Cowboy Troy. Marc explained in 2005:

> They asked us to do "Rollin'" which was amazing. We wanted to do "Rollin'" to open an awards show, any awards show. We just wanted that song to be on TV. The CMA normally wants the single, whatever you have on the radio. They want familiarity; it just makes sense. Robert [Deaton] called me and said, "These guys [CMA producers] are ready to talk about Big & Rich now for the CMAs." They had already confirmed Gretchen. I was expecting "Holy Water." He [Deaton] said, "You're not going to believe this but they want to do the 'Ballad' [of Big & Rich]". I said, "You're shitting me." He said, "I told them that it was going to either happen here [at the CMAs] or the next show they [Big & Rich] were on. It's inevitable how big that's going to be, how big Troy's going to be." They wanted to make sure that that this new form of music got its birthplace at the CMAs and on the Grand Ole Opry stage and not in L.A., in Vegas, or New York City where Nashville couldn't claim it[self] as being a real launch pad. If we had had "Holy Water" on there, we would have ended up doing the "Ballad of Big & Rich" on *Dick Clark's New Year's Rocking Eve* or on the ACM awards [the following spring]. . . .

And they [the CMA] wanted to have a stake in introducing a black act to this format that's going to be a superstar, and I think it's awesome. I think it's amazing that they were thinking that far ahead, because there's a lot of risk in that for them . . . not only a black act, but also Big & Rich that are on the rockin' side of country, and we still hadn't had a hit on the radio. . . . They [the producers] wanted the whole thing with Fred, Troy, and everything, the whole freak parade. It was inspirational.

The CMA's decision to have Big & Rich perform "Rollin'" on its award show that year was significant. Troy's added presence on the Grand Ole Opry stage was unique not only because he is black, but also because he is a rapper. In addition, Troy was the second black musician ever to be featured on the CMA Awards; the first was Charlie Pride, some thirty-eight years prior. It is improbable that Troy would have had as much effect in Nashville without his association with the MuzikMafia. By November 2004 the MuzikMafia had become a metaphor for change in the institution of commercial country music, and artists who were associated with the MuzikMafia were likewise part of that change.

The following day, the online edition of the local newspaper, the *Tennessean*, contained comments from sixty-eight of the show's viewers. Although Gretchen received much praise for her performance of "When I Think about Cheatin'," comments about John, Kenny, and Troy were mostly negative. One person referred to Big & Rich as "a mess of mixed up music." Another individual asked what a rap singer in a Superman T-shirt—a reference to Troy—had to do with country music. One viewer provided an even stronger opinion: "Big & Rich was absolutely abominable. Just awful—the worst performance in the history of the show. I'm pretty conservative when it comes to country music, but even the most wide-ranging fans would have to agree that what Big & Rich played last night could not possibly be considered country music."

Despite the backlash from many country music fans following the show, Big & Rich's performance of "Rollin'" gave the MuzikMafia considerable exposure. The performance also introduced Cowboy Troy and "hick-hop" to country music fans, setting the stage for Troy's upcoming album scheduled for release in summer 2005.

By the time of Gretchen and Big & Rich's appearance at the CMA Awards, the two acts were already scheduled to co-headline the Chevrolet American Revolution Tour. The MuzikMafia received sponsorship for thirteen performances in nine states between November 5 and December 15, 2004. The controversial awards show performance only contributed to the MuzikMafia's popularity, resulting in increased ticket sales for the community's fall tour sponsored by Chevrolet. The tour's convoy comprised at any given time at least six tour buses and four tractor trailers.

Ticket sales for the fall tour also increased because Big & Rich and Gretchen had been nominated for a total of eight CMA awards. Big & Rich were nominated for awards in two categories: the Horizon Award and Vocal Duo of the Year. John received an individual nomination for Song of the Year for co-writing "Redneck Woman." Gretchen was nominated for awards in five categories: the Horizon Award, Single of the Year, Album of the Year, Music Video of the Year, and Song of the Year for "Redneck Woman" that she had co-written with John. Gretchen won the Horizon Award for the being year's best new artist.

The show featured most MuzikMafia members. Jon and James, seated next to each other at center stage, opened each show for thirty minutes, after which there was a brief intermission and set change. Big & Rich performed for fifty minutes; there was another set change, and then Gretchen's fifty-minute portion. Each concert's finale featured the entire MuzikMafia on stage with individual artists performing songs in rotation.

The artists contributed much to the development of their own staging for the tour. John admitted on Episode 1 of *MuzikMafia TV* that neither he nor Gretchen had ever been involved in the staging process prior to this tour. Gretchen acknowledged in the same episode that this was a daunting task: "It was definitely a wake-up call for me. I just sat down at home as quickly as I could and started scratching out some ideas and figuring out exactly how much of that stage I was gonna use and whether or not I had the balls to do it."

There was no organized staging for the show's finale. Instead, the MuzikMafia attempted to re-create the impromptu atmosphere of its earlier Pub of Love shows. The stage props included several couches occupied by friends and family, numerous candles, incense, assorted percussion instruments, bar stools, lamps, and Rachel's easel. The finale's musical content comprised extended jams, solos, duets, and variations on hits by Gretchen and Big & Rich. Kenny often took advantage of the opportunity to include a sermon or two, in addition to prompting the audience to sing the national anthem. At one point during a show that I observed on November 20 in Johnson City, all MuzikMafia members were either singing or playing an instrument. The result was "organized chaos." Backstage, Kenny described the finale of the show as "the galactic Pub of Love . . . or the Pub of Love Superbowl." However, *New York Times* music critic Kelefa Sanneh described the finale as a "radical, anticlimactic way to end an arena show."

MuzikMafia members made numerous televised appearances in 2004 in addition to the ACM and CMA Awards shows. Big & Rich appeared on NBC's *The Tonight Show* with Jay Leno on July 21. CMT documented the history and growing popularity of the MuzikMafia in a three-part series from July 23 to August 6 as part of the weekly show *CMT Insider*. Big & Rich performed on ABC's *Jimmy Kimmel Live* on July 26 and on *Good Morning America* on August 25, the same week that *Horse of a Different Color* reached Number One on *Billboard*'s Country Album chart. On October 25 the MuzikMafia performed with Big & Rich and Gretchen in a five-minute segment on the *Radio Music Awards,* broadcast live by NBC from Las Vegas. CMT produced two hourlong documentaries, *In the Moment: Gretchen Wilson* and *Total Access: Big & Rich,* that both premiered on September 24. CMT also included Big & Rich and Gretchen in a televised concert on October 29, *CMT Outlaws,* that included performances by Hank Williams Jr., Kid Rock, Montgomery Gentry, Tanya Tucker, Lynyrd Skynyrd, Jessi Colter, and James Hetfield. On December 8, Big & Rich and Gretchen appeared on FOX's *Billboard Music Awards*; Big & Rich received the award for New Country Duo/Group Artist of the Year and Gretchen received awards for best Female Country Artist of the Year and New Country Female Artist of the Year. CBS's award-winning news program *60 Minutes* dedicated a ten-minute segment to Gretchen and the MuzikMafia on December 19. Big & Rich closed out the year with a performance on *Dick Clark's New Year's Rockin' Eve* broadcast live on ABC from New York City.

MuzikMafia also received public exposure in 2004 via the print media. Articles on Gretchen, Big & Rich, or the MuzikMafia appeared in the *Wall Street Journal, Rolling Stone,* the *Los Angeles Times, USA Today, Entertainment Weekly,* the *Tennessean, Country Music Today, Billboard,* the *Washington Post, Blender,* and the *New York Times.*

MuzikMafia fans are widespread and as diverse as the artists themselves, so in summer 2005 I conducted a survey of 425 MuzikMafia fans at the annual CMA Music Festival (formerly known as Fan Fair). I chose the festival because it attracts large numbers of country music fans from most of the fifty states and beyond. In 2005 over 145,000 people attended the event over a four-day period from June 9–12 in downtown Nashville. A significant part of the survey focused on fans' knowledge of the MuzikMafia itself.

The survey took place daily from 10:00 a.m. to 4:00 p.m., and only with individuals who visited the MuzikMafia booth in the Nashville Convention Center. I approached those who a) were waiting to purchase MuzikMafia merchandise, b) had already purchased merchandise, or c) were waiting in line for an autograph or photo with a MuzikMafia personality.

I wanted to examine what MuzikMafia fans knew and did not know about the community. Questions included a description of their understanding of the MuzikMafia, how they first heard of the community, their favorite artist, and the names of the founding godfathers.

I began by asking each fan to define what the MuzikMafia actually was. Common responses included "group of something," "awesome," "country music," "diversity," "support group," "friends," "freedom of expression," and "a social movement with a message." Some fans just provided the name of a specific artist such as Gretchen or Big & Rich.

In another question I asked how each fan had first heard of the MuzikMafia. Not surprisingly, many fans initially encountered the MuzikMafia through the visual broadcast media. About 37 percent of the fans interviewed (174 people) said that they had heard of the MuzikMafia through television, with CMT being the most significant source at 23.4 percent. Only 7.4 percent of fans had first become aware of the MuzikMafia through radio. A significant number of people said that they had first heard MuzikMafia artists from buying albums, with Big & Rich at 21 percent and Gretchen Wilson at 11.9 percent.

I also asked MuzikMafia fans to select their favorite artists. Big & Rich were the most popular among 44.4 percent of fans, while Gretchen received 31.7 percent of the votes. Cowboy Troy was third with 78 votes, or 11.8 percent. Oddly enough, three people named Hank Williams Jr. as their favorite MuzikMafia artist. Hank Williams Jr. has never been member of the

MuzikMafia, although he did make a cameo appearance in Gretchen's video for "Redneck Woman."

In another question, I asked fans to name the MuzikMafia's godfathers. There were 766 responses. Most people listed two or more names as godfathers. John and Kenny received a majority of the votes with approximately 250 each, totaling 64 percent of the total names listed. Only thirty-nine people, or 5.1 percent, accurately identified Jon Nicholson as a godfather. Cory Gierman received only twenty-four votes, or 3.1 percent. Only eighteen respondents, or 2.3 percent, correctly identified all four godfathers. (I suspect that this figure is inflated; on the tables and countertops at the MuzikMafia booth were copies of a one-page history and explanation of the MuzikMafia that included the names of all four godfathers.) The question was left blank by 149 respondents, or c. 19.5 percent. Needless to say, the MuzikMafia's fanbase actually knew very little about the MuzikMafia in 2004, despite the national popularity of several of its artists.

The MuzikMafia's widespread success from April through December 2004 raises several questions: Was the sudden increase in commercial country's popularity a result of Big & Rich and Gretchen's contributions—or was their celebrity made possible by a surge in the popularity of commercial country music? What was the media's role in constructing the MuzikMafia's "outlaw" image in 2004, and what was the media's influence on MuzikMafia fans? What changes did the MuzikMafia undergo as a result of its widespread media success? Did the MuzikMafia lose its purely local Nashville identity while part of the national scene?

The MuzikMafia simultaneously influenced and was influenced by changes that the commercial country music industry was undergoing in 2004. The MuzikMafia's entrance into the popular mainstream in 2004 occurred during a time in which commercial country, according to the RIAA, was already experiencing its own surge in popularity. Album sales by country musicians went from a little over 69 million units in 2003 to almost 78 million units in 2004, an increase of about 12 percent. Kenny Chesney, Tim McGraw, Shania Twain, Toby Keith, George Strait, Jimmy Buffett, and Brad Paisley each sold a minimum of one million albums that year. Combined with platinum sales by Big & Rich and Gretchen, the above artists collectively sold approximately 20.8 million albums, comprising 28 percent of all country album sales. It is evident that commercial country's increase in popularity allowed for safe inclusion of atypical acts such as Gretchen and Big & Rich who had been marginalized or excluded in years prior by the commercial music industry.

The MuzikMafia's designation by CMT as the Number One hit of 2004 probably had more to do with the changing image of commercial country than album sales or concert tours by MuzikMafia artists. On the other hand, both Gretchen and Big & Rich added a much-needed flavor to the apparent standardization of Nashville commercial artists. Gretchen's redneck woman persona provided an alternative to the sex symbol image cultivated by Faith Hill, Shania Twain, and Sara Evans. Big & Rich's flamboyant costumes and "Love Everybody" motto gave the growing number of Nashville's "hat acts" more diversity while adding a sense of pride in being lower class.

The MuzikMafia also affected the sound of commercially produced music in Nashville. Gretchen's hardcore lyrics and rough, edgy timbre compared more with Hank Williams Jr., Kid Rock, Willie Nelson, Merle Haggard, Waylon Jennings, and Tanya Tucker than with current artists atop the country charts. Big & Rich's combination of various genres, namely rock and country, compared somewhat with what Johnny Cash was doing musically in the 1960s and what Garth Brooks was attempting in the early 1990s. Many fans described MuzikMafia in 2004 as new, innovative, and forward thinking, but in reality, MuzikMafia artists were really demonstrating their affinity for musicians from earlier eras.

The MuzikMafia's auxiliary members had their own views on the community's success. Max attributed the sudden popularity of Big & Rich and Gretchen in 2004 to "all of the planets being in alignment." Paul Worley took a different approach. When asked why the MuzikMafia had emerged from the Nashville scene instead of from some other musical center like New York City or Los Angeles, he replied: "The music scenes up there [NYC] are too big and too far flung. This is more like L.A. in the 1960s where everybody lived in Hollywood and Laurel Canyon, where everybody hung out and played on each other's albums, creating a lot of great music. It started to die when everybody moved out to Encino, the Valley."

Another underlying question concerned the MuzikMafia's "outlaw" image as portrayed by the media during the second half of 2004. A significant example took place on September 9, when CMT sponsored a concert called the CMT Outlaws at the Gaylord Entertainment Center in downtown

Nashville. The event was edited into a two-hour television show of the same name that premiered on October 29 on CMT. The concert's roster included performances by Montgomery Gentry, Kid Rock, Hank Williams Jr., Jessi Colter, Tanya Tucker, Shooter Jennings, Lynyrd Skynyrd, James Hetfield, Big & Rich, and Gretchen. The concert was an obvious acknowledgement of hardcore country music's significance and the style's apparent revival since the release of Gretchen's album *Here for the Party*.

Participation in the concert by MuzikMafia artists was puzzling. No MuzikMafia member had ever characterized themselves individually or collectively as outlaws in personal conversations with me, live stage performances, quotes in published articles, televised interviews, or televised awards show appearances. In fact, at the after-party held at the Fontanel estate (now the Plowboy Mansion) following the above performance, I did not hear the term "outlaw" at all when discussing the evening's music with the artists themselves. In spite of this, both CMT and Chevrolet described the MuzikMafia as "country's newest outlaws," specifically in television promotions for the American Revolution Tour in fall 2004.

In fact, in 2005 John and Kenny expressed their opposition to Muzik-Mafia being described as outlaws. Both agreed that outlaws want to break the rules by going against an institution. According to John, "We [the MuzikMafia] don't want to *break* the rules; we just don't think that there *should* be any rules." Here, John's use of the outlaw image compared more closely with that of the rebel rather than with that of an anarchist. It is significant that, even though they disavowed both rebel and outlaw images, MuzikMafia artists certainly benefited financially from such an image in the media. Most members of the MuzikMafia, John included, were not dissatisfied with the entire system of commercially produced music but rather were displeased with only certain widely accepted rules, namely those pertaining to genre classification and radio's "consistency of format" programming guidelines. This shared musical and social ideology created a bond between MuzikMafia artists—and that bond, or rather its commodification, transformed the MuzikMafia into a significant component of the commercial music industry.

To my knowledge, the outlaw moniker caused no significant tension between the MuzikMafia and the media. Many MuzikMafia members disagreed with their public image as outlaws, but at the time each artist was benefiting financially from the association. Most MuzikMafia artists accepted such distortions of image as an unfortunate aspect of the commercial music industry. Max told me in a 2005 interview:

> I'm not so nuts about it [the term *outlaw*]. I understand that it's like a sales pitch. It's a little hyperbolic for my taste. Talk about the cultural baggage of a word . . . It just seems a little trite. John got thrown out of Lonestar. I guess that "outcast" would be more accurate. . . . The term *outlaw* is a very effective sales tool to make people buy something. People like to define themselves as being an outlaw if they do something differently. But if you're really an outlaw, you probably wouldn't sell 2.5 million of jack shit. And if you were breaking all the rules, you probably wouldn't have a major label record deal. We're not breaking a lot of rules, here. If anything, we know the system so well that we own it.

For Max many other MuzikMafia musicians, financial gain and the dissemination of the music and its message trumped any inaccurate representations of image.

Max's comments raise an important point: MuzikMafia members knew how to work within Nashville's commercial music system. Prior to founding the MuzikMafia, John, Kenny, Jon, and Cory had learned much about the music industry from their respective experiences with major labels on Music Row. Each godfather was aware of the conflict between artistic creativity and the business of selling records. Max confirmed that, although the MuzikMafia was somewhat unorthodox compared to many other commercial acts, it was far from being outside the mainstream:

> You're looking at people who understood the system and knew how to distill that change into someone who made decisions at a record store. The *outlaw* term has always bugged me. We don't break rules. For Heaven sakes, we were on CMT! We have a major record deal. We are all using the system. A road is still a road, from Roman times to today. We're still making records and playing the music. It might be distributed differently. The ideas behind it might be a little different, but we're still working within a framework. . . . You can use the

momentum and power of the system as your tool if you understand it, and you are smarter than it, and if you work harder than it. John Rich is a great example of someone who saw a tool and fit it to his own hand.

Here, Max confirmed the MuzikMafia's ability to function within the broader system of the commercial music industry, albeit with a sense of false consciousness. The system of the commercial country music industry already incorporates if not expects "outlaws" in a variety of forms to rock the boat every once in a while.

The fan survey I conducted at the CMA Music Festival showed that, by summer 2005, only few of the MuzikMafia's fans understood what the community actually was about. The survey supported the assumption that most fans received their knowledge of the MuzikMafia directly from the mass media. Very few fans knew the names of the godfathers and why the MuzikMafia had been founded. An even smaller percentage of fans had experienced the MuzikMafia through its free, regular Tuesday night shows in Nashville. The result was two MuzikMafias: a) the public, mass-marketed, mass-mediated image of several multi-platinum selling musicians, and b) the group of marginalized artists who had once celebrated their collectivity and musical diversity at the Pub of Love.

Another underlying question concerns changes that the MuzikMafia underwent in 2004 as a result of widespread media success. First and foremost, the MuzikMafia's local dynamic changed drastically. As a single musical collective in Nashville, they previously had a strong base of MuzikMafia fans as such. This changed when the MuzikMafia toured across the United States and found Gretchen fans or Big & Rich fans, few of whom knew (or cared) about the MuzikMafia.

While on the Chevrolet American Revolution Tour in fall 2004, I interviewed concert attendees who identified themselves specifically as "Gretchen fans" or "Big & Rich fans." Most audience members, with whom I spoke, had little or no idea who Jon Nicholson, Chance, Pino Squillace, Rachel Kice, James Otto, or other MuzikMafia members were. Many attendees did not even know what the MuzikMafia was but had come to the concert to see a specific act, namely Big & Rich or Gretchen.

The result was an unfortunate but observable separation between the famous and non-famous members of the MuzikMafia. Although no lesser-known MuzikMafia member was willing to go on record with their displeasure with the situation, I often sensed considerable tension in conversations about the more popular MuzikMafia artists.

Of significance was the MuzikMafia's retention or loss of its purely local Nashville identity on the national stage. I described how the Muzik-Mafia closed each show of the Chevrolet American Revolution Tour with all members performing together on stage. Unfortunately, the MuzikMafia's attempts to re-create the "open jam" of its Tuesday night shows in Nashville were not as successful in the new, commercial environment. The cacophony coming from the stage's thirty or more microphones was difficult at best for the tour's sound engineers to clarify for live audiences of five to ten thousand people. MuzikMafia artists also spanned the entire length of the sixty-foot stage, creating an overwhelming spectacle that confused many audience members who did not know where to focus their attention. In addition, the mass amount of applause frequently resulted in two or more MuzikMafia artists soloing at the same time, each wanting to have their respective share of the spotlight. The intimacy and informality that had once characterized the MuzikMafia's weekly shows in Nashville had been eclipsed by the community's national popularity and considerable financial gain. For many MuzikMafia members, fans, and critics, the coming year would prove whether the MuzikMafia was just a temporary fad or a semi-permanent fixture of the popular mainstream.

Chapter Five

INTERLUDE

Meet the MuzikMafia of 2004

The MuzikMafia's membership has changed somewhat since the community officially began in October 2001. However, there was a core roster of MuzikMafia members that remained relatively stable in 2004 and 2005 and contributed much to the community's rise to national popularity. You will find, among the following bios of those core members, similar experiences and common threads growing up that facilitated the strong bond of friendship that they eventually shared: age, eclectic musical tastes, working-class upbringing, connection to the South, religion, relocation to Nashville, and negative experiences with formal institutions such as school or the music industry.

The members appear here according to the length of time that they were with the MuzikMafia. I should point out that James, Gretchen, Brian, Max, Pino, and Rachel began their association with the MuzikMafia either at its first performance or shortly thereafter. Their order of appearance here is purely arbitrary. Adam Shoenfeld appears first because he was already performing with Kenny and John before the idea of MuzikMafia was conceived.

Known by friends and fans as Atom, Adam Shoenfeld has a unique role in the birth, growth, and development in the MuzikMafia. As an established Nashville session guitarist, he was already performing and recording with Kenny and John several years before the MuzikMafia began and was an active member of the MuzikMafia throughout its brief history.

Adam was born on April 29, 1974, to Cookie and Andy Shoenfeld in Huntington, on New York's Long Island. His family moved when he was three years old to Blairstown, New Jersey, where Adam spent the rest of his childhood and adolescent years.

Adam inherited many of his childhood musical influences from his parents, whose favorites included rock acts such as the Beatles and Blood, Sweat, and Tears; jazz saxophonist Paul Winter; and Motown legend Stevie Wonder. Adam's interest in electric guitar began at age five, and he still remembers jumping up and down on his mattress and playing air guitar to Peter Frampton's album *Frampton Comes Alive!* (1976). Adam's parents were inspired by his enthusiasm for music and subsequently purchased him his first guitar in 1979. Adam later adopted a fascination with heavy metal guitar technique, especially that of the Swedish virtuoso Yngwie Malmsteen.

With the support of his parents, Adam pursued his interest in electric guitar throughout middle school and high school. He played trumpet in school band in fifth and sixth grade, but sold his trumpet shortly thereafter and purchased his first Fender electric guitar. At age fourteen he began writing songs, and performed them as a member of a local heavy metal band called Morehead Fonster, a word play on "forehead monster." While attending a private high school called the Blair Academy, Adam enrolled in the school's jazz/rock band class and continued to broaden his musical horizons in addition to the experience he was acquiring with his own band, Exit. Adam's training as a session guitarist began at home with his own four-track recorder. Later, while a senior in high school, he performed and recorded music with a local ensemble called the Nathan Lee Band. Adam graduated from the Blair Academy in 1992, having been voted by his peers Most Likely to Succeed in Music. He spent the year following graduation in Blairstown working for a local wildlife photographer.

Adam moved to Nashville in January 1994 with the Nathan Lee Band. Unfortunately, within six months the band had broken up, and Adam found himself working as a waiter at Ruby Tuesday while supplementing his income through sporadic gigs as a rock-blues guitarist around town. By 1995 Adam's luck had changed; he began working at the well-known Woodland Studios, a state-of-the-art recording facility in Nashville. Although he was paid primarily for answering the phone, Adam was invited on numerous occasions by the studio's owner Bob Solomon to play on various artists' albums. In addition, when the studio was not booked at night, Adam and his friends would frequently record their own music.

Adam's professional relationship with Kenny Alphin began in 1998 when Adam was asked to audition for Kenny's band, Big Kenny. Adam had known Kenny's music from the band's numerous performances at 12th & Porter and the Exit/In in Nashville and was friends with Kenny's keyboardist Stevie King. The audition was for a possible tour for Kenny's upcoming album on Hollywood Records, *Live a Little*. Adam performed several shows with Big Kenny in 1999 before Hollywood shelved the record and ultimately dropped Kenny from the label. His band members went their separate ways.

However, it was only a few short months before Adam and Kenny reconnected in the form of Kenny's new band luvjOi. The two had continued to write songs following the demise of Kenny's earlier band and decided to team up again. According to Adam:

> He [Kenny] had some songs, and we had written some together, so we started putting the first luvjOi record together. It was just he and I and our friend Chris Stone, who engineers almost everything we do, and a couple of hired session musicians, and it was great. So I was like, "dude, we need to make this a band." So we got Larry Babb, who's the current [2009] Big & Rich drummer, and one of our good friends Justin Tocket to play bass. We decided to call it luvjOi; John [Rich] came up with it [the name].

LuvjOi experienced moderate success in Nashville and beyond, the height of which was the band's 2000 appearance at Rockfest, along with Metallica, Stone Temple Pilots, and Kid Rock. Following their appearance on the Rockfest stage, luvjOi performed frequently to packed clubs in Nashville and Knoxville.

Unfortunately, luvjOi's success was short-lived. John Rich and Cowboy Troy began making appearances with luvjOi at Kenny's request in 2000 and 2001. Although the presence of guest artists on stage was, in itself, not unusual for luvjOi, the musical contributions by a cowboy and a rapper did not sit well among luvjOi's members, who considered themselves purely a rock band. As a result, luvjOi produced only two albums before disbanding, a self-titled first album in 2000 and *volume 2* in 2001.

Despite his brief stint as lead guitarist for luvjOi, Adam continued to perform with Kenny in fall 2001 and spring 2002, primarily at MuzikMafia shows at the Pub of Love. He also accompanied John and Kenny during 2001 Christmas visits to Vanderbilt Children's Hospital in Nashville, where the three met and befriended cancer patient Katie Darnell, whose song "Rescue Me" was later recorded by John, Kenny, and Adam in 2002. That same year, Kenny surprised Adam with the news that Big & Rich had gotten a recording contract with Warner Bros. Adam played lead guitar on many of the duo's hits, including "Save a Horse (Ride a Cowboy)." Adam has served as lead guitarist for Big & Rich ever since.

James Otto was with the MuzikMafia at its first performance in October 2001 and remained a significant figure in the community's political structure. James is one of several MuzikMafia artists who closely identify with commercial country music. James's style is also influenced by rhythm and blues.

James was born on July 29, 1973, on an army base in Benton City, Washington. His father, a career military man and also a musician, contributed much to James's musical growth and development. Following his parents' divorce when he was three, James spent his youth in numerous areas of the country, including North Dakota and Alabama with his mother, followed by a return to Washington to his father.

James's formal musical training consisted of violin in second grade, voice in third grade, and saxophone in sixth grade; not until high school did he develop an interest in electric guitar. His musical interests have included the Beatles, the Rolling Stones, Led Zeppelin, Judas Priest, Ozzy Osborne, Steppenwolf, Bob Seger, Travis Tritt, Garth Brooks, Hank Williams Jr., Willie Nelson, Van Halen, and Prince.

Disinterested in college, James found gainful employment in other areas. In 1993 he enrolled in the United States Navy, spending the bulk of his two-year enlistment period as a deck seaman. Following his discharge from military service and a series of menial jobs in Seattle, James moved to the Nashville area in 1998, where he spent his days driving an oil truck and his nights performing music in local clubs. He eventually secured a record deal with Mercury Records, who released his debut album *Days of Our Lives* in 2004. He reached considerable nationwide exposure with the release of his 2008 album *Sunset Man* that included the Number One hit single "Just Got Started Lovin' You."

Gretchen Wilson was arguably the best-known member of the MuzikMafia in 2004, largely the result of her multi-platinum debut album *Here for the Party* on Sony/Epic, released that May. Gretchen's emergence onto the national scene, her hit song "Redneck Woman" and her hardcore lifestyle contributed greatly to changes in sound, image, and direction of commercial country.

Born June 26, 1973, in Pocahontas, Illinois, Gretchen experienced a difficult childhood. Her mother, a high school dropout, was sixteen years old when Gretchen was born, and Gretchen's father left when she was two. Consisting of Gretchen, her mother Christine, and her younger half-brother Josh, the family relocated frequently after being evicted from various trailer homes for nonpayment of rent. By the time Gretchen dropped out of school in eighth grade to tend bar full time, she had attended approximately twenty different schools. By age fifteen, Gretchen was living on her own, supporting herself with money earned from bartending and singing with various bands.

Gretchen moved to Nashville in 1996. She worked as a bartender at the Bourbon Street Blues & Boogie Bar in Printer's Alley, and supplemented her income by singing demos for various Nashville songwriters. It was in March 1999 at the Bourbon Street Blues & Boogie Bar where Gretchen first met John Rich, who later marketed Gretchen and her music to various record labels on Music Row.

Brian Barnett is most recognizable as the bare-chested drummer in Gretchen Wilson's video for her Number One single "Redneck Woman." Brian toured regularly with Big & Rich from summer 2004 through summer 2006, and he was among the MuzikMafia's original members.

Brian was born on the south side of Chicago on February 27, 1962, into what he described to me as a "blue-collar family." His father regularly worked sixty hours a week in a machine shop, and Brian's mother had worked since she was sixteen for International Harvester. Brian began learning drums at age eight, and spent his formative years listening to Bob Dylan, Chicago, Neil Young, Led Zeppelin, Machine Head, and Rush.

Brian experienced many difficulties in life. He was expelled from Catholic school in eighth grade for smoking marijuana, and he dropped out of high school during his sophomore year to pursue music full-time with his band. By age eighteen, Brian was married and had two children. He received his General Equivalency Diploma (GED) in 1988, four years after moving to Nashville. During his early years in Nashville, Brian—then divorced—supported himself by performing at the Opryland theme park and with numerous performances with his own band Exit 65.

In 2004 Max Abrams's roles in the MuzikMafia were threefold. Known as "Max the Sax," he was first and foremost the lead saxophone player, contributing that timbre to the texture of most songs at live MuzikMafia performances and many studio recordings. Second, Max monitored and directed, when necessary, the flow of each stage performance. His duties as stage manager, with the assistance of Cory, involved regulating the order and sometimes the length of solos as well as who performed and when. Third, Max was a regular touring member of Jon Nicholson's band.

Max was born November 10, 1977, in Lexington, Virginia. His family resided in several cities in the area, including Sweetbriar, Monroe, and Amherst, before moving to Lynchburg in 1983. Max's slight New York accent reveals his parents' Long Island background and the influence of his grandparents, who are from Brooklyn. Max experienced a somewhat difficult childhood academically. He struggled while at Sandusky Elementary School in Amherst until fifth grade when it was determined that his academic shortcomings, specifically poor performance in mathematics, were the result of poor eyesight, not a learning disability as suggested by his teachers. Max's physical handicap—he was born with a club foot—had excluded him from sports as a child. He later underwent surgery to correct the condition. His academic performance began to show promise while attending Heritage High School in Lynchburg where he took advanced placement courses in European history, consistently making the honor roll.

Despite taking piano lessons beginning in third grade, Max did not begin to enjoy music until age eleven. Max's godfather Robert de Maria supplied him with numerous vintage recordings that, according to Max, spawned his interest in jazz and in saxophone. Max was also exposed to jazz through his father, who was chairman of the board for a nonprofit performing arts center in Lynchburg named the Ellington. In 1990 Max attended a summer music program at the Eastman School of Music and a similar program at the University of Massachusetts the following year. During his high school years Max rode two hours by car each way with his parents every second Tuesday to James Madison University in Harrisonburg, Virginia, where he took private saxophone lessons with Gunnar Mossblad.

In fall 1995 Max continued his education at Princeton University, majoring in history. Max described his course of study at the Ivy League institution as "rigorously difficult, with little room for individuality or diversion." According to Max, his classmates comprised the elite of American society with surnames such as Forbes and Firestone. Dissatisfied with his academic performance in the History Department and his presence among the culturally elite, Max changed his major to music during his junior year at Princeton.

After changing his major, Max attended classes in jazz history taught by adjunct instructor Phil Schaap. In addition, he studied applied saxophone with Rick Margitza and Walt Weiskopf. Max's daily schedule consisted of seven to nine hours of practice and several hours of musical transcription of songs by Lester Young, Count Basie, Stan Getz, Charlie Parker, Sonny Stitt, John Coltrane, and Sonny Rollins. By his final year at Princeton, Max had realized that he did not want to live the life of a jazz musician. He became depressed, discontinuing his rigorous practice schedule. Max graduated in 1999 with his Bachelor of Arts in Music, despite not having played saxophone for over a year.

Wanting to make substantial changes in his life, in May 1999 Max left New Jersey for California. At the behest of close friend and investment banker Aaron Lewis, Max spent three weeks attending interviews in search of employment in San Francisco and Los Angeles. Despite several lucrative offers, he decided to return to music.

Following a five-month return to New Jersey and a brief trip to Europe, Max moved to Nashville in November 1999. He had visited the city several times before at the suggestion of his father. Max arrived in Nashville with the names of two contacts: John Unger and Graham Spice. He had received the name of the former from the Princeton Alumni Association's Nashville branch, and the latter was the name of his godfather's friend. As the manager for well-known commercial country duo The Judds, Unger had numerous connections within the Nashville music industry, and he recommended that Max become a talent agent for the William Morris Agency. After intentionally failing entrance examinations for the William Morris training program, Max decided to return to playing music for his livelihood. The business side of the industry was not for him.

During his first year in Nashville, Max supported himself by performing with numerous musical acts. His jobs included a stint as saxophonist in Infinity, a Top Forty cover band headed by his landlord Warren White, and two annual performances of the *Rocky Horror Picture Show* with a Nashville production company.

Max met and befriended future MuzikMafia godfather Kenny Alphin in October 2000 at 12th & Porter while performing with *The Rocky Horror Picture Show*. Kenny played the role of Eddie in the 2000 and 2001 productions. Impressed with Max's abilities on the saxophone, Kenny asked Max to join his band luvjOi. It was during a luvjOi performance in early 2001 where Max first met John Rich. Max began performing with MuzikMafia in November 2001, several weeks after that now historic first show.

In addition to regular performances with the MuzikMafia, Max continued to pursue a career in the music business. He worked briefly as an assistant to independent producer Fred Mullin. Max recorded for the first time in the studio in 2002 on several projects for Chris Grainger, who played lead guitar in Schfvilkus, a Nashville avant-garde jazz group founded in summer 1996. Max's income from music afforded him only a modest lifestyle, but he continued to perform without payment at MuzikMafia shows because of his closeness with the musicians, his identification with their values of acceptance and inclusivity, and his own previous negative experiences with the musical and social mainstream.

Max made inroads as a Nashville saxophonist and entertainer in 2003, preventing him from attending many MuzikMafia performances. Beginning that February, Max coordinated his Circvs Maximvs, which combined live music, poetry, dance, painting, spoken word, and film in an unrehearsed performance setting. The name derived from the use of three plastic cups, signifying a three-ring circus, in which pieces of paper were kept. Audience members were instructed to submit slips of paper that contained words associated with particular styles of music, a specific Circvs Maximvs performer, a unique mood, tempo, tonalities, topics for poetry, subjects for artistic recreation, and dramatic scenes. Max coordinated each evening's program as "ringmaster" by randomly selecting pieces of paper from each cup. He based his idea of structured improvisation on similar processes in the aleatoric music of composer John Cage. Circvs Maximvs promoted the interrelationship between the audience and the artist, minimizing the cultural distance between the two. According to Max: "When most people think of fine art—jazz, painting, poetry—they think of it as a medium that they can't be involved with. That's absurd. My real hope for the show is that by including people in the creative process they will find that these things are accessible and beautiful."

Regular performers at Circvs Maximvs included visual artists Robert Ellis Orrall, Marvin Posey, Rachel Kice, and Paul McLean; composer, poet, and musician Marcus Hummon; MuzikMafia percussionist Pino Squillace; poet Dennis Ongkiko; drummer Johnny Rabb; Gypsy Hombres violinist Peter Hyrka; and spoken word poets Liszen and Pampata. Through stylistic diversity and interaction between the audience and performers at Circvs Maximvs, Max reinforced similar fundamental aspects of MuzikMafia performances.

Giuseppe "Pino" Squillace is the only member of the MuzikMafia who was born in Italy. Despite popular belief, he exerted no influence on the godfathers in selecting the community's name, nor does he claim to have any association with organized crime in the United States or in Italy. He is an auxiliary percussionist, specializing in the conga drums and *djembe*.

Pino was born on January 15, 1962, in the small town of Savelli in the province of Catanzaro in the Calabria region of southern Italy. His parents affectionately referred to him in childhood as Giuseppino and later Peppino. As a teenager he adopted the derivative Pino, which is how he has been commonly known since. As a child Pino took interest in the folk music of the Calabria region, especially the tarantellas he observed at a young age. He still maintains an affinity for what he describes as "roots music" because of its lively rhythms and its close connection to the people.

When Pino was two years old, his family moved to northern Italy; he lived for twenty years in Milan. During his teenage years Pino developed a destructive addition to cocaine and heroin, for which he spent thirteen months in a rehabilitation clinic in the town of Asti, located two hours southwest of Milan. Pino attributes his successful completion of the program to divine intervention, which provided him with renewed spirituality and a desire to help others.

In 1983, at age twenty-one, Pino moved to Florence, where he enrolled in the Mac Poldo School of Music in Prato, a town located approximately twenty kilometers northwest of Florence. He studied percussion with Mac Poldo and music theory with the school's co-founder Ginger Baker, well-known as the former drummer for Cream. Concurrent to his musical studies, Pino established outside of Florence a rehabilitation program that housed at-risk youths. Pino's partners comprised individuals whom he had befriended in the rehabilitation clinic in Asti. The program consisted of numerous employment opportunities, including the construction of display booths for expositions and trade fairs as well as a record label known as La Sorgente Music. The goal of both ventures was to teach responsibility and values to youths through productive contributions to society. La Sorgente's catalog consisted of imported North American music such as gospel, blues, and jazz as well as music by local acts. Pino and La Sorgente conducted business with over fifteen distributors throughout Europe. The staff comprised at-risk youths, all of whom lived on a farm operated by Pino and his co-founders outside the city.

After selling La Sorgente Music to an Italian publishing company in 1986, Pino left the recording business and founded in Florence a cosmetics company entitled Sally's Line, named after his one-year-old daughter. Sally's Line specialized in the sale of women's cosmetics, competing primarily with L'Oreal for the Tuscan market. Pino's success in the cosmetic industry afforded him many luxuries, including a five-bedroom apartment in the historic district of downtown Prato across the street from the Duomo Prato. Unfortunately, his success lasted only for a few years. Pino lost most of his wealth in an attempt to buy out his supplier, who accepted payment and declared bankruptcy. The business deal forced Pino to liquidate his assets in order to fulfill numerous contractual obligations, leaving the family almost bankrupt. With little opportunity in Florence, Pino, his wife, and their daughter emigrated to the United States.

In December 1989 Pino and his family arrived in San Francisco with six suitcases and two hundred dollars to their name. They moved into a garage apartment owned by his wife's family in Crescent City located on the coast approximately twenty miles south of the Oregon state line. In spring 1990 the Squillaces moved to Los Angeles, where Pino found employment in numerous fields. After a brief stint with Gina's Pizza, Pino sold aluminum windows for Superior Engineering Products. His relative success in the latter allowed Pino and his family to move out of the small L.A. apartment they had been sharing with another family into more spacious accommodations.

By 1993 Pino had decided to leave Los Angeles for Nashville. He was already familiar with the Nashville area through a friend named Rick Cua who had been the bassist in a country rock group known as the Outlaws from 1980 to 1982. Cua had known Pino since 1985, when Pino organized Cua's first tour of Italy. While Pino was living in Los Angeles, Cua contacted him to request his assistance on another tour of Italy, both as an organizer and as a performing percussionist. Cua had Pino flown to Nashville for five days of rehearsals immediately preceding the tour that took place during three weeks from late June to mid-July 1993. While Pino and Cua were on tour, Cua's wife collected numerous job advertisements from Nashville newspapers. Upon his return, Pino responded to several of the ads, eventually securing a position selling aluminum windows on commission for a Nashville company known as Ameritech. The family officially moved to Nashville on August 25 that year. Their first apartment was located in the second story of a house at 1514 Demonbreun Street where Randy Travis had supposedly once resided.

Pino became a successful entrepreneur in the Nashville area. Within a few months of his arrival, he had saved enough money to place a down payment on a commercial property in nearby Franklin, Tennessee. He transformed a guitar store into a small coffee shop known as Caffee Milano that opened its doors on February 28, 1994. In 1996 he relocated Caffee Milano to a much larger building at 174 3rd Ave North off of Lower Broadway in downtown Nashville.

Pino first performed with the MuzikMafia in October 2001. He was playing conga drums with a group at nearby 12th and Porter when a friend invited him to perform across the street at the Pub of Love. Pino remembers seeing more musicians there than audience members. He reports that it was Jon Nicholson who first asked him to join the jam session. Pino accompanied the group of musicians that night on the house conga with a head that had been pierced with a drumstick during a previous performance. The following week, Pino brought his own congas, and has been at every MuzikMafia performance thereafter.

Rachel Kice was born April 29, 1977, in Wichita, Kansas. Through her mother, a graphic designer, she was exposed to the arts at an early age along with her twin younger sisters, who are also artists. Rachel remembers many art projects that occupied her time prior to entering elementary school. While attending Wichita Southeast High School from 1993 to 1996, she took lessons in classical piano and voice while cultivating a strong interest in opera.

Rachel was disinterested in the formality of art music by her senior year of high school, and she decided to apply to the Berklee College of Music to cultivate her enthusiasm for contemporary music. In fall 1996 she left Wichita for Boston, where Berklee had offered her a merit scholarship to study voice, although she continued taking piano lessons. Toward the end of her first semester, Rachel returned to Kansas to give birth to her daughter. Rachel did not take final exams that year at Berklee and subsequently withdrew from the school.

After returning to Wichita from Boston, Rachel found employment in numerous fields such as theater, television, and modeling. Her jobs included actress and set designer with the Wichita Children's Theater and Dance Center, performer with the Wichita production company Stage One, a television commercial actress, moderator for a television show on respiratory ailments entitled *A Breath of Fresh Air*, and poster woman for the portrait photography studio Glamour Shots Inc.

In August 2001 Rachel moved to Nashville at the suggestion of mentor and Berklee professor Pat Pattison. One of Rachel's first jobs was at music publisher Warner/Chappell Music at 20 Music Square East; her tasks included, among others, hanging and positioning award plaques in the lobby. As menial as her job appeared, Rachel had the opportunity to meet each songwriter as they entered the building, including John Rich who introduced himself to Rachel in October 2001. She met Kenny at the Warner/Chappell Christmas party that year, at which John and Kenny invited Rachel to attend MuzikMafia performances at the Pub of Love.

Rachel's earliest experiences with the MuzikMafia were in December 2001. She attended Tuesday night shows at the Pub of Love whenever she could afford a babysitter for her five-year-old daughter. Rachel told me that she had been deeply moved by the environment at the Pub of Love, and her experiences there "touched her heart." Although Rachel did paint at early MuzikMafia performances, she did not paint on stage in an official capacity until several years later.

Rachel's active involvement with MuzikMafia began serendipitously through Max Abrams, whom she formally met in January 2003. Rachel and Max had been introduced to each other by mutual friend and Nashville song writer Doug Levitt, who arranged for Max to babysit Rachel's daughter. At the time, Max was in the process of organizing his Circvs Maximvs and had organized the show to include well-known cubist painter Marvin Posey, who had shown an interest in Max's ideas.

While discussing Rachel's participation in Circvs Maximvs, Max received a phone call from Big Kenny. Surprised by the fact that they were both acquaintances of Kenny, Rachel and Max conversed about their mutual connection to the MuzikMafia and their common interest in musical and artistic experimentation.

Rachel participated in Circvs Maximvs in February 2003 as the "lovely assistant" to Max, the "ringmaster" of the event. Two weeks after the death of artist Marvin Posey, Max asked Rachel to fill the position; she agreed. Rachel began capturing the event's atmosphere on canvas the following week. John and Kenny, who frequented and often performed spoken word for Circvs Maximvs, admired Rachel's talent as an artist and performer. After John and Kenny signed their recording contract with Warner Bros. in August 2002, they invited Rachel to paint during several of their performances that fall. She has since remained a regular fixture on the MuzikMafia stage.

Commonly known by his stage name "Cowboy Troy" and for his close association with Big & Rich, Troy Coleman contributed to the MuzikMafia's diversity his own combination of country and rap, which he describes as "hick-hop." In contrast to Chance, who considers himself to be primarily a hip hop artist who identifies with Southern culture, Troy identifies himself as a country artist who performs rap music, among other styles.

At six feet five inches tall and 250 pounds, Troy is a dominant figure on stage, complete with cowboy boots, a large belt buckle, a T-shirt, and a black cowboy hat. Although these images are common among commercial country artists, the fact that Troy is African American raises many questions about the role of race in commercial country music and MuzikMafia's response to the Anglo-American dominance over the genre.

Troy was born on December 18, 1970, in Victoria, Texas. His family moved to Ft. Worth when he was five years old and to Dallas when he was thirteen, where he remained throughout high school. In 1989 Troy began his undergraduate studies at the University of Texas–Austin; he graduated in 1993 with a Bachelor of Arts in Psychology. Troy began a master's degree in economics at Texas A&M University in 1998. He took an extended leave of absence in 1999, returned to his studies in 2000, and left the graduate program in 2001 twelve credits shy of graduation. He told me in 2004 that his decision had been the result of his growing interest in pursuing music professionally and his disenchantment with a future career in academia.

Troy's diverse musical interests are similar to those of many MuzikMafia members. He received much exposure to jazz and blues from his father, who had studied music in college. Troy remembers listening as a child to artists such as Maynard Ferguson, Chuck Mangione, Branford Marsalis, Ray Charles, and Tom Brown. Troy's mother exposed him to commercial country artists of the time such as Kenny Rogers, Dolly Parton, Charlie Daniels, John Denver, and Jerry Reed. During the late 1970s and early 1980s, Troy's interests diversified to include music by Foreigner, Boston, Kansas, Steely Dan, the Eagles, Kiss, and Def Leppard. The first album that Troy purchased with his allowance was ZZ Top's *Eliminator,* released in 1983. After moving to Dallas in 1984, Troy began listening to rap and hip hop music by Run-D.M.C., the Fat Boys, the Beastie Boys, and Whodini.

Although classified legally as an African American, Troy's ethnic background is as diverse as his musical interests. According to family members, Troy's heritage includes, to varying degrees, Caucasian, African American, Native American Choctaw, Chinese, and Mexican ethnicities. In addition to being fluent in English and Spanish, Troy has taken courses in Chinese language. When asked to describe Troy's background in November 2004, John Rich humorously referred to him as being "Afro-Cauca-Choca-Nese." However, Troy discourages the use of ethnic labels in his case, describing himself first and foremost as "an American."

Troy actively began to pursue his interest in performing rap music in 1989 while a freshman in college. In an attempt to emulate their favorite artists on MTV's show *Yo MTV Raps*, Troy and his two roommates composed their own songs. Troy's friends encouraged him to perform his musical publicly, which he did at various fraternity parties and local Austin clubs. Troy described to me his personal rap flow as, "Sometimes in 4/4 but not always; some songs are more syncopated than others; my flow varies from song to song and sometimes it changes within a song; this way I keep the listener's attention." He also revealed that his flow is primarily a combination of two sources: rhythmic complexity from rap artists such as Ice Cube, Everlast, Public Enemy, Run-D.M.C., LL Cool J, and Kid Rock; and lyrical and tonal influences from the 1970s band sound defined by Kansas, Boston, and Foreigner.

Troy first met John in 1993 at a Dallas music club named the Borrowed Money Saloon. John was performing with the group Lonestar. The two became friends and remained in contact with one another for several years. At John's invitation, Troy made brief visits to Nashville in 1998, 1999, and 2000 in search of employment. During his first trip, Troy met and befriended Kenny who, at the time, was performing regularly with his rock band luvjOi. John and Kenny invited Troy to make guest appearances at their respective venues when Troy was in town. Most shows took place at 12th & Porter in downtown Nashville.

Troy first performed with the MuzikMafia on December 10, 2001. Thereafter he either drove or flew to Nashville once each month from Dallas for such appearances. In 2002 Troy independently released an album entitled *Beginner's Luck* that included contributions by godfathers John, Jon, and Kenny. Troy's Dallas job at a Foot Locker shoe store from April 2003 to June 2004 kept him from attending Nashville shows more frequently. Troy finally moved to Nashville in summer 2004, enabling him to attend Tuesday night shows whenever he was not on tour with John and Kenny.

John and Kenny signed a contract with Warner Bros. in fall 2002 to record *Horse of a Different Color*. The duo included a rap interlude sung by Troy on "Rollin' (The Ballad of Big & Rich)," the album's first track. Troy accompanied John and Kenny on their 2004 summer tour with Tim McGraw and performed at each show on the Chevrolet American Revolution Tour in fall 2004. Within a period of five months, Troy's life transformed from working at Foot Locker in Dallas to performing on a national tour for crowds in excess of ten thousand fans with the MuzikMafia and regular appearances on national television.

Also known as Mista D, Damien Horne started performing regularly with the MuzikMafia in August 2002, although he did not become an official member until early 2005. His musical style includes strong influences from R&B, gospel, and pop.

Damien was born July 14, 1978, in Hickory, North Carolina, into a low-income family. Damien is one of twelve siblings: four by his parents, Barbara Horn and Charles Semmes, and eight whom his father sired with other women. Damien grew up largely influenced by his mother, who encouraged his participation in the local church choir. His father, an alcoholic for much of Damien's life, played a lesser role in Damien's early development.

Damien's musical interests centered on gospel and R&B throughout much of his childhood and early adult years. He began learning to play piano at age seventeen by copying church musicians. Following high school graduation in Hickory and a two-year stint at Guilford Tech in Greensboro, Damien moved to Hollywood, California, where he became homeless for a year before returning home to North Carolina. In the summer of 2002 he moved to Nashville and immediately started learning guitar in addition to his seminary studies at Freewill Baptist College. While performing one night on the corner of 2nd Avenue and Broadway, Damien caught the attention of John Rich, who invited him to perform the following week with the MuzikMafia.

Jerry Navarro described his role in the MuzikMafia as "sideman." As the primary bassist for the collective, Jerry's duties were twofold. From January 2004 through December 2005 he accompanied the MuzikMafia during most Tuesday night shows in Nashville. However, Jerry was also bassist for most of Jon Nicholson's solo endeavors, including his 2005 debut album entitled *A Lil' Sump'm Sump'm*. His Hispanic background contributed much to the musical and racial diversity of the MuzikMafia, and, like many members, Jerry had overcome numerous obstacles.

Jerry was born on March 1, 1976, in Oxnard, California, a small farm-
ing community between Los Angeles and Santa Barbara. His father Phillip,
a professional guitarist, introduced Jerry to music at a young age. Jerry's
mother, a Mexican immigrant with only a sixth-grade education, inspired
her son, among other ways, through her entrepreneurial achievements,
including her own cleaning business in Oxnard with approximately twenty-
five employees.

Jerry was exposed to music throughout his childhood. Jerry began
guitar lessons at age five with his father, and by age six was regularly performing traditional Mexican music with his family at local restaurants and
churches in Oxnard. Introduced to him by his aunt Terry, the bass became
the focus of Jerry's interests at age twelve. Jerry's father asked Terry to
teach Jerry bass to fill a vacant position in Satin Soul, a local band that comprised members of the Navarro and Preciado families. Jerry later admit
ted that the instrument "spoke" to him, and he has remained a bass player
since.

At age fourteen Jerry met Toby Preciado Sr., with whom he formed
Satin Soul II. Toby had assembled the original Satin Soul some twenty years
prior. The other members of Satin Soul were Jerry's uncle David, aunt Terry,
and his father Phillip, as well as friends from the Preciado family. Headed by
Toby Preciado Sr., Satin Soul II featured the next generation of musicians
from both families, mostly between the ages of nine and fourteen.

Although Jerry began performing with his family using an acoustic guitar with nylon strings, he later switched to electric guitar while in middle
school. The change in instrument resulted in changes in Jerry's musical
interests. In high school Jerry focused on styles that emphasized electric
guitar, especially heavy metal and a host of popular hard rock groups of
the 1980s and early 1990s. Jerry's favorite groups included Slayer, Metallica, and S.O.D. (Stormtroopers of Death). Throughout high school Jerry
complemented family performances at local restaurants with brief stints in
Oxnard punk and ska bands.

Jerry attributes much of his current musical philosophy to his experiences with Toby and Satin Soul II. According to Jerry, Toby instilled in
each band member a dedication to perfection through often painstaking
attention to rhythm, timbre, and musical expressiveness. Jerry describes

an important lesson that he learned from Toby: "[In order to play bass well] You can't be a frustrated guitar player; you have to accept your role as a sideman. It's not about you; it's about the music." Jerry's musical influences from his teen years include John Coltrane, Tito Puente, Machito, and a local Latin jazz sextet known as the Estrada Brothers that included Rubin "Cougar" Estrada.

Jerry has overcome numerous obstacles in his life, especially in regard to difficulties in education. He attended Port Hueneme High School in Oxnard, with approximately eighty percent of its student body being of lower to middle class and of Hispanic descent. Describing his education there as of "poor quality," Jerry dropped out of high school in 1993 at age seventeen to pursue music professionally. However, his uncle, who had attended college, encouraged Jerry to enroll at Ventura College in nearby Ventura, California, to learn music theory and ear training and to gain piano proficiency before depending on music as a sole source of income.

Without notifying his high school or his parents of his decision, Jerry enrolled at Ventura College with the assistance of a counselor with Extended Opportunity Programs and Services (EOPS), a department that facilitated a college education for underprivileged minorities. Jerry had lied on his application by stating his age as eighteen instead of seventeen, and the college did not require that he submit high school transcripts. While at Ventura College, Jerry took a standard battery of music courses in addition to private lessons from jazz guitarist and friend Mathew Greif. Meanwhile, his former high school had not noticed his truancy, and in the spring before his expected graduation, Jerry received from his school order forms for a cap and gown for his graduation, which he did not attend. Jerry later received his GED as a result of accumulated college credits.

In 1996 Jerry transferred to Belmont University in Nashville on the advice of Steve Spittle, an Oxnard bass player and friend who had taught bass guitar at several music stores before moving to Nashville in 1995. At Belmont, Jerry studied bass guitar with Roy Vogt. Jerry funded his education with college loans and income earned performing on weekends with local music groups. By August 1998 Jerry had decided to leave Belmont. Following a brief semester of study at Middle Tennessee State University in nearby Murfreesboro, Jerry left higher education in January 1999 without completing his degree in order to pursue music full time in the Nashville area.

Jerry's first significant contact with the MuzikMafia occurred in December 2003 when godfather Jon Nicholson invited Jerry to join his new group that fused rock and roll, rhythm and blues, and soul. Jon had heard of Jerry through a mutual friend, MuzikMafia percussionist Pino Squillace, whom Jerry had met on numerous occasions at Pino's Nashville club Caffee Milano. Following several telephone conversations and a brief audition, Jon asked Jerry and newly hired drummer Elijah "D.D." Holt to perform at a MuzikMafia show on Tuesday, January 6, 2004, at the Dan McGuiness Pub.

Elijah "D.D." Holt was known by MuzikMafia members and fans as Jon Nicholson's drummer and keyboardist. Pino contacted both D.D. and Jerry in early 2004 for the purpose of filling vacancies in Jon's band. The Muzik-Mafia had resumed performances in January 2004 at Dan McGuinness Pub, and the weekly event gave Jon the opportunity to experiment with new band members.

D.D. was born Elijah Demond Holt in Nashville on September 19, 1973, and grew up in nearby Hendersonville. He started taking drums lessons at age nine at a local music store. When D.D. was fourteen years old, his uncle introduced him to the basics of gospel-style organ. In 1993 D.D. became the regular organist with the famed Born Again Church in Nashville, a position that he has held ever since. D.D. is an accomplished percussionist and organist, and he has performed with many well-known artists independent of his MuzikMafia affiliation. According to D.D., his first professional experience as a musician was at age seventeen when he began performing regularly with gospel legend Bobby Jones, including national tours and several broadcast performances on Black Entertainment Television (BET). From 1997 to 2002 D.D. toured with seven time Grammy Award winner CeCe Winans, also a member of the Born Again Church.

A native of Taylorsville, Kentucky, Shannon Lawson is the only MuzikMafia member whose musical style contains considerable ties to bluegrass. In addition, he incorporates other influences such as blues, rhythm and blues, funk, and commercial country, separating him stylistically from many bluegrass artists.

Shannon's exposure to bluegrass began at an early age. He was born on July 12, 1970, in Taylorsville, Kentucky, thirty-three miles southeast of Louisville. His childhood was spent working on the family tobacco farm and playing bluegrass music. Shannon's family includes numerous musicians dating back several generations to a Confederate fiddle player named Elihu Green Lawson who performed regularly while incarcerated at Andersonville Prison in Sumter County, Georgia. Shannon's father Bob Lawson, who is proficient on the guitar, mandolin, banjo, bass, and Dobro, taught Shannon how to play guitar at age seven. Bob Lawson and Shannon's uncle Glenn formed their own bluegrass band in the early 1970s known as the Lawson Brothers. Glenn was later invited to tour with J. D. Crowe & the New South. Glenn also performed for several years in Spectrum, a bluegrass group that included Bela Fleck, Mark Schatz, and Jimmy Gaudreau. In a 1997 interview with *Louisville Magazine*'s Bob Bahr, Shannon recalled, "All my uncles used to practice with my dad at my grandma's on the front porch outside at night, and my cousins and I used to dance around and in between them while they were playing."

In high school Shannon set aside his interest in bluegrass to pursue rock, blues, and rhythm and blues. His strongest musical influences at that time were Pink Floyd, Led Zeppelin, Jimi Hendrix, Stevie Ray Vaughn, Lead Belly, and Richard "Kush" Griffin, who had been a member of George Clinton's band Parliament. Shannon's first professional engagement came at the age of eighteen, when Kush Griffin invited Shannon to play with his Sunstroke Blues Band. At the time, Shannon's father was experimenting with more complex styles of guitar technique associated with Andrés Segovia and Chet Atkins. According to Shannon, both influences contributed much to his own eclectic style.

After graduating from high school in 1988, Shannon briefly attended the University of Kentucky at Louisville. He left the university when Chicago blues musician Burt "Top Hat" Robinson invited him to perform regularly with his club act in Louisville. Shannon remained with Top Hat's band for three years before returning to his bluegrass roots.

In 1993 Shannon founded the Galoots, a bluegrass-based band that became well-known in the Louisville area. According to Shannon, the group marked a return to his bluegrass roots but with stylistic influences from rock, blues, and rhythm and blues. The Galoots included Dennis Talley on upright bass, Todd Osborne on banjo, Mike Schroeder on mandolin, and Shannon on lead guitar and vocals. The experience provided Shannon with an outlet for his growing interest in songwriting, eventually resulting in three relatively successful self-distributed Galoots albums. The group's live performances were well-known for their inclusion of roots covers of popular tunes, namely "Whippin' Post" by the Allman Brothers, "All Along the Watchtower" by Bob Dylan, "Let's Get It On" by Marvin Gaye, and "Ring of Fire" by Johnny Cash.

Shannon moved to Nashville in 1998 with his wife Mandy, a Louisville disc jockey whom Shannon had met in May 1996 when she invited him to appear on her radio show. Shannon's first job in Nashville included regular performances at the Station Inn, a well-known venue for bluegrass and acoustic music. The exposure led to Shannon's publishing contract with Extreme Writers Group and, eventually, a record deal with MCA.

Shannon's debut album, *Chase the Sun*, was released in spring 2002 by MCA and led to several appearances at the Grand Ole Opry that year. Although Shannon likes his first album, he felt that its commercial sound was not what he would have created without the influence of MCA producer Mark Wright. For example, the album's eleventh track contains a cover of Marvin Gaye's 1973 soul classic "Let's Get It On." The version that appears on the album—with moderate tempo, relatively small tessitura, and relaxed Latin drum rhythm in the background—contrasts greatly with the version that Shannon had been performing live since 1993. Shannon's original cover of the tune comprises slow and fast tempos, country and funk rhythms on the drums and bass, a broad vocal range with numerous blues-influenced fills, vocal cadenzas, and numerous instrumental solos. At Shannon's request, included on the album as a hidden track was a gospel song, "They Hung Him on the Cross," that Shannon had learned in his youth from a Lead Belly recording.

Following considerable artistic dispute with MCA Records for a possible second album, Shannon left the label to produce his own music. In 2004 he independently released a follow-up album, *The Acoustic Livingroom Session*. Recorded at the home of friend Dan Friszell in Franklin, Tennessee, the album features all-acoustic instrumentation and stronger bluegrass influence. He told me that much of his fanbase preferred *The Acoustic Livingroom Session* to the commercial sound of his first album with MCA, which had been produced for and marketed to radio audiences.

As an active performer within the Nashville music scene, Shannon was well aware of the birth, growth, and development of the MuzikMafia from its origins at the Pub of Love in October 2001. However, it was not until

January 2004 that he performed on stage for the first time with the Muzik-Mafia. Shannon had known godfathers John and Jon from their Nashville performances and through mutual connections to Extreme Writers Group. Shannon frequented John's shows at the Exit/In, where Jon also performed on occasion. In addition, Shannon had written many songs with Rodney Clawson, John's former baseball coach from high school. Jon invited Shannon to attend a MuzikMafia show in January 2004 at the Dan McGuiness Pub. Shannon was inducted into the MuzikMafia in November that year.

Dean Hall's virtuosic guitar style—a synthesis of blues and southern rock that distanced him from the attention of major labels on Music Row—was attractive to the MuzikMafia from his first appearance with them in 2004. His position as the lead electric guitarist for the MuzikMafia spotlighted his musical talent and provided him with a creative outlet for individual musical expression.

Dean was born on June 11, 1961, in Grayson, Kentucky, the son of well-known commercial country entertainer Tom T. Hall. Dean began his musical training on drums at three, largely influenced by his uncle Harold McKinney, who lived in nearby Flatwoods, Kentucky. However, within two years Dean had developed a fascination with guitar through much exposure to records by Johnny Cash, B.B. King, and Jimi Hendrix that he listened to on the family's phonograph and, on occasion, live bluegrass music of the region. He remained in Grayson throughout his childhood, leaving only after high school graduation in spring 1979 for college.

In fall 1979 Dean attended the University of Kentucky–Lexington on a football scholarship. At six feet three inches and 215 pounds, and with a muscular build, Dean adjusted well to college athletics. His girlfriend and future wife Carol described Dean at the time as being "clean cut with short hair . . . self-confident."

After his freshman year, Dean transferred to Vanderbilt University in Nashville. In addition to his plans to study medicine at the well-known university hospital, Dean wanted to get to know his father, who was residing in Nashville at the time. Dean had had relatively little contact with Tom T. Hall since his parents' divorce in 1962. Dean was ten years old when he met his father, at which time Tom T. Hall gave him his first guitar. Dean first became aware that his father was a well-known entertainer during a junior high talent show; a student sang "Harper Valley P.T.A.," after which Dean's teacher told him that his father had written the song. After transferring to Vanderbilt, Dean reconnected with his father. Tom T. Hall emphasized the importance of education to his son by financing Dean's studies while at Vanderbilt. Dean later assumed the costs of tuition, room, and board after transferring to Middle Tennessee State University twenty-five miles southeast of Nashville. He had heard of the Recording Industry Program at MTSU and wanted to pursue a career in the music business. Dean took courses in music theory, music history, music copyright, and music publishing.

In 1983 Dean left MTSU to tour with his father's band. There he learned the music business from the ground up—selling T-shirts, carrying equipment, repairing the bus, and playing guitar from time to time. However, Tom T. Hall advised his son against being a sideman in someone else's band, urging Dean to learn how to write his own songs and to perfect his guitar skills.

Dean spent the next few years between school and the road. After a two-month stint touring with Marie Osmond in 1983, Dean returned to MTSU, only to leave again the same year to fill a sudden vacancy in his father's band. Dean toured with his father until 1989. Dean viewed his experiences on the road with his father as a training period for his future career in music. In 1989 Dean accompanied country singer Bobby Bare on tour for approximately one year. Dean returned to his father's band later that year before embarking on his own solo career.

By 1993 Dean was well-known in the Nashville area. Regular performances at Rivalry's Sports Bar on Murfreesboro Pike, where he performed every Tuesday between 1994 and 2004, and at 3rd and Lindsley led to significant career opportunities. While performing at Rivalry's in 1997, Dean caught the attention of NASCAR executives who had been invited to attend the show by Benny Quinn of Masterfonics, the Nashville studio that had mastered Dean's second album, *The Ghost of James Bell*. Quinn had discussed with Dean the possibility of performing at NASCAR races, and when the executives offered to let him headline his own show, Dean accepted the job with the stipulation that he would not endorse cigarettes. According to Dean, he had reservations about Winston cigarettes' sponsorship of NASCAR because of his dislike for tobacco products. He advocated personal choice in the matter of tobacco use or non-use, but did not want his position as entertainer to endorse the tobacco industry or its products.

While touring with NASCAR, Dean's popularity as an entertainer grew significantly. Approximately three hundred people attended Dean's first show in 1997, and a crowd of 5,000 were at his show the following evening. Dean began touring with his own bus and staging for NASCAR events that soon averaged 10,000 to 18,000 people per performance. Winston pulled its sponsorship of Dean's show in 2000 due to governmental regulations regarding cigarette advertising at NASCAR events, and Dean's contract was not renewed. Soon thereafter Winston discontinued its overall sponsorship of NASCAR, and the circuit eventually underwent a name change to the Nextel Cup.

Shortly after resuming regular performances at Rivalry's Sports Bar that same year, Dean was discovered by a production crew in town for the filming of *The Last Castle*, starring Robert Redford and James Gandolfini. Friend Chet Frist, who was director of the Tennessee Film Commission at the time, invited the production crew to Rivalry's to see Dean perform. Dean's large stature and shaved head made him appropriate for a movie filmed at the former Tennessee State Prison, and the film's production crew invited him to audition. Dean did not get the part but was asked to remain as an extra. While on set, Dean composed a blues song titled "Chiseled in Stone," describing the hardships associated with prison life. Director Rod Lurie heard about Dean's musical abilities and solicited examples of his work. Lurie asked if he could use "Chiseled in Stone" for the scene following the death of inmate Aguilar. The song appears again during the closing credits.

Dean confirms that his musical style is deeply rooted in blues, but he was not exposed to traditional blues music until after he left Kentucky for Nashville. He affirms that he learned blues chords listening to the music of Led Zeppelin, the Allman Brothers, ZZ Top, and Eric Clapton, which explains the considerable rock influence in Dean's music. After becoming an accomplished guitarist, Dean sought out recordings by Robert Johnson, Freddie King, Elmore James, and Muddy Waters, and eventually incorporated their sounds into his own blues-rock style.

Dean's association with MuzikMafia musicians began in the late 1990s at Rivalry's, where he often performed when not on tour with NASCAR. Jon Nicholson frequented Dean's shows, occasionally joining him on stage. Nicholson was sharing an apartment with Big Kenny at the time; he brought his roommate to Rivalry's to make introductions but the three engaged in no professional collaborations until several years later.

Dean did not perform on the MuzikMafia stage until March 2004. Dean had been recently fired for playing too loud at his regular Tuesday night gig at a club called the Box Seat in the Green Hills area of Nashville, so with an unexpected opening in his schedule, he decided to attend a MuzikMafia show at the Mercy Lounge. Godfathers Jon, Kenny, and John already knew of Dean's musical abilities, having heard him perform at Rivalry's Sport's Bar. He underwent formal initiation into the MuzikMafia on June 23, 2004, in New York City, where the collective performed at CBGB and the Cutting Room. The purpose for the trip was to promote Big & Rich's album *Horse of a Different Color*, which had been released the previous month.

In fall 2004 Dean experienced numerous career successes. In September he received three nominations for the 5th Annual Music City Blues Awards: Blues Guitarist of the Year, Entertainer of the Year, and Electric Act of the Year. In October he performed with Gretchen Wilson and Big & Rich on the Radio Music Awards that was televised live on NBC from Las Vegas. Dean accompanied the MuzikMafia on the Chevrolet American Revolution Tour in thirteen cities from Charleston, South Carolina, to Fresno, California. In February 2005 Dean performed with Gretchen Wilson as part of the pre-game concert for Superbowl XXIX broadcast live on Fox. That year he toured regularly with Wilson as her lead guitarist. Dean's invitation to join Wilson's band was highlighted in Episode 6 of *MuzikMafia TV*, which first aired on Country Music Television (CMT) on February 5, 2005.

Timothy C. Smith, known among friends and fans as Chance, contributed much to the MuzikMafia. Although Chance's time with the MuzikMafia was brief (2004–2006), he played a significant role in the community as an example of musical excellence and stylistic diversity. He described to me his own style of music as "southern hip-hop: a combination of country, rap, and southern rock." Unlike Cowboy Troy, whose music has been marketed primarily to commercial country audiences, Chance appeals more to hip hop enthusiasts.

Born Timothy Cheth Smith on September 4, 1980, in Huntington, West Virginia, Chance received his future stage name in elementary school in Nashville. In contrast to many rappers who receive their aliases from peers or through self-proclamation, his teachers consistently mispronounced his middle name. The misnomer has since become a metaphor for his personal and professional approach to overcoming life's challenges.

Chance was exposed to commercial country and rap music from early childhood. His parents, a regional country music duo known as Tim and Pauline, brought Chance with them on the road two weeks after his birth. Consisting of the father, mother, and one backup singer, the act traveled via tour bus for five years from 1980 to 1985 along the East Coast, performing alternative styles of commercial country with such artists as Willie Nelson, David Allen Coe, and Tanya Tucker. Musical performance afforded the family only a modest lifestyle, despite two Top Twenty hits in the mid-1980s, "Dreamy Eyes" and "Cowboy Boots and Soft Blue Denim."

The early years of touring prepared Chance for his future profession in music through constant contact with the public, numerous stage appearances, widespread travel, and regular exposure to hybrid styles of music such as country-rock. Chance was also influenced musically by amateur rapper Rio Clemmons, the older brother of Kenyatta "Kenny" Clemmons, one of Chance's close friends from elementary school. The presence of commercial country and rap music in Chance's early childhood explain the symbiosis between the two in his professional career in the form of Southern hip hop.

The divorce of his parents in 1985 and his mother's eventual death from cancer in 1993 contributed to Chance's difficult childhood. He recalls attending twelve different schools from Tennessee to Virginia throughout his educational career, remaining in one place no longer than two years at a time. As a result of ongoing problems at school and at home, Chance was sent by his father and stepmother to Fork Union Military Academy in Virginia in 1993, where he reached the rank of battalion training officer by the time of his graduation in spring 1998.

In fall 1998 Chance continued his education at Austin Peay State University in Clarksville, fifty miles northwest of Nashville. Majoring in English and business, Chance pursued hobbies such as emceeing, basketball, and football. He supported himself with monies earned from the Bates Motel, the former fraternity house of Sigma Phi Epsilon that Chance rented and operated to provide musical entertainment and "refreshment" to university students. He left Austin Peay in 2003 twelve credits shy of graduation and returned to Nashville to pursue music professionally.

Since 1999 he had been organizing and hosting battles during weekly trips to Nashville. After the move Chance dedicated himself full-time to developing the relatively small hip hop scene. His battles provided an outlet for local artists such as 187 Blitz, Boom Bap, Kyhil, Father Abraham, T-Tone, and Afro Pic; turntablists United Crates, DJ Kutt, and DJ Chosen; and Chance's own collective, known as the Dragon Farm Project and including POW Shadows, Jelly Roll, and RPM. Numerous public performances by these artists contributed to the establishment of a comparatively stable Nashville hip hop scene by 2004.

Chance first became acquainted with the MuzikMafia in winter 2001 through Isaac Rich, a close friend at Austin Peay and brother of godfather John Rich. Isaac was a member of Alpha Gamma Rho (AGR), whose fraternity house was adjacent to the Bates Motel. Chance had cultivated numerous friendships with members of AGR, known to many university students as the "redneck" fraternity. Chance and Isaac attended the first MuzikMafia session at the Pub of Love, where Chance met godfathers John, Kenny, and Jon. While studying at Austin Peay, Chance's weekly visits to Nashville included regular attendance at MuzikMafia shows.

Chance's performance debut with the MuzikMafia took place in the spring of 2004 at the Mercy Lounge. MuzikMafia Mizfit member SWJ had seen Chance perform previously at the well-known Tootsie's Orchid Lounge on Lower Broadway in downtown Nashville. Chance also performed with the Mafia Mizfits on occasion. SWJ recommended to MuzikMafia member Damien Horne that he invite Chance on stage. During a Tuesday night show, Damien did so in mid-song, providing Chance with an opportunity for an impromptu performance of his local favorite "I Came to Drink" for the first time in front of a MuzikMafia audience. Three weeks later John, Kenny, and Jon invited Chance back to perform for a second time on stage.

In between MuzikMafia shows, Chance engaged in promoting his own career as a southern hip hop artist. Chance's close friend, Nashville music promoter Jekorie "T-Tone" Eason, shared some of Chance's demo recordings with Sony Records. The label subsequently requested a showcase to hear Chance in a live setting. The showcase segment took place at the Mercy Lounge on May 25, 2004, during a MuzikMafia performance and consisted of Chance's most popular songs of the time: "I Came to Drink," "Eyes of a Dead Man," "Ridin' on Chrome," and "Four Shots of Jack." Although the performance did not lead to a record deal with Sony, Chance's performance was well received by the audience as well as among MuzikMafia musicians. He underwent formal initiation into the MuzikMafia several weeks later.

In addition to performing at weekly MuzikMafia sessions and unscheduled appearances at numerous Mafia Mizfits shows, Chance celebrated various successes throughout fall 2004 and 2005. On November 18, 2004, Chance was named Crossover Artist of the Year at the 14th Annual L.A. Music Awards in Los Angeles. His appearance at the awards ceremony was recorded by a film crew for the *MuzikMafia TV* series and aired on Country Music Television (CMT) in spring 2005. In October 2004 Chance competed in and won the preliminary round for *MTV's Battles*, qualifying him for the finals to be held in spring 2005. In November and December 2004 Chance performed with the MuzikMafia at the last five of its thirteen scheduled performances as part of the Chevrolet American Revolution Tour.

On October 26, 2004, Chance organized the first performance of the Tennessee Trailer Choir, a weekly concert whose diverse format was similar to that of the MuzikMafia, highlighting talented local artists of varying genres. The show had actually begun under the name the Trashville Music Choir at Bluesboro Rhythm and Blues Co. in Murfreesboro. In December 2004 the Tennessee Trailer Choir released a Christmas album titled *Mistletoe Belt Buckle Christmas,* underwritten by the MuzikMafia and whose proceeds were donated to Nashville's Angel Tree program sponsored by the Salvation Army. By 2005 Chance's collective had become the Nashville Trailer Choir but no longer included Chance, who was busy working on his album with Raybaw Records. The Trailer Choir caught the attention of country music superstar Toby Keith, who invited the group to perform with him on tour. The Trailer Choir also appeared as the house band in Toby Keith's 2008 movie *Beer for My Horses.*

Fred Gill is among the most recognizable members of the MuzikMafia, having received national attention as the dwarf who appeared in Big & Rich's video for the hit song, "Save a Horse (Ride a Cowboy)." Although Fred is three feet two inches tall, he is known by friends and fans as Two Foot Fred or The Deuce.

Born July 27, 1974, in Seymour, Indiana, Fred experienced considerable health problems early on in life. He was born with a form of dwarfism known as diastrophic displaysia. His other ailments from birth included a cauliflower ear, a cleft palate, two club feet, and scoliosis; he endured multiple surgeries throughout his childhood. He graduated from high school in 1993 and began his studies at Ball State University, where he graduated in 1997 from the Entrepreneurship Program with a Bachelor of Science in Business with a concentration in entrepreneurship. Today, Fred's corporation, Gill Enterprises, LLC, owns a Seymour pub called the Funkey Monkey, 259 rental properties, and a spice company called Phat Freddie's Seasonings.

Fred became a member of the MuzikMafia through John, whom he met at a Nashville bar during Fan Fair in 1998. The two corresponded with one another every few months until February 2004, when John approached Fred about appearing in the video. In 2004 and 2005 Fred appeared with Big & Rich on their tours with Tim McGraw, Brooks & Dunn, and the Muzik-Mafia, as well as in a parody video of Toby Keith's song "Never Smoke Weed with Willie."

The "godfathers." Front row: Cory Gierman and John Rich. Back row: Jon Nicholson and Kenny Alphin. Courtesy of Cory Gierman.

The godfathers at the Pub of Love 2001–2: John Rich, Kenny Alphin, and Jon Nicholson. Courtesy of Cory Gierman.

James Otto, Jon Nicholson, and Max Abrams
at the Pub of Love, March 27, 2002. Courtesy of
Cory Gierman.

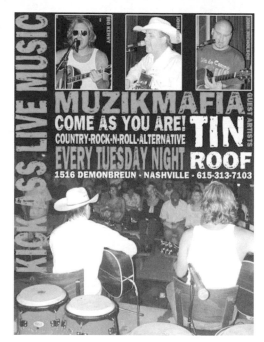

Advertisement for MuzikMafia Shows at the
Tin Roof, 2002–3. Courtesy of Cory Gierman.

MuzikMafia Hits L.A.

Songwriter Acoustic Jam Session
Featuring:
John Rich
Big Kenny
Jon Nicholson

Sunday May 19th 9 p.m.
at the Lil Wonder Bar
2692 S La Cienega Blvd
310-837-7443

Monday May 20th 9-11p.m.
at the Martini Lounge
5767 Melrose Ave
323-467-4068

MuzikMafia.com

Advertisement for MuzikMafia show in Los Angeles, 2002. Courtesy of Cory Gierman.

Gretchen Wilson and John Rich at Dan McGuinness Pub, January 27, 2004. Courtesy of Cory Gierman.

Cowboy Troy, Jon Nicholson, and Kenny Alphin at the Hideout in Chicago. Courtesy of Cory Gierman.

Collective jam at the Mercy Lounge, June 15, 2004. Left to right: John Rich, James Otto, Jerry Navarro, Kenny Alphin, and Damien Horne. Jon Nicholson is standing behind James Otto.

John Rich and Gretchen Wilson on stage at the Mercy Lounge, July 13, 2004.

Rachel Kice paints at MuzikMafia show at Bluesboro, July 27, 2004.

Concert with Kid Rock. Left to right: John Rich, Kid Rock, and Kenny Alphin. Courtesy of Nancy Gierman.

The "godfathers." Kenny Alphin, Jon Nicholson, Cory Gierman, and John Rich. Courtesy of Deanna Kay.

Adam Shoenfeld on tour with Big & Rich. Courtesy of Cory Gierman.

Shannon Lawson and Dean Hall. Courtesy of Cory Gierman.

Two-Foot Fred on tour with Big & Rich
(Deuces Wild Tour with Brooks & Dunn).
Courtesy of Cory Gierman.

Downtown Nashville skyline as seen
from the MuzikMafia's former offices,
February 2006.

Chapter Six

2005
The Second Wave

By the end of 2004 the MuzikMafia had created a significant niche for itself in commercial country music and American popular culture. However, the this success represented only a portion of the community's potential. Much to the delight of its fans and the music industry in general, the MuzikMafia began 2005 with several bangs.

MuzikMafia TV, a six-part television series that CMT broadcast weekly from January 15 through February 19, 2005, was both a television documentary and a reality show. The series included behind-the-scenes footage of life on the road with the MuzikMafia interspersed with information on its history. Ivan Dudynsky of Live Animals Productions had approached the godfathers in late summer 2004 with the idea of creating a television series on the Muzik-Mafia for CMT. He had already been slated to produce the CMT Outlaws, featuring Gretchen and Big & Rich and scheduled for taping on September 7. Live Animals Productions created MuzikMafia TV to document the community's rise to national prominence.

A significant portion of the show's content focused on the Chevrolet American Revolution Tour. Although the series clearly emphasized the tour's headliners Gretchen and Big & Rich, many episodes also contained segments featuring other artists, namely Jon, James, Troy, Dean, Max, Rachel, and Chance.

Episode One provided a general overview of the MuzikMafia and the meaning behind its motto "Music without Prejudice." Episode Two documented the community's invitation to visit and perform with Willie Nelson in Austin, a discussion about bringing Chance on tour, and the drama that followed Gretchen's winning the Top New Artist award over Kanye West at the American Music Awards. Episode Three featured Gretchen and her return home to sing the national anthem for a St. Louis Cardinals baseball game; Big & Rich recuperating in Deadwood, South Dakota; and Jon and his band recording his debut album in Woodstock, New York.

The show's producers included an even greater variety of themes in Episode Four. There were brief segments on James, Max, and Dean. In addition, the episode highlighted the MuzikMafia's excursion to Fort Benning Army Base in Columbus, Georgia, to experience the ranger training course. MuzikMafia members acknowledged the toughness of the course and paid their respects to the armed services. The patriotic aspect of Episode Four resurfaced when Kenny led a concert audience in the singing of the national anthem. The episode also included the sentimental story of a sixteen-year-old cancer patient whom Big & Rich had invited on stage at a show on November 16 in Hidalgo, Texas. The episode concluded with Gretchen firing her lead guitarist and Dean's quick preparations to fill the vacancy.

Episode Five was more lighthearted than the others. The viewer was able to observe Jon preparing a new dressing room with tie-dyed blankets and Lava Lamps, the trials and tribulations of living on a tour bus, James's problems with his hair, Kenny's parents joining the tour with homemade baked goods, and James's marriage proposal to his girlfriend on stage in Las Vegas.

The series concluded with Episode Six, which featured Troy and Gretchen. A brief discussion of Troy's background as a shoe salesman for Foot Locker prepared the viewer for the significance of a later scene in which Troy received news of his record deal with Raybaw. The episode concluded with a feature on Gretchen and her winning the Horizon Award at the CMAs.

In many ways, *MuzikMafia TV* was a double-edged sword for the community. On the one hand, the show introduced the next wave of artists—Jon, James, Troy, and Chance—whose careers would greatly benefit from the national television exposure. The series also confirmed Gretchen and Big & Rich's significance to commercial country music. In addition, Max, Rachel, and Pino's segments reinforced the idea of MuzikMafia as an artistic collective rather than just a few platinum-selling musicians.

On the other hand, several members were displeased with the series' shortcomings. For example, drummer Brian Barnett and guitarist Adam Shoenfeld appeared only infrequently and always in the context of their association with Big & Rich. Both Brian and Adam had played integral roles in the MuzikMafia since the Pub of Love. Moreover, Adam had been Kenny's lead guitarist in luvjOi for two years prior to the MuzikMafia's inception. In addition, the television series emphasized the more sensationalist aspects of the MuzikMafia in 2004, including attendance at awards shows, the tension with Kanye West, thousands of screaming fans, visits with Willie Nelson, the trip to Fort Benning, and James's wedding engagement. More than one member expressed to me their dissatisfaction with *MuzikMafia TV* because the series included little or no discussion of the actual music.

In January 2005 the MuzikMafia founded its own record label, Raybaw Records, a co-venture with Warner Bros. An acronym for "red and yellow, black and white," *Raybaw* came from the text of "Jesus Loves the Little Children," a Christian hymn particularly popular among Southern Baptists.

Jesus loves the little children,
All the children of the world.
Red and yellow, black and white,
All are precious in His sight,
Jesus loves the little children of the world.

The words had been written by a Chicago preacher named Clare Herbert Woolston (1856–1927) and set to a Civil War folk tune titled "Tramp, Tramp, Tramp," composed by George F. Root (1820–1895). John thought the text would appropriately reflect the ideas behind the record label's founding and the MuzikMafia's motto "Music without Prejudice."

Raybaw Records' relationship with Warner Bros. was that of a custom imprint: in the music industry, an imprint is usually started by a successful artist, management company, or label, and is pressed, distributed and promoted (and sometimes later purchased) by a larger label. Although Raybaw was a joint venture between Warner Bros. and the MuzikMafia, Raybaw did not cultivate the fully subordinate relationship to Warner Bros. that many imprints do with their parent companies.

Plans for Raybaw had begun in mid-2004. Paul Worley contacted the godfathers in late summer about starting a MuzikMafia-led record label associated with Warner Bros. John, Kenny, Jon, and Cory liked the idea. However, the godfathers insisted that "MuzikMafia" not appear in the label's official title. According to Cory: "We wanted to stay untouched by the music industry. We wanted to keep a bubble around it [the MuzikMafia]. . . . We went back to Warner [Bros.] and told them that Raybaw was the name. It was obvious that they were shocked by us not wanting to call it MuzikMafia Records."

Unfortunately, the MuzikMafia did not remain "untouched by the music industry." From the beginning, Raybaw Records caused significant changes to, and considerable tension within, the MuzikMafia's social structure.

The first hurdle was who Raybaw's principal owners would be. The four godfathers were obvious choices; however, none of them had experience running a record label or knew about the logistics of signing and promoting artists. The godfathers asked Dale Morris and Marc Oswald in as principal owners because of their many years of experience in the music industry. Dale's artist management company handled clients including Alabama, Kenny Chesney, and Louise Mandrell. Dale's business associate Marc managed Gretchen, Big & Rich, and Cowboy Troy. Dale and Marc were friends of the MuzikMafia and were enthusiastic about Raybaw's potential.

John, Kenny, Cory, Jon, Marc, and Dale spent fall 2004 working out the details of Raybaw's incorporation. By December Raybaw had begun to take shape. Warner Bros.' roles included financing album projects, marketing, and publicity. Raybaw would be responsible for artist research and development. After all, MuzikMafia had a reputation for attracting and showcasing some of the best talent in Nashville. Warner Bros. wanted the MuzikMafia to retain authority over the creative aspect of the label to ensure a continuous flow of talented artists.

The first visible presence of the MuzikMafia at Warner Bros. occurred in fall 2004, when Cory moved into his new office in the Warner Bros. building located at 20 Music Square East. Cory's third-floor corner office was slightly larger than Paul Worley's and overlooked both Music Row and the Demonbreun Street Roundabout. Warner Bros.' hiring Cory in September, as an independent consultant to handle all MuzikMafia-related matters, eventually led to the creation of Raybaw.

Raybaw was created with its first signed artist already in mind: Cowboy Troy. Cory later explained to me in a 2006 interview:

> We knew we had something with him [Troy]. We knew what type of record could be recorded: one that had never been done before. We knew that [with Troy] we could knock one out of the park. And he was already out on the road touring, and it was a great story, and with a label called "red and yellow, black and white," a black rapping cowboy was a great choice to start it off with. Our whole thing has been going against the industry and Music Row. By putting a black rapping cowboy in there, we were making a statement. We had no hesitation in that decision.

Troy signed his contract in January and began work on his debut album, which was scheduled for release in early summer.

James Otto was the second artist to sign with Raybaw. He had been experiencing considerable tension at Mercury. James's first album did not sell well, and his second (then under way) was not what Mercury had envisioned. James had asked John Rich to produce the album. John allowed James to be himself, including James's numerous influences from the Muscle Shoals Sound, the Alabama version of the Stax Sound in Memphis that James had demonstrated at MuzikMafia shows since the Pub of Love. James submitted five completed tracks to Mercury in January 2005, and was dropped from the label that month.

James's move from Mercury to Raybaw was not immediate. After his departure from Mercury, James received offers from Sony, Warner Bros., and Raybaw, each wanting to take over his contract. Cory described the situation to me as a "weird conflict of interest, with Warner Bros. and Raybaw bidding for James's contract, but that kind of got worked out." James signed with Raybaw in May, and the label purchased James's completed tracks from Mercury. James's completed album, *Sunset Man,* was finally released in 2008.

In November 2005 Chance became the third artist to sign with Raybaw. Contract negotiations had been under way since early spring. Chance's song "Pauline" convinced John, Paul, and the rest of the decision makers at Raybaw to offer Chance a deal. In 2006 Paul Worley described Chance's success at Raybaw:

> You ask me if Chance is going to be successful, and the answer's "yes." How it unfolds will be like everything else that unfolds from the MuzikMafia, because every one of the artists in the Mafia is unique. Chance's hip hop music falls outside that genre and certainly falls outside anything that has to do with country. The bottom line is that it shouldn't matter. In the old days, record labels found geniuses and supported them and figured out how to carry their music forward. And that's what we want to do. That's what MuzikMafia is all about, and that's what Raybaw is all about. That's what we're going to do for Chance. "Ridin' on Chrome" and "I Came to Drink" were what got me interested in Chance, but when I heard "Pauline," I realized that here's an artist with depth and one who is able to express everything about life.

Chance's album was tentatively scheduled for release in late 2006 or early 2007, and he recorded much of his debut album under Raybaw's budget. However, Chance left Raybaw in early 2007, before the album was completed, primarily because of ongoing tensions between him and Raybaw's management, namely John Rich.

Raybaw's first significant public exposure came with the release of Cowboy Troy's album *Loco Motive* in May 2005. John produced the album and also co-wrote most of its songs with Troy, whose goal with *Loco Motive,* as he described to me back in 2004, was to include "instrumentation from classic rock, a timeless sound comparable to Steely Dan and the Eagles, the flow of rap . . . and traditional country themes presented in a vastly different way." The album's first single "I Play Chicken with the Train" was a metaphor for a rapper going against the norms of commercial country music.

Loco Motive was a relatively successful debut when one considers the fact that Troy's self-titled version of rap known as "hick-hop" fit nowhere in radio's prescribed format categories. The album debuted at Number Two on *Billboard*'s Country Album chart, Number Thirteen on the Rap Album chart, and Number Fifteen on Billboard's Top 200, all of which were the album's peak positions. The single peaked at Number Eighteen on *Billboard*'s Bubbling Under Hot Singles chart the week of the album's release; "I Play Chicken with the Train" did not fare well on the country charts primarily because the single received relatively little radio airplay.

Troy's success in 2005 had little to do with radio or chart positions. Because of Troy's widespread exposure touring with Big & Rich and Tim McGraw in 2004, Raybaw shipped 400,000 units of *Loco Motive* prior to the album's release. Marc Oswald reported to the International Entertainment Buyers Association (IEBA) annual meeting in Nashville in October 2005 that plans were already in the works to do a second shipment. According to Cory, Troy's album had sold approximately 450,000 copies by spring 2007. On April 15 "I Play Chicken with the Train" for a brief time reached the Number One Download spot from the online digital music store iTunes.

Troy's television appearances in 2005 included a performance and interview on NBC's *The Tonight Show* with Jay Leno on May 19, ABC's *Good Morning America* May 30, and MSNBC's *Imus in the Morning* June 1. Troy also performed with Big & Rich in the *Boston Pops Fireworks Spectacular* broadcast live on CBS on July 4, the *CMA Music Festival* that CBS aired on August 2, the premiere of ESPN's *College Game Day* on September 3, and the *39th Annual Country Music Awards* broadcast live on November 15 on CBS.

In addition, articles on Troy appeared in print and online media throughout 2005, including features in the *Arizona Daily Star*, *AOL Entertainment News*, the *Tennessean*, *Country Weekly*, *New York Daily News*, *The Arizona Republic*, *Rolling Stone*, *Time*, and *USA Today*. In October 2005 Troy accepted an offer from the USA network to cohost with Wynonna the fourth season of *Nashville Star*, scheduled to air in spring 2006.

Raybaw underwent considerable change in fall 2005. First, Cory decided to move out of his office at Warner Bros. He told me that his decision was based mainly on his displeasure with corporate life. Cory had entered the music business as a song plugger and music publisher, working closely with the artists. His duties at Warner Bros and Raybaw concentrated largely on budget meetings and marketing strategies, none of which he was trained for. Second, Cory's role as godfather required that he tend to many MuzikMafia-related matters that were often beyond the scope of his duties at Raybaw. The result was some minor tension between Raybaw, Warner Bros., and the MuzikMafia.

Raybaw's creation also resulted in tension among MuzikMafia artists who were not in the running to receive record deals. An anonymous staff member of MuzikMafia, LLC, the MuzikMafia's own commercial entity, shared with me in 2006, "The [MuzikMafia] members need to understand that everyone won't get a record deal with Raybaw. That's not how things work around here." This statement is particularly meaningful when one takes into consideration that the "here" to which the staff member referred was the commercial music industry and Raybaw's involvement in it.

Finally, the MuzikMafia had become a significant component of something that it had originally opposed: Nashville's commercial music culture. According to Cory, "It [MuzikMafia] wasn't about the music anymore. [Muzik]Mafia needed to exist outside the walls of corporate Nashville." Raybaw's principal owners solved the dilemma by hiring an independent publicist named Virginia Hunt-Davis to take over as director of operations. Virginia's job was to oversee Raybaw's daily functions and to report to the godfathers, Marc, and Dale on a regular basis. Cory and the godfathers moved their offices across town to 1305 Clinton Street and began operations there in January 2006.

In an attempt to examine the changes in the MuzikMafia's fanbase and its views of the community in 2005 and partly in 2006, I repeated my MuzikMafia fan survey. As with the previous year's survey, I chose the CMA Music Fest in downtown Nashville, held June 8–11, 2006. I strove to maintain as much consistency as possible with the year before: location at the MuzikMafia booth in the exhibit hall at the Nashville Convention Center, approximate number of fans surveyed, the same questions, and the same manner of collecting and evaluating data.

In response to the question, "In your opinion, what is the MuzikMafia?" the number of duplicated responses increased from 499 in 2005 to 719 in 2006. This was owing to additional categories such as "musicians/artists," "Musically Artistic Friends in Alliance," and "virtuosic/talented." A large percentage of fans understood the MuzikMafia to be a "group of something" in both 2005 and 2006. However, the number of fans who described the MuzikMafia strictly as "country music" decreased in 2006 to 5.6 percent. The fans who described MuzikMafia as a "support group" decreased in 2006 to 4.2 percent. Those who viewed MuzikMafia as a family decreased to 1 percent. The number of people who left this question blank—55 people in 2005 and 67 in 2006—is significant, because the lack of response indicated continuing difficulty defining the MuzikMafia even one year later.

Another question that produced significantly different responses in 2006 from the year before was "Who is your favorite MuzikMafia artist?" The number of answers decreased from 662 to 638. Although Big & Rich remained the favorite MuzikMafia group with around 44 percent of all votes, 12 respondents listed their favorite as John Rich as a solo act/songwriter. Gretchen's popularity decreased from 31.7 percent in 2005 to 23 percent in 2006, probably because she did not appear at the CMA Music Fest in 2006. James Otto's popularity nearly doubled in 2006 to 4.9 percent as did Two Foot Fred's popularity (2.8 percent). Rachel's popularity increased dramatically from 0.5 percent to 1.9 percent. Each of these artists had spent considerably more time in the media than the year before. Of considerable significance is the surprisingly large number of non-MuzikMafia members who made this list: Hank Williams Jr., the Trailer Choir, Shannon Brown, Shanna Crooks, Willie Nelson, Tanya Tucker, Toby Keith, Van Zant, and Shania Twain. In 2006—two years after the MuzikMafia emergence onto the national stage—fans were still unclear as to the MuzikMafia's membership.

I also re-examined fans' knowledge of the MuzikMafia's godfathers. The total number of responses to this question increased from 766 in 2005 to 804 in 2006. A majority of fans still identified John and Kenny as the MuzikMafia's godfathers: about 32 percent of the total names in 2005 and 2006. The number of fans who listed Jon Nicholson as a godfather increased from 5.1 percent in 2005 to 6 percent in 2006. Cory's recognition as godfather actually decreased slightly. Gretchen's identification as godmother increased among fans from 0.9 percent in 2005 to 2.7 percent in 2006. Out of 403 survey participants who answered this question, only 4.4 percent of the respondents correctly identified all four godfathers by name; only 1.9 percent included Gretchen as a fifth godmother. Surprising is the number and diversity of responses that included the names of non-MuzikMafia artists: Hank Williams Jr., Willie Nelson, Marc Oswald, Charlie Daniels, Waylon Jennings, Kid Rock, Al Pacino, Johnny Cash, Merle Haggard, and David Allen Coe. It is safe to assume that relatively few people knew who the MuzikMafia's godfathers were, even as late as 2006.

Of particular interest to me were fans' responses to the question, "Where/when have you seen live performances by MuzikMafia artists?" The number of responses that included dates rose from 319 in 2005 to 373 in 2006. The 2006 survey identified performances at large Nashville locales, small Nashville locales, and non-Nashville venues. In both surveys, a majority of fans had attended performances from the previous year. From the 405 responses in 2006 that identified specific cities/locales, 42.2 percent were from large venues in Nashville such as the CMA Music Festival. Only 5.3 percent of MuzikMafia fans had seen a live show at a small Nashville club such as the Mercy Lounge or Bluesboro. This figure is significant because MuzikMafia musicians closely identified with their origins among Nashville's smaller clubs. Approximately 58 percent of MuzikMafia fans had seen live performances only outside of Nashville.

Gretchen's success touring with Kenny Chesney in 2005 almost equaled that of the 2004 tour. Chesney's Somewhere in the Sun Tour contained two parts: March 11 through May 14 and May 26 through August 28. Gretchen opened twenty-four performances for Chesney during the first half of the tour and thirty-five performances during the second half. Total ticket sales of 1,131,326 for Chesney's 2005 tour compared closely with the 1,143,909 tickets sold in 2004. Chesney's 2005 tour ranked Number Four in concert attendance among all music genres, just behind U2, Dave Mathews Band, and the Rolling Stones, and Number One among tours by country music artists.

Big & Rich made career inroads in 2005 by touring with Brooks & Dunn, country music's most popular duo act since 1991. Brooks & Dunn's Deuces Wild Tour comprised thirty-two performances from August 6 through October 30 and featured the Warren Brothers, Big & Rich, and Brooks & Dunn.

Reviews of tour concerts were mixed, but most critics preferred Big & Rich to the tour's headliners. Werner Trieschmann of the *Arkansas Democrat Gazette* wrote about a performance in Little Rock on August 7: "There was a spark missing from Brooks & Dunn's show, and perhaps it was the overemphasis on guitars. Big & Rich, however, were on fire." The fire reference is appropriate given the fact that Big & Rich's fifty-minute set contained various pyrotechnics, including numerous controlled explosions and nine-foot-high columns of flame. The tour sold 489,239 tickets, making it the Number Six best-selling tour by a country act in 2005.

The rest of the MuzikMafia opened four concerts for Hank Williams Jr. from July through September 2005. The MuzikMafia's one-hour opener featured James, Jon, Shannon, Damien, Rachel, and Chance. Each act performed two or three songs—except Rachel, who painted at stage right during the entire set.

Touring with Hank Williams Jr. was a learning experience for the MuzikMafia. The tour was the first time that the MuzikMafia had regularly opened for a major act other than Big & Rich or Gretchen. The crowds were smaller at first, and Hank Williams Jr.'s fans were quite different from those of Big & Rich, Gretchen, or the MuzikMafia. Most obvious were the numerous Dixie flags hanging from cars in the parking lot and the various racial slurs used by fans before and after the MuzikMafia's set.

The MuzikMafia's first concert with Hank Williams Jr. took place at the DTE Energy Music Theater on July 9 in Clarkston, Michigan. The venue was about a quarter full when Jon and James took the stage at 7:00 p.m. The flow between artists during the MuzikMafia's opening act was unsteady and awkward, and the crowd's response was unenthusiastic to moderate. James offered some constructive advice to the other artists backstage after the show:

We need to get the band to do some interludes while people are coming up to play. Like when Chance gets up there, we need to get that beat going right away. We only have an hour, and we need to keep everybody moving. Make sure that we rev that show up, instead of up and down, up and down. By the last song, everyone needs to be going crazy. We still got some learning to do. It [the show] can be good, but we have to make sure that the placement is all right: a steady build-up to hysteria at the end.

This demonstrates how the MuzikMafia was consciously improving their show for public consumption.

Audience members offered varying comments to me following the Clarkston performance. Some enjoyed the show and mentioned the names of specific artists, especially Chance. Others described the music as "different" or "weird." One man expressed his displeasure with the MuzikMafia because he had come to hear an act similar to Hank Williams Jr. A bald man with several tattoos and wearing no shirt made several derogatory racial comments about Damien and D.D. who were the only black people on stage and, possibly, at the entire venue.

The MuzikMafia's final performance with Hank Williams Jr. took place on September 23 in Pelham, Alabama, just a few miles south of Birmingham. By this time, the MuzikMafia had refined its show considerably. The artists exhibited much more enthusiasm on stage, which I attributed to the positive crowd response from the nearly sold-out venue. Stage lighting accompanied the MuzikMafia set and lighting changes often corresponded to musical cues. The flow from artist to artist had also improved. The one-hour set contained few if any musical gaps between artists. Another crowd-pleaser was Shannon Lawson's addition of the "Star Spangled Banner" on electric guitar modeled after the version that Jimi Hendrix had played at Woodstock back in 1969. All comments from fans, with whom I spoke following the MuzikMafia's set, were positive if not enthusiastic.

The MuzikMafia reconvened with Big & Rich and Gretchen in November for a second run of the Chevrolet American Revolution Tour. The 2005 tour began on November 4 in Woodlands, Texas, and comprised fourteen performances in Texas, Connecticut, New York, Pennsylvania, Michigan, Minnesota, Wisconsin, Tennessee, Louisiana, and Alabama. Jon and James opened each show as they had done in the previous year followed by fifty-minute sets by Big & Rich and Gretchen, respectively. Each show's finale included all MuzikMafia artists on stage in an effort to re-create the community's earlier performances at the Pub of Love.

While on tour, the MuzikMafia contributed to several charities. The community donated 100 percent of the proceeds from its performance on December 1 in Jackson, Mississippi, to CMT's One Country campaign. CMT divided these funds among the American Red Cross, America's Second Harvest, Habitat for Humanity, the USO, Boys and Girls Clubs, and Hands

On America. The $75,000 that the MuzikMafia show generated was to go toward assisting victims of Hurricane Katrina.

Proceeds from a MuzikMafia show at the Ryman Auditorium in Nashville went to the Country Music Hall of Fame and Museum. Included in the 2005 All for the Hall fundraising series, the show had originally been planned to take place on November 30 but was eventually rescheduled for February 19, 2006. Aside from ticket sales, additional funds were generated through V.I.P. packages that included airfare to and lodging in Nashville, a private dinner with Gretchen and Big & Rich at the Plowboy Mansion, an autographed Epiphone guitar, admission to a pre-concert reception, front row seating, a signed print by Rachel, and a post-concert party with the artists at the Country Music Hall of Fame and Museum. Some V.I.P. packages sold for as much as $10,000. According to Marc Oswald, who booked the event: "I had been approached by several [record] labels to do some charity stuff with the Mafia. Many suggested that we release a single whose proceeds would go to the Hall [of Fame]. I said, 'no'; a concert would be better. We made some calls and made it happen." The event generated approximately $180,000 for the Country Music Hall of Fame and Museum.

The MuzikMafia took part in several other fundraisers in 2005. On March 10 they provided the entertainment for Ringside: A Fight for Kids, an annual fundraiser for the Charley Foundation, a nonprofit organization that provides support to charitable agencies addressing the critical needs of children. Event guests included Joe Frazier, Darrin Humphrey, Barbara Mandrell, Shannon Brown, Big & Rich, Troy, James, Chance, Damien, Fred, and Dean. Ringside generated over $100,000 to help children in need.

On May 10 the MuzikMafia held a benefit concert at the Cannery Row Ballroom for the Nashville Songwriters Association International (NSAI). The concert's list of performers included the entire MuzikMafia, Kid Rock, Shooter Jennings, Jessi Colter, and Chicago bluesman Ty Stone. The event raised more than $25,000 to assist Nashville songwriters with copyright protection. On August 23 the MuzikMafia returned to the Cannery Row Ballroom for its second annual benefit concert for the Crohn's and Colitis Foundation of America. The three-hour show included all MuzikMafia members except for Gretchen and raised a total of $30,000.

MuzikMafia members made numerous television appearances in 2005. On January 15 CMT launched the first of six weekly episodes of *MuzikMafia*

TV. Each episode re-aired numerous times following its premiere, and by the series' sixth week, several episodes of MuzikMafia appeared daily on CMT. On February 6 Gretchen performed with Charlie Daniels for national and international audiences during the Superbowl XXIX pre-game concert, titled Bridging the Generations and broadcast live on Fox. By this time, MuzikMafia guitarist Dean Hall was a permanent fixture of Gretchen's band, and he accompanied her at the performance. On April 1 CNN aired an eleven-minute segment on Gretchen for the show *People in the News*. Big & Rich gave Katie Couric a tour of downtown Nashville for a segment on the *Today Show* that NBC broadcast on April 28. Big & Rich joined Jessica Simpson in Rammstein, Germany, for *Nick and Jessica's Tour of Duty,* which ABC aired on May 23. Cowboy Troy joined the talk show circuit with appearances on ABC's *Good Morning America* on May 30 and MSNBC's *Imus in the Morning* on May 31. Big & Rich, Gretchen, and Troy teamed up to sing an arrangement of the national anthem for the *Boston Pops Fireworks Spectacular 2005* that CBS broadcast live on July 4. Big & Rich and Troy performed a special version of their newly released single "Comin' to Your City" at the premiere of ESPN's *College Gameday* on August 1. Fred, Troy, and Big & Rich made a five-minute appearance with dialogue in the premiere episode of NBC's popular mini-series *Las Vegas* on September 19. CMT dedicated a one-hour primetime slot on September 24 for a documentary, *Gretchen: Undressed,* in which Gretchen performed acoustic versions of songs from her upcoming sophomore album *All Jacked Up*.

All this exposure fueled the MuzikMafia's ever-growing popularity and increased album sales for Gretchen, Big & Rich, and Troy. The RIAA certified Big & Rich's *Horse of a Different Color* as double platinum on January 11. Gretchen's album *Here for the Party* was certified as quadruple platinum on February 22, 2005.

In 2005 Big & Rich and Gretchen shadowed their previous year's list of awards and nominations. Their first appearance of the year took place at the *47th Annual Grammy Awards* on February 13 in Los Angeles. John and Gretchen received a joint nomination for Best Country Song for "Redneck Woman" but lost the Grammy to "Live Like You Were Dying" that Tim Nichols & Craig Wiseman had written for Tim McGraw. Gretchen received three additional nominations: Best New Artist, Best Country Album, and Best

Female Country Vocal Performance. She won the award for Best Female Country Vocal Performance, the first award of its kind for Gretchen.

Big & Rich, Gretchen, and Troy all appeared on the *40th Annual Academy of Country Music Awards,* broadcast by CBS on May 17. Gretchen opened the live show with her Number One hit song "Here for the Party." Later in the broadcast Troy introduced Big & Rich, who performed their latest single "Big Time." Gretchen was nominated for awards in five categories: Top Female Vocalist, Top New Artist, Single Record of the Year, Album of the Year, and Video of the Year. Big & Rich were nominated for Video of the Year for "Save a Horse (Ride a Cowboy)," Top New Artist, and Top Vocal Duo. John received additional nominations for Single Record of the Year for co-producing Gretchen's song "Redneck Woman" and Album of the Year for Gretchen's *Here for the Party.* Gretchen amazed the audience with her wins for both Top Female Vocalist and Top New Artist.

Gretchen, Troy, and Big & Rich's successes continued at the *39th Annual Country Music Association Awards,* which CBS broadcast live from Madison Square Garden on November 15. The CMA's decision to move the show from Nashville to New York met with considerable controversy among country audiences. However, the CMA wished to expand the genre's marketability and subsequently launched its Country Takes NYC campaign to re-energize current country listeners while attracting new ones. Gretchen was nominated for three awards: Female Vocalist of the Year, Song of the Year for "Redneck Woman," and Music Video of the Year for "When I Think about Cheatin'." She won for Best Female Vocalist. Troy joined Wynonna to present the award for Album of the Year. Big & Rich won no awards, although they received nominations in two categories: Horizon Award and Vocal Duo of the Year. John received an additional nomination for Song of the Year for "Redneck Woman." In addition, Big & Rich performed "Comin' to Your City," the title track from their sophomore album.

On December 8 the National Academy of Recording Arts and Sciences announced nominations for the *48th Annual Grammy Awards.* Sony/Epic had released Gretchen's second album *All Jacked Up* on September 27, three days before the deadline for eligibility. Gretchen received nominations in four categories: Best Female Country Vocal Performance for the album's title track, Best Country Collaboration with Vocals for her duet "Politically

Uncorrect" with Merle Haggard, Best Country Song for "All Jacked Up," and Best Country Album. John received a nomination for Best Country Song for co-writing "All Jacked Up" with Gretchen and Vicky McGehee.

Reflecting the growing popularity of MuzikMafia and its member artists, five MuzikMafia acts had albums released in 2005: Big Kenny, Troy, Big & Rich, Gretchen, and Jon. Each experienced its own level of relative success. Hollywood Records finally released Kenny's 1999 solo project entitled *Live a Little*. Gretchen's album *All Jacked Up* celebrated high chart placement as did Big & Rich's *Comin' to Your City*. Both generated considerably high sales. Troy's *Loco Motive* epitomized the eclectic sound of newly formed Raybaw Records. Warner Bros. released Jon's debut album *A Lil Sump'm Sump'm,* which unfortunately experienced low sales and relatively little radio airplay.

In March 2005 Hollywood Records released Kenny's album *Live a Little* that he had actually recorded in 1999. Unfortunately, Hollywood had dropped Kenny from the label prior to the album's scheduled 2000 release date. Hollywood eventually released the album on March 1, 2005, with an added sticker that read, "Big & Rich's Big Kenny: The legendary solo album by Mr. Universal Minister of Love." The decision to release the album and its "stickered" cover had obviously been influenced by Big & Rich's ongoing commercial success since summer 2004.

It is not difficult to understand Hollywood Records' hesitation about releasing *Live a Little* in 2000. The album was an experiment in creativity, and few labels are willing to take such chances on a relatively unknown artist. An anonymous reviewer at *Billboard* described the album: "It's too damn weird to market, particularly to an audience that has no idea who Big Kenny is. [*Live a Little* is] a swirling, pastel-colored collage of psychedelia, bombastic album rock, swinging British Invasion harmonies, and post-alternative pop, all packaged in an ultra-slick, cavernous production."

Kenny was disheartened when Hollywood canceled his contract and even more so after the album was finally released. In 2005 Kenny told me: "Yeah, they [Hollywood] dropped me, and never released the record. Now John and I hook up and are making music which is rock and roll, country, and other influences just slammed together. Then we [Big & Rich] come out, and they finally release that record based upon our success. We're still doing the same

thing now as we were back then." Kenny seldom promotes the album in public and has performed few if any of its songs at MuzikMafia shows.

Sony/Epic released Gretchen's album *All Jacked Up* on September 27 as
her follow-up to *Here for the Party*. The album was an instant success on the
Billboard charts. *All Jacked Up* debuted at Number One on *Billboard*'s Top
200, Top Country Album, and its Top Comprehensive Album charts.

Gretchen's musical style and working-class social messages in *All Jacked
Up* compared closely with those on *Here for the Party*. She retained her rough,
edgy vocals on hardcore country songs such as "Skoal Ring," "Rebel Child,"
and "Not Bad for a Bartender." *Stylus* magazine's Scott Inskeep described
the album's title track as a "rowdy, beer drinking song." The video for "All
Jacked Up" features Charlie Daniels, Kid Rock, Larry the Cable Guy, and
Hank Williams Jr. The single peaked at Number Eight on *Billboard*'s Hot
Country Singles chart on October 1.

Many reviewers were unimpressed with *All Jacked Up*. Rob Sheffield of
Rolling Stone described the album as "a mediocre follow-up with nothing as
great as "Redneck Woman" or "Here for the Party." An anonymous reviewer
for the *New York Post* (online edition) remarked: "After her inspired debut
last year, it seemed like Wilson would be the redneck woman who was going
to shake up Nashville. But on her sophomore disc she proves herself to be a
pretty ordinary twanger." Most reviewers based their critiques of *All Jacked
Up* on the sound and success of *Here for the Party*, ignoring the fact that
Gretchen and *Here for the Party* emerged during a specific cultural context
that had changed somewhat by 2005. In addition, Gretchen had undergone several changes as a musician by the time she recorded *All Jacked Up*.
The album sold well: the RIAA certified *All Jacked Up* as gold and platinum
on October 27, one month after the album's release. According to Nielsen
Soundscan, *All Jacked Up* was sixth best in country album sales in 2005.

Warner Bros. released Jon Nicholson's debut album *A Lil Sump'm
Sump'm* on September 27, the same day that Sony/Epic released Gretchen's
All Jacked Up. Unfortunately, Jon's album did not meet with the same success as Gretchen's. In fact, by industry standards, *A Lil Sump'm Sump'm* was
a commercial flop, having sold as few as 3,700 copies by February 21, 2006,
according to Kat Chandler of Scott Welch Management, Jon's managing
agency at the time.

Jon's low record sales resulted in considerable tension between him, Warner Bros., and the MuzikMafia. Warner did not release a single, nor did the label promote the album with the same intensity it had done with Big & Rich's *Horse of a Different Color*. Warner Bros.' former senior vice president of publicity Jules Wortman revealed to me in 2005 the label's difficulty:

> He [Jon] is one of those who has done great touring and is out there getting exposure, but there's not a real target where we can play it on the radio. We don't know which format he's going to gravitate to. So we're just exposing him through major touring. . . .We all know it's [*A Lil Sump'm Sump'm*] a brilliant piece of work, but those are sometimes the hardest ones to market. Honestly, we're doing everything we can to give it the right opportunities; it's just where it's gonna fall where masses can hear it, that's still a big question mark.

Jon's touring schedule in 2005 included a lengthy stint with jazz/funk innovators Karl Denson's Tiny Universe and numerous solo concerts. His February 27 performance at Nashville club 3rd & Lindsley was broadcast live on the local progressive rock radio station WRLT. Jon appeared with Karl Denson at the internationally known Bonnaroo Music and Arts Festival on June 11. On July 25 his concert at Nashville's 12th & Porter was broadcast live on Jimmy Buffet's satellite station, Radio Margaritaville. The release party for *A Lil Sump'm Sump'm* took place at the Mercy Lounge on September 27.

A Lil Sump'm Sump'm was significant despite the album's low sales. Jon insisted that his own band accompany him on the album, a request that is rarely granted in Nashville by a major record label, especially for a relatively unknown solo artist. In addition, Jon recorded the album with little or no input from Warner Bros. Instead, the label hired Jon's band and a well-known independent producer named Angelo Petraglia to accompany him to the well-known Allaire Studios near Woodstock, New York, from early November to mid-December 2004. As Jon told me in 2005:

> I didn't give them [Warner Bros.] a choice in the matter. I said that we were going to go cut a record, and we're not going to take any input from anybody. We just went and did it. Paul [Worley] is on our team.

He always has been. I didn't even talk to the label about it. Paul knew what I was going to do. I just went up [to Allaire] and did it without any label representation, without any A&R. Cory [Gierman] was the A&R. He was up there with us, but he was just up there for support and to hang out, you know. We just went up and made music however we wanted to make it without worrying about what anybody thought, and trying to make the best record that we could.

By the time Jon signed his contract with Warner Bros. in August 2004, the MuzikMafia had considerable influence over Music Row. Jon's request to be in charge of his own recording project was supported by John, Kenny, Cory and the rest of the MuzikMafia; Warner Bros. acquiesced.

Warner Bros. released Big & Rich's sophomore album *Comin' to Your City* on November 15. The album debuted at Number Seven on *Billboard*'s Top 200 chart and at Number Three on the Country Album chart, both of which were the album's peak positions. The album's title track debuted on September 10 at Number Fifty-Two on *Billboard*'s Hot Country Singles chart. The song peaked at Number Twenty-One on December 17, 2005.

Comin' to Your City generated considerable press several months before the album's release. Big & Rich opened each performance of the Deuces Wild tour with the album's title track. The duo also performed "Comin' to Your City" at the premiere of ESPN's *College Gameday* on August 1. In addition, CMT broadcast a one-hour concert special entitled *Wanted: Big & Rich—Alive in Deadwood* on October 22. The show featured many songs from *Comin' to Your City* and several audience favorites from *Horse of a Different Color*.

Comin' to Your City contained more stylistic diversity than the duo's first album. The various styles present on the album included soul/funk rock with "Soul Shaker" and "Jalapeño," country with "20 Margaritas," Dixieland jazz with "Filthy Rich," easy listening with John's ballad "Never Mind Me," a slow waltz entitled "8th of November" that shared the story of a Vietnam veteran's experiences, and rock, the latter exemplified by Kenny's tunes "Leap of Faith, "Slow Motion," and "Blow My Mind," which compare stylistically with songs from his solo album *Live a Little*. *Comin' to Your City* begins with a brief, childlike prelude entitled "The Freak Parade." The album ends with a bonus track entitled "Our America" that Big & Rich, Gretchen, and Troy performed on CBS's *Boston Pops Fireworks Spectacular* on July 4. The RIAA certified the album as both gold and platinum on January 17, 2006, approximately two months after its release.

John Rich's reputation as a Nashville songwriter and producer grew considerably in 2005 and independently of his association with Big & Rich or the MuzikMafia. John boasted in October 2005 at an ASCAP reception in his honor that he had written over nine hundred songs since age twenty. In 2005 alone, ninety-six of John's songs were recorded, seven of which appeared in the Top Ten of *Billboard*'s Country Singles chart. ASCAP named John as the Country Songwriter-Artist of the Year. His credits included three songs for Faith Hill's 2005 album *Fireflies*. Hill commented on John's abilities in an interview with Beverly Keel in 2005 for *Country Music Today*: "John's contribution to this album is huge. I believe he is an extremely talented writer, producer, and musician. There are no limitations to the measurement of his abilities. He is surprising, and that reflects in his music."

Twelve songs that were either written or co-written by John and that peaked high on *Billboard*'s Country Singles chart in 2005 include, along with their peak position, "Mississippi Girl" for Faith Hill (#1), "Here for the Party" for Gretchen Wilson (#3), "When I Think about Cheatin'" for Gretchen Wilson (#4), "Like We Never Loved At All" for Faith Hill and Tim McGraw (#5), "Pickin' Wildflowers" for Keith Anderson (#8), "All Jacked Up" for Gretchen Wilson (#8), "Hicktown" for Jason Aldean (#10), "Why" for Jason Aldean (#14), for Big & Rich "Holy Water" (#15), "Big Time" (#20), and "Comin' to Your City" (#21), and "I Don't Feel Like Loving You Today" for Gretchen Wilson (#22).

John also established himself as a competent producer in 2005. After producing or co-producing in 2004 Gretchen's *Here for the Party* and Big & Rich's *Horse of a Different Color*, in 2005 he produced Cowboy Troy's *Loco Motive*, Shannon Brown's *Corn Fed*, Keith Anderson's *Three Chord Country and American Rock & Roll*, James Otto's *Sunset Man*, Billy Joe Shaver's *The Real Deal*, Big & Rich's *Comin' to Your City*, and Gretchen Wilson's *All Jacked Up*.

The MuzikMafia's presence at the International Entertainment Buyers Association (IEBA) annual meeting in October 2005 was a milestone in the community's gradual transformation from a group of once marginalized artists into a single, marketable commodity for national consumption.

The IEBA meeting took place October 2–4 at the Nashville Hilton Downtown. Most events were held in the hotel's lavish ballroom. The conference attracts a variety of entertainment industry personnel including booking agents, record company executives, arena owners, managers, tour promoters, radio conglomerate executives, producers, and talent agents. Artists on hand to perform included Martina McBride, Dierks Bentley, Buddy Jewell, and MuzikMafia members.

The MuzikMafia's contribution to the conference was a panel titled "Music without Prejudice," organized and moderated by Greg Oswald, senior vice president of the William Morris Agency–Nashville. By October 2005 most MuzikMafia members were receiving their booking engagements through the William Morris Agency, one of the largest talent and literary agencies in the world. The panelists were Kenny, John, Cory, Jon, Troy, Shannon, Rachel, Greg, Marc, and Bill Moore.

The panel included a variety of topics that Greg had briefly rehearsed with the artists in the green room. Each artist received a six-page list of themes that Greg intended to discuss during the presentation. Greg also assigned specific topics to several people. Marc and Kenny discussed the history of the MuzikMafia; John and Kenny introduced all artists and discussed how each had become a member. Shannon and Jon each performed one or two musical selections, and Marc addressed the topic of the MuzikMafia and the media. Greg had Cory discuss the community's notable business relationships, the story of Raybaw Records, and the MuzikMafia's incorporation of various media technologies. Greg asked Bill Moore to describe the activities of the Mafia Soldiers, the MuzikMafia's official fan club.

The most significant element of the panel was Greg and Bill's contribution, "Can You Buy the MuzikMafia?" Greg divided the presentation into two parts: a) "What Is the Hidden Value of Buying a Mafia Artist?" and b) "What Makes a MuzikMafia Artist Valuable?" According to Greg, the hidden value of a MuzikMafia event arises from the Mafia Soldiers, a web-based community whose members are on hand at various performances to distribute promotional materials such as free recordings, stickers, and wearable gear. Bill described how the fan club's membership, approximately 3,000 across the United States, is notified when the community will be performing in a specific area, and nearby fan club members are invited to attend. The Mafia soldiers work for and with the MuzikMafia at each event.

Greg and Bill described the high value of MuzikMafia's team of managers and the quantity of albums sold. MuzikMafia managers Dale Morris and Greg have worked with artists such as Alabama, Kenny Chesney,
Luther Vandross, Michael Bolton, Gretchen, Big & Rich, and Cowboy Troy
and have been involved in the sales of hundreds of millions of albums. Warner Bros., Sony/Epic, and Raybaw together shipped approximately eleven
million albums by MuzikMafia artists in 2004 and 2005. Greg emphasized
to IEBA attendees the direct correlation between album sales and concert
ticket sales.

Greg also announced that Troy would be touring with Big & Rich in
2006 and that Troy's album was approaching gold certification. He ended
his presentation by reiterating, "The MuzikMafia can be bought." If a venue
owner or booking manager could not afford Big & Rich, Gretchen, or Troy,
Greg suggested the following:

> If the event is right, and it's going to be a fun, tasteful thing, you
> [IEBA members] can talk to William Morris [Agency] and they'll try
> to help you sort out a MuzikMafia that you can have for an hour or
> so with Shannon, Chance, Jon. . . . You can book Otto and Nicholson
> alone or as a duo, or you can add Chance to the bill. . . . For once we're
> avoiding the homogenized packaging of artists. There is an alterna-
> tive. We'll create something, a package, that fits what you're trying to
> do. . . . It's not about making money for us; It's usually a "break-even"
> proposition for us. It's all about spreading the word. We like to do it,
> because it exposes the public through you [IEBA members] to what we
> hope is the next stuff [upcoming MuzikMafia artists].

Greg's statement that MuzikMafia "can be bought" was significant in
that it contradicted the reasons for the community's founding in 2001.
Ironically, several MuzikMafia members were on stage at the IEBA meeting, embracing Greg's comments and the panel's original purpose: to present the MuzikMafia as a marketable, highly valued commodity for public
consumption.

By the end of 2005 the MuzikMafia had experienced stark changes on
several levels. Audience reception played a significant role in how MuzikMafia members constructed their public images. Nowhere is this more evident

than with John and Kenny. After all, the two had spent more time in the public eye than any other MuzikMafia artists. In addition to appearances on televised award shows, talk shows, radio interviews, music videos, and concert tours, John and Kenny appeared in a variety of television commercials, television mini-series, fundraisers, sporting events, and car rallies.

Big & Rich's live show was the best example of how performers construct and re-negotiate their public image on stage. John and Kenny performed for their audiences while at the same time reacting to the audience's reception of the music. I observed Big & Rich's opening set for Brooks & Dunn on two different occasions as part of the Deuces Wild tour: August 25, 2005, in Pelham, Alabama, and October 28, 2005, in Atlanta. The two shows were almost identical in flow, staging, lighting, song tempos, verbal commentary between songs, physical movement, length, and song choice. The similarities seemed remarkable and unnatural for a live show.

Later that year Max Abrams provided me with an explanation. In early 2005 he had observed Big & Rich's manager Marc for three days. Max reported how Marc methodically analyzed each aspect of Big & Rich's set. For Max and many others, Big & Rich's performances are exciting. However, by observing Marc, Max realized that much thought lay behind each performance and that every detail had been carefully rehearsed. According to Max, "He [Marc] nipped and tucked that show every day. That's the best part of it: demystifying the action. There is logic behind these actions. These aren't just random occurrences. There is a method that enables it to work consistently."

But Max's observations did not stop with Marc. Max also analyzed Big & Rich's staging himself, and in doing so deduced the multidimensional planes that existed. Max elaborated:

The most important thing 90 percent of the time is the vocal plane. Working your way back you've got Adam [on electric guitar] and Ethan [on electric bass]. Those guys are always moving. If people get tired of focusing on Big & Rich, they can focus on Adam for a while. He communicates so well with the motion of his playing [and] what he's trying to communicate. Dean Hall is great at that too. Ethan jumps up and down. In the back plane there is Brian. This is the John and Kenny show up front, but it's the Adam show on stage right.

The reason that I started paying attention to it is because it worked. I saw the difference in how people reacted during a Big & Rich show compared to other shows. People go crazy for Big & Rich. People get excited. By the end, people are going crazy. I bet that if you sat John Rich down, he could tell you every event on the stage.

I observed such multidimensional planes in action in the two Deuces Wild performances. During any given song's verse, Big & Rich were the focal point for the audience. However, during a song's bridge or chorus, the audience's attention moved to any one of the stage's other planes. Guitarist Adam Shoenfeld emphasized his up-and-down motion and often walked behind John and Kenny to bassist Ethan at stage left. Ethan often retreated to drummer Brian at the rear of the stage during a song's verses or one of Adam's solos. Ethan sometimes joined Brian on his riser during a drum feature to draw the audience's attention further in that direction. The diversity of focal points contributed to an unusually consistent flow throughout the performance. The experience was similar to observing a circus or the inside of a beehive. Each musician performed specific tasks toward a common goal: providing an entertaining show for the audience.

Most MuzikMafia members agreed that they had observed the most artistic development in Max. When Max began performing with the MuzikMafia in late 2001, he considered himself a timid performer who did not think about stage presence at all. In fact, he admitted to me in 2005 that John and Kenny had discussed with him on numerous occasions the matter of being a better communicator. For Max, there was no problem with communicating his message in the recording studio. However, while on stage, he had to employ all of his senses in order to convey musical meaning to the audience.

Max admitted that physical motion played a much greater role on stage than he had previously imagined. According to Max, "Cameras don't like me sitting here talking. That's really boring after a while. Cameras like John pouring beer on Dean Hall's head." Max continued: "I've actually experimented with stuff like this on stage. 'Cause you can tell by how many flashes go off if people think something is cool. Sometimes I'll stand for a while and nothing happens. Then, if I run to the front of the stage and jump, then all the flashes go off. Everything pops. That's what I got from watching John Rich in every single one of those Big & Rich shows on tour, all of them."

However, musical communication is not exact. Max described to me in May 2005 the accuracy of his messages and the relationship between audience and performer:

> Sometimes I'm a sender, and sometimes I'm a receiver. The question is: "When I'm sending, is it being received the way that I intended?" Sometimes you have to bring in other tools than what's coming out of your instrument in order to get your point across. It's a visual medium. You have to encode and decode. You're always looking for ways to insure that the message is getting across as accurately as possible. The task is enormous.

There is fundamental difference between MuzikMafia musicians and, say, a local rock band. Artists like Big & Rich and Gretchen Wilson receive feedback from managers, publicity agents, record label executives, tour personnel, television footage, and millions of fans in addition to their own observations during live performances. A purely local band, by contrast, has to "self-adjust" based upon their own interpretation of audience responses.

It is not surprising that I witnessed little musical change in my observations of individual MuzikMafia artists in 2004 and 2005; the MuzikMafia was a commercial endeavor almost from its beginning in 2001. Performances by each MuzikMafia artist in 2004 and 2005 included noticeable consistency in repertoire, stage comportment, reactions to audience participation, vocal range, instrumentation, and style.

The differences that emerged during any given performance in 2004 or 2005 can be best described as variations or innovations. For example, John and Kenny told me that they had performed an audience favorite entitled "Limo Larry" at the Pub of Love with only guitar accompaniment. By fall 2004 the song was accompanied by the entire band. Such additions did not change the meaning of the song. Nor did the audience's dramatic increase in size and composition lessen the sense of togetherness that the singalong encouraged.

Likewise I noticed few social changes in individual MuzikMafia artists. For example, John's large ego, which he acknowledges, was similar among performances that I attended from 2004 through 2008, that Paul Worley had described to me of his experience with John in 2002, and that I observed in video footage from Pub of Love shows in 2001 and 2002. In a 2005 interview, Max supported these conclusions about the absence of significant change in John or Kenny:

> Those guys have always worked this hard. Even back in 2001 they were doing some production stuff, and even then it still took me three weeks to get ahold of Kenny. He was in town, but he was so busy. Now I have the same problem. That's the weird thing: they always acted like millionaires. Things aren't weird now with all the publicity, they're better. Kenny was always on a mission. . . . John Rich is doing the same stuff.

Although Max identified several changes in his own stage persona and musical proficiency, he believed that he was the same person in 2005 as he was in 2001.

On the other hand, I did observe significant change in the MuzikMafia at the group level. Some changes were generated from within, while others came from outside. The primary factor for changes in the MuzikMafia from 2001 through 2005 was the community's growth in popularity.

The significant amount of income generated by MuzikMafia artists such as Gretchen, Big & Rich, and Troy changed the MuzikMafia's group dynamic. Those who had performed at the Pub of Love received no monetary compensation for weekly performances; the emphasis was on the group and its marginalized status within the Nashville music establishment. By 2004 the MuzikMafia was attracting many new artists whose goals included public exposure that might lead to a record deal. Over that time MuzikMafia shows transformed from an escape from the corporate, non-artistic aspects of Music Row to an opportunity for many artists to gain access to Music Row.

The external changes resulted in some internal changes, the most noticeable being Gretchen's change in relationship with the MuzikMafia. Most community members have recounted numerous Gretchen performances with the MuzikMafia from October 2001 through June 2003. However, her Nashville appearances with the MuzikMafia thereafter became sporadic due to the significant amount of time she spent working on her debut album, promotion, interviews, and tours. In fact, from June 2004 through December 2005 Gretchen performed with the MuzikMafia at only four of the community's twenty-two Nashville shows.

It is little known outside the MuzikMafia's inner circle that Gretchen maintained considerable distance from the community after she signed with Sony in 2003. Gretchen's failure to acknowledge the MuzikMafia during several of her televised award acceptance speeches in 2004 and 2005 hinted at such, although Gretchen never publicly addressed this topic.

However, much of what I observed from behind the scenes alluded to this. On November 20, 2004, I observed at a performance on the Chevrolet American Revolution Tour how Gretchen's personal area backstage was on the opposite side of the tunnel entrance from the one labeled MuzikMafia. Access to her green room, where she spent much of her free time, was also limited.

At the community's Ryman Auditorium performance on the 2005 Chevrolet American Revolution Tour, the dressing room for Gretchen and her band was on the third floor on the side of the building, opposite that for the MuzikMafia. My Big & Rich backstage pass did not grant access to Gretchen's green room. In addition, I had received prior notice that Sony had forbidden the videotaping of Gretchen's segment of the show by the MuzikMafia's camera crew, myself included.

Gretchen's social and professional distance from the MuzikMafia was confirmed by several individuals. In 2005 Jules Wortman described to me her experience trying to get Sony to work with Warner Bros on various MuzikMafia-related projects: "When the whole thing started going [Big & Rich and MuzikMafia], I was getting the cover stories for USA Today, etc., and I would call Sony and tell them what we were doing and asked if Gretchen could be a part of it. They were great at first, but they really don't want to do it anymore. They want to keep it [Gretchen and the MuzikMafia] separated." Sony was marketing Gretchen as a hardcore country artist to a conservative fanbase, and wanted to maintain considerable distance from the MuzikMafia, an organization that promoted a "love everybody" liberalism and artistic flexibility.

Another incident involved Gretchen's promotion to the rank of godmother. The four godfathers named Gretchen as an official godmother during a performance that took place on November 20, 2005, in Erie, Pennsylvania. An anonymous MuzikMafia member close to the godfathers described the events surrounding the incident as "weird" and that the announcement had been a surprise to many MuzikMafia artists. Jon Nicholson commented on the event during an interview the following day for a local radio station, intimating that Gretchen had strong-armed her way into the position.

Gretchen's social distance from the MuzikMafia can be explained by examining how she became a member. Gretchen entered the MuzikMafia through her association with John Rich, whom she first met in 1999. It was also through John's influence that Gretchen was granted a meeting with John Grady at Sony, which eventually led to Gretchen's record deal and subsequent commercial success. John also wrote or co-wrote many of the songs that appear on Gretchen's first two albums. Gretchen's professional commitment to John took precedence over her relationship with the MuzikMafia.

The MuzikMafia's influence on change within Nashville's commercial music scene was apparent throughout 2004 and 2005, especially when one considers the popularity of the unified show among Nashville music clubs. Until the MuzikMafia came along in 2001, the general practice was for a venue to hire several acts to perform over the course of an evening. Each act would feature a solo artist or band that would have little to do with the evening's other performers except for perhaps a similarity in musical style. The MuzikMafia created and marketed themselves as a unified show with an announcer—usually a godfather—and a series of artists who were closely related in terms of their stylistic marginality, propensity for improvisation, and their belief in artistic diversity. A MuzikMafia show contained a clear beginning that comprised a gradual, unrehearsed entrance by one or more artists. The show continued with several climaxes among guest artists, at least one of Kenny's sermons, and songs by MuzikMafia members that included favorites such as "Limo Larry."

The idea of a unified show spread throughout the Nashville music scene, especially in 2004 and 2005. In fall 2004 Chance began regular performances of the Nashville Trailer Choir that carried on such MuzikMafia traditions as stylistic diversity and a unified show format. The Trailer Choir eventually caught the eye of Toby Keith, who invited them on tour with him and to make cameo appearances in his 2008 movie *Beer for my Horses*. There was also Alabama Line, a similar phenomenon organized by Jamey Garner that took place at both the Rhythm Kitchen and 3rd & Lindsley. Garner modeled Alabama Line after MuzikMafia shows, at which he performed on occasion in 2004.

The music being created by Nashville's well-known commercial artists in 2004 and 2005 greatly contrasted with that by artists immediately preceding the MuzikMafia's rise to national prominence. I refer to this phenomenon as the "Gretchen Effect," since it was Gretchen's recording of "Redneck Woman" that returned hardcore country musical style to the forefront of Nashville's commercial output. As Paul Worley admitted to me in 2004, country music had been "dead or was in the process of dying" as of 2002. Gretchen's rough, edgy sound and her lower-class, redneck persona energized commercial country's fanbase while promoting an empowering, perhaps even threatening female image.

Gretchen's presence in the commercial mainstream contributed to a resurgence in the popularity of Hank Williams Jr., Willie Nelson, Jessi Colter, Lynyrd Skynyrd, and other "outlaw" music acts. In 2004 and 2005 CMT broadcast two versions of *CMT Outlaws*. The televised concerts confirmed the significance of many once-marginalized artists to the genre of commercial country. In addition, Gretchen's 2006 performance schedule included the Redneck Revolution Tour that featured artists such as Van Zant, Blaine Larson, and Trace Adkins.

Commercial country acts such as Jo Dee Messina reached new popularity in 2004 and 2005 by hardening their image—an obvious result of the Gretchen Effect. Messina released "My Give a Damn's Busted" in January 2005. The song reached Number One on *Billboard*'s Hot Country Singles and Tracks chart twenty weeks later in May 2005. The video features Messina dressed in a maroon leather outfit—a stark contrast both musically and visually to her earlier video for the hit song "Bye Bye."

Another cause for such rapid variation in Nashville's commercially produced music was John's influence—what I aptly call the "John Rich Effect." John co-wrote "Redneck Woman" and many other songs from Gretchen's albums *Here for the Party* and *All Jacked Up*. Dominant themes of John's commercial output included the embracing of one's roots and the life of the average working-class person. "Mississippi Girl," John's Number One hit for Faith Hill co-written with MuzikMafia guitarist Adam Shoenfeld, told the story of a woman who did not change her ways amid wealth and national popularity but maintained close ties to her Mississippi upbringing. Jason Aldean reached *Billboard*'s Top Ten Country Singles and Tracks with John's song "Hicktown" in October 2005. The John Rich Effect is little known outside Nashville's music community, but John's work as a songwriter and producer had a profound influence on Music Row's commercial output during the rise of the MuzikMafia.

2005 proved to be another exciting year for the MuzikMafia. However, the MuzikMafia's commercial success was accompanied by the community's fair share of problems, including a growing tension among its members, a variety of financial disputes, and considerable debate among the godfathers on the direction of the MuzikMafia and its various commercial enterprises. By December 2008, the MuzikMafia would be dissolved almost entirely.

Chapter Seven

THE BEGINNING OF THE END

From 2006 through 2008 the MuzikMafia went from being a major force in the commercial music industry to a disorganized, dysfunctional collection of individuals almost unrecognizable from the close-knit community that had taken Nashville by storm just a few years earlier. This was a period characterized by the addition of new members, the departure of others, the unofficial break-up of Big & Rich, financial problems among the MuzikMafia's various commercial enterprises, and considerable tension among the godfathers regarding the MuzikMafia's vision and direction. The result was the MuzikMafia's eventual downfall which left only a small glimmer of hope for the community's possible resurrection in 2009.

Several MuzikMafia members attributed the downfall of the community to its nebulous, sometimes confusing structure. The fact that there were two MuzikMafias, a social one and a commercial one, did not make things any easier. In order to understand the community's polity, we must first distinguish the MuzikMafia as a social collective from the MuzikMafia as a commercial enterprise. But the MuzikMafia's problems did not begin in 2006. Many fatal flaws were present within the MuzikMafia from its beginnings in 2001.

The social aspect of the MuzikMafia included throughout its brief history the free Tuesday night shows in Nashville in which a group of friends got together and jammed on stage. The MuzikMafia's substantial commercial side, beginning in 2004, included concert tours, mass media exposure, and the community's various publishing companies, Raybaw Records, publicized fundraisers, and MuzikMafia LLC. The social structure of the Muzik-Mafia community from 2001 to 2008 closely resembled that of a family with four parents instead of two.

At the top of the MuzikMafia's original social hierarchy were the four godfathers: John, Kenny, Jon, and Cory. Gretchen was promoted to godmother in spring 2006. From 2001 to 2006, all decisions concerning the MuzikMafia's social activities were the result of the godfathers' collective input. Social activities comprised primarily the community's weekly performances and the process of taking on new members. Most decisions were made by the godfathers after informal discussion and sometimes considerable debate.

I was privy to a conversation between godfathers Cory and John backstage at a MuzikMafia performance in Johnson City, Tennessee. The show was one of thirteen on the Chevrolet American Revolution Tour in November and December 2004. The topic under discussion was how to stage the national anthem for the sold-out crowd of approximately 8,000 fans that evening. Cory began with "And we [Jon, Kenny, and himself] talked about doing the national anthem . . ." before John interjected, "OK, who's gonna do it?" Cory responded, "Everyone . . . [pause] . . . the [Muzik] Mafia choir . . . and like Dean Hall or Adam [Shoenfeld] could take some licks . . . [Cory imitated with his version of air guitar] . . . and Max could take a lick . . ." John interjected, "Well, if we're in a key . . ." Cory interrupted, "That's the thing." John continued, "We have to start off in a key."

Cory took a sip from his plastic cup filled with Crown Royal and Coca Cola and mumbled, "hmmm." John followed with, "I wouldn't . . . you know, it's really not cool, though, to be playing guitar licks while people are singing the national anthem." After a brief pause, Cory defended his position with, "But if there's a way we could feature kind of everyone." John interrupted, "Well, if there's a way, but you got to be able to have some order . . . [pause] . . . you don't want to defile the national anthem by screwing crap up with it." Cory agreed but added, "Well, what I'm thinking is that we'll have everyone sing along and we'll have you guys [John and Kenny] lead it, and we could get a pretty cool . . . [hesitates]." John responded, "I wouldn't let people play during it unless we worked it out, because it could look completely not cool . . . you got the whole audience singing along to the 'Star Spangled Banner' and some of the guys are going 'dah da da dah da da' [plays air guitar] off the top of it." Cory defended his position with, "Well, I think, if we can do it tastefully, you know, like we're . . ." John replied, "I think if we sing it, we should just sing it straight tonight . . . that way we don't need a key. Somebody just starts singing and we just go [with it]." Cory returned to his idea: "OK, but you know how like freakin' Jimi Hendrix did his . . ." John interrupted, "Yeah, but nobody was singing; he just played it." Cory shrugs his shoulders and says, "so what?" John defended his stance: "I'm just saying that you got to be real careful with that song. It can come across like you're jacking with it . . . it's not cool, I'm just saying." Cory responded, "Well, it needs to be gone over, I'm sure." John broke the seriousness of the conversation by lighting a cigarette and waving it around. "That's redneck incense right there," he said as both he and Cory laughed. The MuzikMafia did not play during the singing of the national anthem that evening.

Decision-making among the four godfathers was sometimes a last-minute process, as the above example indicates, and ambivalence has even become a marketing slogan for MuzikMafia performances. In describing MuzikMafia shows at the Pub of Love, John's brother Isaac used the phrase "you never know who's going to be there." This sentiment has often appeared as "you never know who's gonna show" in advertisements for MuzikMafia performances, at MuzikMafia's autograph signing booth in Nashville at the CMA Fest 2005, and in emails distributed to fans from the MuzikMafia website.

The general public seldom knew which artists were going to appear at MuzikMafia shows, because, for much of the MuzikMafia's brief history, the musicians themselves did not know who was going to be at any given performance. In an interview with Cory in August 2004, I asked how he organized each Tuesday night's line-up. According to Cory, he did not usually think about the schedule of each show until the afternoon before an evening performance: "It's like, I call Jon [that afternoon] and ask 'do we have a bass player?' or 'do we have a drummer?' or say that 'Otto is here,' or 'John and Kenny [Big & Rich] are in town so they might be coming by.' It's all pretty much a last-minute thing."

One should keep in mind that in 2004 the MuzikMafia performed every Tuesday night in Nashville from January 6 until August 31, followed by sporadic performances thereafter. Shows were free and open to the public. There was little expectation of or demand for organization. Cory's honest Monday phrase for a Tuesday show, "I don't know who's going to be there," soon became a metaphor for unpredictability that developed into a lucrative marketing strategy for MuzikMafia appearances. (I should point out that the above context relates primarily to MuzikMafia performances beginning in January 2004. In the earlier days of MuzikMafia, namely fall 2001 through fall 2002, there was no need for a formalized schedule. Musicians simply made their presence known to the godfathers upon their arrival at each show and waited to be called upon to perform.)

Aside from the godfathers, several others had relative power inside the MuzikMafia. In 2004 Cory identified James Otto as an "underboss" because of the length of time that James performed with the community. Cory elaborated further: "He [James] is so close with the godfathers that he is almost a godfather [himself]. But he didn't arrive until the first performance and wasn't part of the [earlier] late-night planning sessions." John had met Gretchen in 1999 while she was bartending and singing at the Bourbon Street Blues & Boogie Bar. Although her bar job, a steady boyfriend, and an infant child kept Gretchen from attending every Tuesday night show at the Pub of Love, she rapidly became the best-known MuzikMafia member in 2004 with her multi-platinum debut album *Here for the Party*.

Max's role in the MuzikMafia was twofold until around 2006. First, Max was the lead saxophone player, contributing that timbre to the texture of most songs at live MuzikMafia shows and many studio recordings.

Secondly, Max monitored and, when necessary, directed the flow of each stage performance. His duties as stage manager involved regulating the order and sometimes the length of solos as well as deciding (with Cory) who performed and when. His extensive knowledge of the artists and their respective repertories enabled him better to control to the flow of songs at live performances.

There were also regularly featured artists who had little to do with MuzikMafia's internal decision-making process. These included John Anderson, Cowboy Troy, Shanna Crooks, Chance, and Damien Horne, and a host of auxiliary performers such as percussionist Pino Squillace, bassist Jerry Navarro, graphic artist Rachel Kice, and entrepreneur Two-Foot Fred. In addition, the MuzikMafia maintained a list of "on call" musicians who frequently performed at shows but were not considered by the godfathers to be official members.

MuzikMafia members exhibited varying levels of commitment to and detachment from the community, each having varying degrees of contact with the godfathers and with other members. In other words, the political structure or power distribution directly affected the degree to which MuzikMafia members aligned themselves with or separated themselves from the collective. I observed several members, namely Chance, Two-Foot Fred, Troy, Dean Hall, Brian Barnette, and Rachel Kice, engage their respective solo careers independent of any MuzikMafia affiliation. This was owing to their relative isolation from major decisions that the godfathers made on behalf of the community.

For example, in fall 2004 Chance started his own weekly variety show after regular Tuesday night MuzikMafia performances stopped. On October 26, less than three weeks after the last 2004 MuzikMafia show in Nashville, Chance organized the first performance of the Nashville Trailer Choir. Chance's vision was a weekly concert whose diverse format was similar to that of the MuzikMafia, highlighting talented local artists of varying music genres. The show's regular acts included Chance, the Butter and Sugar Show, Shanna Crooks, and Shawna Pierce. In December 2004 the Trailer Choir released a Christmas album entitled *Mistletoe Belt Buckle Christmas* underwritten by the MuzikMafia, the proceeds of which were donated to Nashville's Angel Tree program sponsored by the Salvation Army.

MuzikMafia members entered the community in a variety of ways, which also affected their level of commitment and detachment. For example, there were artists such as Troy, Gretchen, and Two-Foot Fred whose first association with the MuzikMafia came about through John Rich's influence. John met Troy in Dallas in 1993, discovered Gretchen at the Bourbon Street Blues and Boogie bar in 1999, and met Fred in 1998 at a Nashville bar during Fan Fair. Musicians such as bass guitarist Jerry, guitarist Sean Smith, and drummer D.D. Holt entered the MuzikMafia community as members of Jon Nicholson's band and accordingly, maintained higher levels of commitment to the individual responsible for introducing them to the MuzikMafia than to the MuzikMafia itself. This later presented numerous problems to the MuzikMafia, splitting the community into several disparate parts.

The social structure of the MuzikMafia was complicated by the community's various commercial endeavors. Besides Raybaw Records there was a publishing entity called MuzikMafia Publishing and the corporate face of the social collective, MuzikMafia LLC.

All decisions concerning Raybaw's operations and artist roster included official votes by the MuzikMafia godfathers, Warner Bros.' Chief Creative Officer Paul Worley, manager and entrepreneur Dale Morris, and Marc Oswald, who together comprised Raybaw's board of directors. Marc Oswald, who managed Gretchen Wilson, Big & Rich, and Cowboy Troy, also had additional input into decisions made at Raybaw on behalf of his clients.

Most if not all MuzikMafia acts were booked and promoted by representatives for Greg Oswald, the president of the Nashville branch of William Morris Agency and Marc Oswald's older brother. Although Greg made significant contributions to the MuzikMafia's internal decisions, especially those pertaining to booking and promoting, he had relatively little influence at Raybaw. Marc, on the other hand, asserted considerable authority in MuzikMafia's internal decisions and decisions concerning Raybaw.

According to Max, the inception of Raybaw was when most of the problems with MuzikMafia started. In a 2009 interview he told me:

Raybaw was just a reflection of that fundamental problem. John Rich was the alpha; he was the top. The other guys had to make a decision. They didn't have the intelligence that John did. Legally, everything was equal. It was a failure from conception in that they all had different world views. John and Jon were living in different dimensions, Kenny and Cory, too. The issues over Raybaw . . . it was just a battlefield for a MuzikMafia war.

The "war" to which Max was referring was actually between John and the three other godfathers over the direction of the MuzikMafia—a feud to which I will return later.

Pino Squillace saw Raybaw as a logical milestone on the MuzikMafia's path of development within the commercial music industry:

> When it came to Raybaw, it was a natural consequence, not what happened *to* Raybaw but rather *with* Raybaw, because a lot of artists wanted to be associated with us and recognized the value in musical integrity that they could relate to. Big & Rich was with Warner Bros., and Warner Bros. was supportive of our organization, so a record label was natural. Troy and James are on there and have had great success. Perhaps that was the cause. No matter how much structure you put behind something, it's the individuals who make the difference, and who make the decisions that spearhead everything else. Some choices preserve the endurance and vision, or not.

In addition to being the MuzikMafia's primary percussionist, Pino was also a well-established Nashville entrepreneur and so had an understanding of the commercial music industry inside and out.

As of 2009 Raybaw was still in existence, albeit in a limited and controversial capacity. The label maintained a catalog of three artists: Cowboy Troy, James Otto, and John Anderson. However, according to Jon, John Rich had caused some problems throughout 2008 concerning the label's public image: "That's another sabotage effort, public relations-wise. John sent out a release to *Billboard* . . . that Raybaw was closing its doors. And that was right in the middle of James's single getting big and about to hit. [Sarcastically] So we're the #1 record label that doesn't exist, with the #1 artist, and the #1 song."

Kenny was referring to James's 2008 album *Sunset Man*. The album peaked at Number Two on *Billboard*'s Top Country Album chart and Number Three on the *Billboard* 200 chart. The album's first single, "Just Got

Started Lovin' You," reached Number One on the Hot Country Songs chart in 2008, in addition to having its video in regular rotation on both CMT and GAC. Moreover, James performed part of "Just Got Started Lovin' You" live at the CMA Awards in fall 2008.

Cory, Kenny, and Jon confirmed in an interview with me in early 2009 that Raybaw still existed, but just "on paper." Unfortunately, the label was not allowed to sign any more artists—another sabotage effort on John Rich's part, according to Jon.

Independent of Raybaw, three of the four original godfathers, respectively, also owned and operated at least one independent music publishing company in 2006. Each enterprise maintained a catalog that included its respective godfather's own songs as well as those written by singer/songwriters that each godfather had contracted over the years. The godfathers and their respective music publishing companies were as follows: Kenny: Love Everybody Music and Big Love Music; John: Rich Texan Music and John D. Richafella Music; and Cory: Mo Famous Music.

However, the central corporate entity that bound all MuzikMafia interests was MuzikMafia LLC. Responsible for the MuzikMafia brand name and the development of the community's artists, the company maintained a staff to support artist development, management, marketing, and media (the MuzikMafia website, the MuzikMafia internet radio station, and additional episodes of *MuzikMafia TV*).

MuzikMafia members had mixed emotions about the LLC. To some, the LLC was a stabilizing structure for the community's nebulous existence. The LLC's offices on Clinton Street in Nashville provided a central location from which to organize the community's various social and commercial endeavors. In addition, the LLC legitimized the members' commitment to the MuzikMafia as a whole rather than to individual godfathers.

For other MuzikMafia members, including some of the godfathers, the LLC was a nightmare. The basic problem was that it was a structured commercial entity born from a group of loosely organized artists, each with his or her own vision for their respective careers and that of the MuzikMafia as a whole. MuzikMafia artists like Big & Rich, Gretchen, Troy, James, and Damien experienced considerable success as a result of MuzikMafia LLC and Raybaw, but other MuzikMafia artists told me that they themselves seemed to be "waiting in line," disillusioned with how their careers were progressing under the LLC's direction. Several artists expressed to me their dissatisfaction with the fact that they were being eclipsed by the few select members who consumed the bulk of the Muzik-Mafia's media exposure.

It finally boiled down to money, and MuzikMafia LLC was not making any. The company was generating considerable buzz throughout the music industry vis-à-vis wide-reaching marketing campaigns, sizable sponsorships from well-known corporations, and the Mafia Soldiers, a grass-roots street team that promoted MuzikMafia events around the country. However, these efforts barely produced enough profit to cover the company's expenses.

At one point in 2006 the godfathers held an LLC budget meeting which was, according to one MuzikMafia member, "when the shit hit the fan." Virginia Davis, who was general manager of Raybaw at the time, brought the MuzikMafia LLC budget report to the meeting, which took place at the LLC's offices on Clinton Street. The report showed that LLC had actually been losing money and was habitually in deficit spending. According to an LLC employee who was present at the meeting, Kenny started making cuts, including Deanna Wollenburg, who had been in charge of video and editing for the MuzikMafia for some time. The most shocking result of the meeting was the decision to replace Cory as general manager of the LLC. The other three godfathers agreed that LLC's management needed a change, despite the fact that Cory was a founding godfather and had a 25 percent stake in the LLC. Cory's departure as general manager was awkward and not without considerable controversy.

When speaking with MuzikMafia members several years later, I was told that there had been more to that 2006 meeting than meets the eye. One LLC employee suspected that the budget reports had been incorrect and that LLC had actually been producing some, albeit meager, profits. Jon, Cory, and Kenny later revealed to me their suspicions that John Rich had orchestrated the whole episode in an attempt to marginalize Cory, whose vision for the LLC he did not share. In retrospect, one should not be surprised at Cory's termination and the budget meeting's suspicious results in general, especially given the fact that John had already hand-picked Cory's replacement and that the LLC's direction had moved in the direction of John's vision for the company.

Following that now-infamous meeting, Cory was replaced as general manager of MuzikMafia LLC by Charlie Pennachio. Charlie's claim to fame had been his participation in the boy band Linear, which had achieved relative commercial success in the early 1990s. I first met Charlie backstage when Big & Rich opened up for Brooks & Dunn on August 25, 2005, one of forty performances on the Deuces Wild Tour that fall. Charlie, John, Two-Foot Fred, a few others, and I spent considerable time hanging out on John's tour bus after the show before heading to a local Hooter's restaurant for a few hours. I was surprised to find out later that Charlie had been named general manager of MuzikMafia LLC, because he had such strong ties to John, and none to the MuzikMafia. Cory officially resigned his position at MuzikMafia LLC and dedicated the bulk of his time to his music publishing company.

Many MuzikMafia members viewed the management change at LLC with surprise, others with disdain. According to Max:

> When Charlie was operating MuzikMafia LLC, that was a firestorm. Charlie got things done, but he pushed Cory and Deanna out. That was a bloodbath . . . Cory's income was drawn primarily from John and Kenny's coffers at that point. People just got sideways about money. You had to serve John *and* Kenny, and if you weren't serving them the way they wanted to be served—and believe me, being everything that John and Kenny want you to be is an impossibility. . . . I think that he [Cory] just got drawn and quartered to keep the folks happy who were paying his check.

Bill Moore, one of several original employees at MuzikMafia LLC, described some of the entity's flaws:

> The pecking order was James Otto, then Jon Nicholson. It was all packaging. But Jon didn't have the right team working for him to get things along with Warner Bros. But not everybody got equal space on the marketing posters. It was supposed to be that the time you put into it was the time you got out of it, like a fraternity. The rules of the business [MuzikMafia LLC] were never laid out, which is why John Anderson got moved up so fast. I don't think that the by-laws of LLC

were ever drawn up. Big Kenny never wanted it to be a commercial entity, he just wanted it to be the community; Cory too.

With regard to LLC's funding, Bill continued:

> The LLC was serving at that time [2005–6] only Big & Rich, who were doing things that the record label wasn't doing. That's where most of its funding came in. [Marc] Oswald was feeding it projects, and I was bringing in the other side. That was causing the office's vision to be challenged. Cory was already out, and Charlie was in charge. Cory and everybody else owned it, but Charlie was in charge, and he represented John's interests because of the budget and the funding which was primarily from John. Cory and us just fell under Charlie and John Rich. It caused a lot of tension.

Kenny disliked the whole idea of MuzikMafia LLC from the beginning. In a 2009 interview he told me: "They [we, the godfathers] set up the MuzikMafia LLC office to try to bring all those people [talented artists] in. It was a whole development thing. It don't make no difference. You don't need an office to develop things." For Kenny the essence of the MuzikMafia was the free Tuesday night shows in Nashville where their friends got together and played great music. He relished the communal aspect of MuzikMafia gatherings and the "love everybody" mentality that he promoted there.

Pino had a different opinion of LLC. In a 2009 interview he said: "Obviously, in our society it's necessary to create some kind of a structure behind what you're doing so you can legitimize it and own it. In order to own a brand, you have to have an entity behind it. If we hadn't done that, somebody could have picked up that name and forced us to change it. There were certain things that we had to do." Pino was addressing an unfortunate reality of the music industry: copyright. And Pino knew the music business as well as many other MuzikMafia members. Following the rules was the best and perhaps the only way to get ahead in Nashville.

As of 2009 the MuzikMafia LLC existed only in the form of a website. There was no official office, no support staff, and little if any money.

By 2007 individual members' association with the MuzikMafia's various commercial enterprises was complicated. Shannon Lawson, for example, was an integral performer with the MuzikMafia social collective in its Nashville performances and organized tours. However, his relationship with Raybaw was limited to sporadic backup vocal and instrumental tracks on other artists' albums. Shannon had a publishing contract with MuzikMafia Publishing and John Rich's publishing companies, Rich Texan Music and later John D. Richafella Music, but not with that of any other godfather.

Brian Barnett, who had been a member of the MuzikMafia since its first performance in 2001, had a different story. Brian, the drummer who performed bare-chested in Gretchen Wilson's video for her hit song "Redneck Woman" and toured with Big & Rich from spring 2004 through spring 2006, by the end of 2006 had left Big & Rich, Warner Bros., and MuzikMafia LLC but still performed on occasion at shows in Nashville as a member of the MuzikMafia social collective.

Dean Hall's relationship with the MuzikMafia was problematic at best. Having been a member of the MuzikMafia since spring 2004, Dean became Gretchen's lead guitarist in January 2005. However, like Gretchen, Dean had little contact thereafter with the MuzikMafia social collective, MuzikMafia LLC, or Raybaw. He officially ended his association with the MuzikMafia via formal letter to the godfathers in January 2006 but remained with Gretchen's band for the rest of the year. Anonymous sources suggested several reasons for Dean's separation from the MuzikMafia, including his frustration with Raybaw's management concerning a possible recording contract for him and his personal aversion toward John Rich. Dean left Gretchen's band in 2007 and returned to his life as an independent guitarist in the Nashville music scene.

Max Abrams had undergone a series of functional transformations in the MuzikMafia since 2004. He was already the lead saxophone and stage manager for all MuzikMafia shows in Nashville. In fall 2004 Max added to his duties the role of sax player in Jon Nicholson's band and performed with Jon on tour and on his debut album, *A Lil Sump'm Sump'm*. However, when Jon began distancing himself from the MuzikMafia in 2006 with a move to California, Max remained in Nashville and forged a career as independent artist with numerous non-MuzikMafia related activities that included work as a studio musician and record producer.

Also in 2006, Max began drawing a regular salary as Kenny's executive assistant in a variety of personal projects. Max worked on Kenny's Save

Darfur campaign, his University of Creativity, his Pirate Project, and for Kenny's music publishing company. Max maintained frequent contact with MuzikMafia LLC and MuzikMafia Publishing due to their collaborations on a range of projects. Max had some affiliation with Rich Texan Music and John D. Richafella Music because of their concentrations in pop-rock. However, Max had little or no contact with Cory or Jon in 2007. In addition, Max performed saxophone only infrequently in 2007 because the MuzikMafia seldom convened for shows that year.

Chance's affiliation with the MuzikMafia and MuzikMafia LLC ended in November 2006, although he remained with Raybaw until February 2007. Although Jon and Cory remained godfathers of the MuzikMafia, as of summer 2007 they both had little to do with MuzikMafia LLC, Muzik-Mafia Publishing, or any other MuzikMafia commercial enterprise. Furthermore, Bill Moore, who played an integral, behind-the-scenes role in the MuzikMafia's commercial development from fall 2004, left MuzikMafia LLC in summer 2007.

The MuzikMafia's loss of several artists, namely Chance and Dean, paralleled its addition of new ones. In winter 2007 the godfathers invited well-known commercial country artist John Anderson to join the MuzikMafia; John Rich had been producing Anderson's new album *Easy Money*. John Anderson had been one of John Rich's heroes growing up, and Rich was a major force in signing Anderson to Raybaw.

Shanna Crooks, a backup vocalist for Chance throughout 2004 and a songwriter for John Rich's publishing companies from 2006, was invited to join the MuzikMafia in spring 2007. With John's help, Shanna later acquired a recording contract with Atlantic Records and embarked on a solo career. Jennifer Bain, a.k.a. SWJ, who had performed with the Mafia Mizfits and later worked as a personal assistant to Cory and John, became the MuzikMafia's first official spoken-word artist in summer 2007. Finally, Sean Smith, who had been lead guitarist in Jon's band since fall 2004, became an auxiliary member of the MuzikMafia in 2006. By summer 2007, the MuzikMafia was headed by godfathers John, Kenny, Cory, and Jon and godmother Gretchen. Other primary members included James Otto, Cowboy Troy, Damien Horne, Shannon Lawson, Two-Foot Fred, Shanna Crooks, John Anderson, Jennifer Bain, and Rachel Kice. The MuzikMafia's auxiliary members included Max Abrams, Brian Barnett,

Pino Squillace, Jerry Navarro, Elijah "D.D." Holt, Adam Shoenfeld, Ethan Pilzer, and Sean Smith.

Various changes in the MuzikMafia's social collective became apparent at a show that took place on January 30, 2007. The MuzikMafia was performing that night at Fuel, a club located at 114 2nd Avenue South. Although technically located in SoBro, the club is only half a block from the mainstream commercial music scene of The District on lower Broadway in downtown Nashville. The club's owners advertise live music nightly, specifically Top Forty music from the 1970s, 1980s, and 1990s.

My experiences at Fuel greatly contrasted with those of earlier MuzikMafia shows from 2004 through 2006. First, there was only one MuzikMafia fan whom I recognized from shows at the Mercy Lounge, Bluesboro, or 12th & Porter; this is significant when one considers that MuzikMafia had had a dedicated audience of twenty to fifty people who regularly attended weekly shows in 2004, 2005, and 2006. Second, during Shannon Lawson's set few people, if any, danced as had been the case at earlier MuzikMafia shows; most onlookers stood near the stage drinking alcohol and conversing with friends. Third, Bill Moore, who was still director of brand development for MuzikMafia LLC at the time, focused little of his attention on the club's stage; instead, Bill was concentrating on passing out free samples of an energy drink whose marketing campaign was of interest to MuzikMafia LLC. Fourth, the audience included more well-dressed young professionals than I had observed at previous shows.

Despite the above contrasts in social context, the show's musical flow was quite similar to previous MuzikMafia performances in Nashville. Godfathers John and Jon started the evening and included impromptu dialogue between songs. This performance with the MuzikMafia was a first for Jon in recent months. He had been living and performing in California at the request of Warner Bros./Raybaw in an effort to market his music to different audiences from those found in the South. Each artist, namely John, Jon, Shannon, and Shanna Crooks, played songs that dated from 2004 through 2006. The "open jam" that had been a staple at MuzikMafia shows since 2001 was also included.

The MuzikMafia did not perform again together until later that year on October 19, 2007. Although the show's location was a repeat performance at Fuel, the MuzikMafia had changed considerably. The show did not begin with a godfather on stage as had been the custom since 2001. Instead, a non-MuzikMafia band began the evening around 8:00 p.m., probably at the invitation of the club's owners. Few, if any, MuzikMafia members were there; the MuzikMafia part of the evening did not get under way until two hours later.

I suspected that things would be different when, around 10:00 p.m., camera crews from CMT began setting up and a few large tour buses parked outside. Much to the crowd's dismay, a group of musicians entered the club, including 1990s pop sensation Bobby Brown, Dee Snider of Twisted Sister, Julio Iglesias Jr., former Wilson Phillips singer Carnie Wilson, *American Idol* finalist Diana DeGarmo, former *Brady Bunch* actress Maureen McCormick, and popular R&B artist Sisqó. The evening was not intended to be a regular MuzikMafia show, but rather a taping for John's upcoming CMT reality show *Gone Country* that was scheduled to air January through March 2008.

Although many MuzikMafia artists did perform, including John, Jon, Gretchen, James, Shannon, and Troy, the presence of so many other well-known stars created an awkward atmosphere—provocatively dressed groupies, autograph seekers with cameras in hand, an array of television cameras, and celebrities who attempted to outdo each other on stage for their fair share of camera time. The event was fun and entertaining but disappointing for the only two MuzikMafia fans whom I recognized. I noticed that, by midnight, long before the show's end, the two had gone home.

By October 2007 it was apparent that John Rich's solo endeavors were taking off and that the MuzikMafia, both as a social collective and commercial enterprise, was slipping behind. The godfathers agreed that MuzikMafia needed to get back to its roots. Kenny later described to me what was happening: "By the time of the *Gone Country* shooting at Fuel, most everybody was going their separate ways in rocket ship style. We tried to bring it back together on a somewhat regular basis just to keep everything going, to keep the revolution together, hoping that it wouldn't dissipate."

In an effort to revive the MuzikMafia, John suggested a new beginning for regular, free Tuesday night shows in Nashville. On November 4, 2007, John emailed the MuzikMafia the following message:

Hello everyone! Now that touring season is slowing down, it's time to re-ignite the MuzikMafia Tuesday night muzik without prejudice jam!! Time to get back to the grass roots of what Muzik Mafia really means. It's not about the big time hits, or the famous faces showing up, it's about having fun and providing a stage for ourselves and others in town who want to have a place where quality and uniqueness still reins [sic] king!! The last few times I have been out and about in town, I have consistently seen incredibly talented artists who would benefit greatly from having a stage like the MuzikMafia to showcase their talents. I think it's imperative that we kick our jam back in for AT LEAST 10 in a row, and try to make it a regular thing for the entire year of 2008. I have booked a venue called "Elevation" (the old Code Blue) on Division St. for 10 in a row starting Tuesday, November 13th. I understand that some of us are not in town and can't make it. But I would urge the ones of you who are around to invite friends, invite talent, and show up like we used to in force to spread our philosophy of "Muzik Without Prejudice," and offer our stage and vibe to Music City once again!! Looking forward to seeing you all on Nov. 13th!! Please forward this to anyone you wish, and let's get it rollin'!! All the best, Godfather Rich.

Located at 1907 Division Street adjacent Music Row, the nightclub had undergone a series of metamorphoses in recent years. The two-floor structure had once housed a gym on the bottom floor and a Bikram yoga studio above. George Strait's manager bought it and turned the bottom floor into a strip club, complete with semi-circular vinyl booths and a dancing pole in the middle of the dance floor. The strip club folded and was replaced by a bar/nightclub called Code Blue and, under new management, eventually changed its name to Elevation. MuzikMafia shows reconvened there on November 13, 2007. For a brief period it looked as though the MuzikMafia had a new start, but things are not always as they seem.

I attended a MuzikMafia show at Elevation on December 11, 2007, and was both encouraged and disappointed. Jon and Shannon started the show in traditional MuzikMafia style with some audience favorites from Jon's catalog. Max, Pino, Jerry, and D.D.—Jon's full band—were there and backed him just as they had done on tour promoting Jon's album two years prior. Other MuzikMafia members, including Brian Barnette and Damien, joined in the collective jam as the evening progressed, as did a few newcomers such as Danny Salazar. The schedule was loosely organized at best, but closely resembled the shows I attended regularly throughout 2004 and 2005 during the MuzikMafia's heyday. From a musician's perspective, it was like old times—like a family reunion.

What was disconcerting about the evening of December 11 was the audience. The club's physical space was designed in such a way that attention could be focused on a variety of areas independent of the action on stage. As a result, only about half of the audience that night was near the stage. The other half of the audience was scattered around the club's spacious interior, engaging in a variety of conversations and focusing on things other than the music. In the early days of MuzikMafia, the music had been the focal point for each audience member. By the end of 2007, shows had become a social gathering—a place to be seen—quite independent from what was happening on stage.

MuzikMafia performances at Elevation in late 2007 seemed to be working. After all, MuzikMafia artists were doing just what had defined their collectivity since 2001: performing together at Tuesday night shows in Nashville. They were also including in Tuesday lineups a series of well-known artists, including Brad Arnold of 3 Doors Down, Black Flag Militia, Jewel, Billy Dean, Marty Stuart, Jay DeMarcus of Rascal Flatts, Lauren Lucas, Randy Houser, and Kink Ador. John did his fare share of emceeing the Tuesday shows in November and December 2007 at Elevation, but I do not remember ever seeing Kenny perform there. Perhaps Kenny foresaw the firestorm among MuzikMafia members that would tear the community apart less than a month later.

Although the problems at MuzikMafia LLC in 2006 had caused considerable tension among the community's members, it was the events surrounding a single, scheduled MuzikMafia performance in January 2008 in Muscle Shoals, Alabama, that ripped the community apart entirely. Godfather Jon referred to the gig as "D-Day" for the MuzikMafia. The occasion was the Third Annual Sam Phillips Music Festival that had been started two years prior to honor the "Father of Rock and Roll" who had owned and operated legendary Sun Records in Memphis from January 1950. Sun Records' roster had included musical greats such as Elvis Presley, Carl Perkins, Jerry

Lee Lewis, Johnny Cash, Roy Orbison, B.B. King, Charlie Rich, and Howling Wolf, contributing much to the development of American popular music in the twentieth century.

The MuzikMafia had been booked to headline the four-day festival (January 2–5) by Jerry Phillips, son of the legendary Sun label owner, who resides in Muscle Shoals. Phillips's decision to include the MuzikMafia at the 2008 festival was a logical choice for several reasons. The MuzikMafia had performed at the Second Annual Sam Phillips Music Festival the year before with considerable success, and Jerry Phillips had been a fan of the MuzikMafia for several years. I remember seeing Jerry at a MuzikMafia show at Bluesboro on September 14, 2004. MuzikMafia musician James Otto had strong ties to Muscle Shoals: the R&B-inspired "Muscle Shoals Sound" had inspired much of his music, and he had spent considerable time there collaborating with local artists and friends Gary Nichols and James LeBlanc.

As general manager for MuzikMafia LLC, Charlie Pennachio had tended to the contract between MuzikMafia and the festival's organizers. However, Charlie had included in the contract the names of specific performers such as John, Gretchen, Troy, etc. that, according to Jon, was something that the MuzikMafia had seldom done before. Usually, it had been the case to specify "MuzikMafia" as the artists of contract because, as their slogan stated, "you never know who's gonna show." Nevertheless, the contract was signed, the festival's organizers paid LLC a sizable five-figure deposit for the MuzikMafia's appearance, and promotional materials were disseminated.

This is where the plot thickened. Unbeknownst to many MuzikMafia members, including godfathers Jon, Kenny, and Cory, John Rich had previously made several deposits to the LLC bank account (eventually totaling a five-figure amount) that was used to cover operating expenses such as salaries and inventory. John intimated to the other godfathers that the money made from the Muscle Shoals gig in January 2008 was supposed to pay him back. To make matters worse, John had offered Jon, Cory, and Kenny a buyout of their shares of MuzikMafia as repayment for his loan to the LLC. According to an LLC employee: "Everything that was going on was the John Rich show. He [John] didn't like Kenny, and he didn't trust Cory. . . . So John offered to buy the MuzikMafia [name and the LLC] and put a price on the table. They [Kenny, Cory, and Jon] turned down his offer."

Jon later expressed to me his surprise about John's offer:

That [John's potential buyout] was just a hysterical idea in itself. That doesn't make sense. None of us has ever made a penny off of Muzik-Mafia. It's an idea. How are you going to buy out an idea? It's not just us, either. It's everybody who participates in the MuzikMafia. James Otto is just as much a part of this as I am or we are, or Shannon Lawson, or Rachel Kice; it's about us getting together. You can't buy that out, so that's what started the tension.

According to Cory, "It was just a crazy deal. Of course, there's a lot more to it, details that we haven't even figured out." Jon continued Cory's sentiment: "It's like a Dr. Evil, Darth Vader, good side/bad side kind of thing to me in some ways. There was a lot of planning of a coup for control of the Mafia in a lot of ways. We didn't realize that until a little later on. And the money had already been spent." Needless to say, tensions were high during the weeks leading up to the scheduled show date. However, the firestorm that happened among MuzikMafia members the day of the show was a turning point in the community's downfall.

In the early morning hours of the show date, several MuzikMafia members met in Nashville to catch the tour bus that would take them down to Muscle Shoals, approximately 125 miles away. Kenny had been planning on taking his own car but Jon, Cory, and a few other MuzikMafia members arrived at the bus only to find that half of the scheduled performers were not there. According to Jon:

Everyone was getting ready to go get on the bus to go down there early morning the day of the show, and half the people who were supposed to be on the bus aren't even there, including the full production staff: front end staff, monitoring engineer, lights, and the band that was supposed to playing with everybody . . . No Two-Foot Fred, Cowboy Troy; no Gretchen or Max. But we didn't know about Gretchen yet; she had her own bus. So we get on the bus and red flags started going up, so I started calling people. A couple people said that John had told them that the show was canceled. I heard that from the front house engineer.

One can imagine the dismay that Jon and the others felt. According to Kenny: "That's the same thing I got. I started calling around, too. Jon and I spoke. I was getting ready for somebody to come pick me up. All the guys I talked to said that the thing had been called off. And I said that we couldn't just cancel; we're under contract. We are going to play this show tonight."

There were potentially major problems for the MuzikMafia. The show was sold out, and much of the promotional materials mentioned the names of the best-known MuzikMafia artists, none of whom were on the bus to the gig. To make matters worse, John was not answering any phone calls from the other godfathers. Frustrated and disappointed, the remaining godfathers assessed the situation and decided to proceed to Muscle Shoals. According to Jon: "It was a total sabotage effort, and so at that point we said, 'OK, we're going to fucking do this show. We're going to rock the show, and it's going to be great.' There were lots of people coming to jam, so we hooked up production, we hooked up front house, we hooked up the whole deal, independent from the other crews. We hooked up other friends and allies from the past."

John had apparently pulled out of the show at the last minute, without informing the other godfathers. Cory, Kenny, and Jon later discovered that John had called many people and deceptively told them that either the gig had been cancelled or had simply told them not to go. Either way, the remaining godfathers and other MuzikMafia personnel and friends went to the gig and, according to Kenny, put on "a great show . . . Mafia style."

Kenny was bitter about the whole situation. He later discovered that many of the guys had been told by John not to show up or that they would lose their jobs. To make matters worse, Cory, Kenny, and Jon also found out that John had invited much of the MuzikMafia to his own private club the Spot that night to watch a football game and to celebrate his birthday.

From an outside perspective, the incident seems almost out of place for the MuzikMafia. However, the Muscle Shoals debacle was a culmination of considerable tension that had been brewing among MuzikMafia's membership. According to Max, who did not attend the Sam Phillips Celebration show:

That gig was pretty much the line in the sand for me and Mafia. I missed the bus to Muscle Shoals, but still I didn't want to be in the same room with Kenny. That [also] wasn't too long after the Nicholson thing. Jon functionally ate my life from age 26 to 29. The [record] deal was bad to begin with. I remember after the meeting with Warner Bros.' marketing guys, I looked to Jerry [Navarro] and Sean [Smith] and said that this was a dead letter. We've already lost. There weren't any early ripples of publicity. Nobody knew what to do with the album. Had Nicholson been the politician that John Rich is, had he been savvy enough, maybe we would have made it to a second record.

Max's estrangement from Kenny resulted in Max leaving Kenny's employ in December 2007. Max was also still on poor terms with Jon after Jon's move to California following the decline in sales of his first album and subsequent breakup of his band, which had been a major source of income from 2004 through 2006 for his band members, including Max, Jerry, Sean, and D.D. Max continued:

> Then [when Muscle Shoals came up] I thought, "Fuck, I'm not gonna go to Alabama with Big Kenny and Jon Nicholson. . . . And I was working on a record that was going to pay my bills for that month. It became clear, too, that there was a John side of the camp and a Kenny side of the camp. People have strong opinions about John Rich, but in all the time I knew him, we never got sideways about anything once. We always were on good terms. There's never been anything between us but friendship and respect. So my choice was between going to Alabama with these guys (Kenny, etc.) or getting together with John Rich and his club later that night. I said, "Fuck, I'm staying here." That was the last time I saw Kenny.

For Max, the Muscle Shoals performance was also a question of his financial future. He could have risked estrangement from John by playing the gig against John's wishes, or remained in Nashville and taken advantage of numerous benefits that came with being close to John. According to Max: "I love Big Kenny, and I understand him in a lot of ways. I have tremendous respect for how he sees the world . . . a very basic need to remake the world in the image of Heaven. *But* it was John Rich who gave me my MuzikMafia ring. Each one cost $5,000."

Despite the tension surrounding the performance and the absence of many of their MuzikMafia friends, the MuzikMafia members who did show up still had a great time. According to Pino: "That gig was a great gig, because it sounded awesome despite the fact that John and Gretchen didn't show up, and all that. I got a little bit involved at the last minute the day of the show, because some band members weren't showing up. I was calling guitar players at the last minute. We didn't stop. We were making calls and getting it done."

The absence of John, Gretchen, and Troy in Muscle Shoals caused seemingly irreparable damage to relationships among the MuzikMafia's inner circle of members. Pino later said:

> It was a turning point particularly because of the fact that certain individuals made some choices in terms of boycotting the show: John, Troy, Gretchen, Max. . . . It strengthened my relationship with those who were there. It certainly increased my respect level for them. It obviously disappointed us. I was disappointed in those who didn't show up. It brought some ego into play. I don't know what the fuck it was. When that was put in play, it was like disowning the name of the family. It let everybody down. They didn't keep their commitment, and it affected the name of the family. I would have dealt with it a lot differently. Even if there had been good reasons, I would never have done something like that. I would have confronted the circumstances. In the name of MuzikMafia, I would have been there. I would have dealt with the issues, even if that had been our last gig.

One should keep in mind that the MuzikMafia was, in the beginning, a social collective of like-minded artists. Pino's frustration with those who did not attend the Muscle Shoals gig reflected his relationship with the MuzikMafia's members as close friends and family rather than as a commercial enterprise.

By the time of the Muscle Shoals gig, godfathers Jon and John had been experiencing their own difficulties with one another, the most significant of which surrounded Jon's DVD shoot that had taken place in September 2007 in Nashville. John had approached Jon to shoot a live DVD to promote Jon's album that Warner Bros. had abandoned the year before. John offered to finance the project that comprised a week of paid rehearsals, a full production crew from Tacklebox Films, a six-camera shoot, and the renting of well-known club Exit/In, all of which totaled a six-figure price tag. At first, Jon was enthusiastic about the DVD:

> He [John] came to me and asked me if I would do this DVD shoot, and I though that it was a good-hearted deal. He said that it would be a great way for people to see me live. He said that he would finance it. He suggested that we do it 50/50, so I said sure, why not? So we set up the show to do, and pulled it all together, and we recorded a beautiful night of music with some really great content.

However, soon after production ended, things became tense between the two godfathers. Jon elaborated to me in a 2009 interview:

> As soon as we got it done, we started editing and stuff and wrapping it up, and tensions were starting to come. John had just spent a chunk of money on this DVD, and he wanted to start getting it back. So this 50/50 started going to 80/20 then 95/5, and then he just wanted it all. He had plans for this and that, and I didn't want all of that. I was just doing a show. So it never went anywhere. My tensions with him started at that point. He [also] wanted me to do some publishing stuff with him that I wasn't willing to do. . . . Because before that, John really didn't have anything on me in any way where he could feel like he could tell me how to make my music or tell me who to talk to or get directly involved in a benefit with.

The DVD has been not been released, other than a few excerpts that were posted to YouTube. Needless to say, the events surrounding the DVD shoot caused significant financial and emotional tension between the two godfathers—tension that, as of early 2009, had not been resolved.

It was no secret among MuzikMafia that friction had existed between John and Kenny for several years and for legitimate reasons. According to several members, Big & Rich were "doomed from the start." A former employee of William Morris Agency overheard Greg Oswald telling John early on that he and Kenny needed to "put all that shit aside" because Big

& Rich were always fighting. A former MuzikMafia employee described the difference (or indifference) between John and Kenny as follows:

> John is the kind of guy who would walk into a place and shake a wine bottle all over everybody and ruin someone's shit. And Kenny would bring a wine bottle and give it to someone and say, "Hey, this is for you." John would rather piss on the floor and raise a ruckus than have a meaningful relationship with someone. It's the John Rich show; it's selfish. That tension has always been there. If you had a partner who was acting like an asshole all of the time, it reflects upon you.

At one point Cory, Kenny, and Jon called a godfather meeting to discuss the problems with John. Of major concern was an episode that occurred while Big & Rich were on tour. According to Kenny, "John walked right out after the show, got in his Corvette with some young girl, and started doing burnouts in the parking lot as 50,000 people were leaving the show." In regards to the above incident, Jon later told me, "The godfathers all had a sit-down about that, and the consensus was to suspend John and that he needed to chill the fuck out." The idea to "suspend" John never came to fruition, because as Kenny later told me, "You can't talk to somebody who ain't listening."

For other MuzikMafia members, the beginning of the end for Big & Rich was a failed European tour with Bon Jovi in 2007. Big & Rich had been featured earlier that year in a duet entitled "We Got It Going On" with Bon Jovi on their album *Lost Highway*. In addition, Big & Rich had opened two performances in New Jersey for Bon Jovi in late October 2007. By the time of the Bon Jovi gigs, tensions were reaching a boiling point between John and Kenny. According to Max: "Several folks on the Big & Rich staff realized that this thing [Big & Rich] is folding and started looking at other options. When they shut down the Bon Jovi tour in Europe, that was the beginning of the end. They were going to do the tour but got cancelled. A lot of friends pulled me aside and told me to really start thinking about what I was doing next. John was one of them."

Tension existed between John and Kenny almost from the beginning and resulted in a gradual separation of their personal and professional lives over time. Kenny married and had a child while engaging in various commercial and humanitarian efforts that were independent of Big & Rich and the MuzikMafia. According to Max, who was Kenny's assistant in 2007, "Kenny's vision was to work both side of the books: to have a for-profit entity independent of Big & Rich that funded his non-profit entity and that was separate from MuzikMafia." Among Kenny's many activities were his Pirate Project, a CD compilation of children's songs, and his Save Darfur campaign that, with the assistance of the National Geographic Society, resulted in a video documentary about the genocide taking place in the Darfur region of the Sudan.

At some point early on, John realized what was happening between him and Kenny and between him and the MuzikMafia and made some fairly significant decisions. His popularity as a serious Nashville producer, songwriter, and performer had been steadily growing for some years, and in 2007 he decided to branch out in several different directions.

John's accomplishments over the next few years were significant. In 2008 and 2009 John hosted two seasons of *Gone Country* on CMT, the highest-rated show in the history of the network. In 2008 he was one of three judges on the sixth season of NBC's *Nashville Star*. John also recorded his solo album *Son of a Preacher Man,* which was released in March 2009. As a songwriter or performer, John had charted thirty-six Top Forty country hits by the end of 2008.

John's producing credits were equally significant. In 2008 he produced James Otto's album *Sunset Man,* whose single "Just Got Started Loving You" was the most-played country song of the year. John also produced two tracks with Jimmy Jam and Terry Lewis on Ruben Studdard's last album. In addition, John produced Randy Owen's first solo record, an album entitled *One on One* that ultimately resulted in three singles on *Billboard*'s Hot Country Songs chart. Randy was famous as a longtime member of the legendary country group Alabama.

The corporate entity of Big & Rich continued vis-à-vis album sales, an official website, and a fan club, but for all intents and purposes John and Kenny unofficially disbanded in late 2007. However, the duo still performed together sporadically. As of January 2009, future concert dates were still in the works, including a summer 2009 tour scheduled from mid-June to late August.

By the beginning of 2009 the MuzikMafia was almost unrecognizable from its earlier form at the Pub of Love or even its heyday in 2004 and 2005. John and Kenny had not spoken in months; John had stopped returning

Kenny's emails and phone calls. Max had not spoken to Kenny or Jon in over a year. James and Damien were experiencing considerable success as solo artists with little publicity from their MuzikMafia affiliation. Shannon Lawson was making most of his income as a Nashville songwriter with cuts appearing on Gretchen's third album *One of the Boys*, John Anderson's Raybaw album *Easy Money*, and Randy Owen's debut solo album *One on One*. With John Rich's help, Shanna Crooks had secured a recording contract for a pop album with Atlantic Records. Jon had not spoken to his former band members in a long time. The emotional wounds from the Muscle Shoals gig in January 2008 ran deep. For much of 2008, I thought that MuzikMafia had simply folded like many other entities do in Nashville's commercial music industry. Much to my surprise, I received an email from Jon on November 27, 2008, telling me, "The revolution has only just begun." The MuzikMafia was reborn—a phoenix, if you will, from the ashes of the old—in the form of Mafia Nation.

Mafia Nation was the brainchild of Jon and a few other MuzikMafia members and comprised both a "return to roots" for the MuzikMafia and an expansion of MuzikMafia's ideals and beliefs. According to Jon: "Everybody was doing their own thing and there was all this turmoil, and I was out in California at the time, and everything was really getting scattered. . . . it's what happened when Mafia ideas and mine molded together to try to encompass more that just MuzikMafia, more groups."

Jon wanted to get back to the ideas upon which the MuzikMafia was founded: friends getting together to play music, learn from each other, and support each other in a nonterritorial, noncombative, and nonrestrictive environment.

More importantly, Jon was adamant about not using the MuzikMafia name. He later explained to me:

> It's a little different than your standard Mafia gathering, because it encompasses a lot more than the standard MuzikMafia artists, a lot of great people who just want to gather together in the scene. The idea was to expand into a larger thing. because we kind of closed Muzik-Mafia off. We said [a few years ago] that these were the artists of the MuzikMafia, and it doesn't go beyond this, and John was a real proponent of that and tried to keep it all in a box.

Jon, Kenny, and Cory agreed that John Rich was the driving factor behind transforming the MuzikMafia into an elite society, comprising "the best of the best of the best" among Nashville talent. John was a major financier of the MuzikMafia rings, handcrafted by well-known Nashville jeweler "Diamond Dave" and each worth approximately $5,000. The MuzikMafia website also boasted its rather closed membership of thirteen principal artists plus a host of auxiliary performers. In contrast, Jon, Kenny, and Cory wanted to have Mafia Nation jam sessions be inclusive rather than exclusive. Pino, who was alongside Jon in the planning of Mafia Nation in 2008, later told me, "Jon felt the need to build something on his own with his brothers [MuzikMafia, excluding John Rich], just keeping the same nucleus, but still having the freedom to make decisions like the original vision that he had, like we all had."

After about a year of informal planning among Jon, Kenny, Cory, and a few other MuzikMafia members, the Mafia Nation's first performance took place on January 6, 2009. The show had been scheduled to take place at the historic Ryman Auditorium in downtown Nashville. However, due to low ticket pre-sales, the venue was changed to the Cannery Row Ballroom in the same building as the Mercy Lounge—both former hangouts for the MuzikMafia. The Mafia Nation's advertisement flyer mentioned nothing of the MuzikMafia, but rather contained a list of artists who would be performing that evening. The roster included Brad Arnold and Todd Harrell of 3 Doors Down, Buddy Jewel, Seven-Day Binge, Kenny Olsen, Danny Salazar, Shannon Lawson, Anthony Gomes, Bobby Bare Jr., Randy Houser, James Otto, and SWJ. Most significant was the presence of two band names that had not appeared in Nashville in quite some time: luvjOi and Stroller.

Both bands were legendary among MuzikMafia members. LuvjOi was Kenny's band before Big & Rich, and Stroller was Jon Nicholson's band before he went solo in 2004. Both were rock bands and shared electric guitarist virtuoso Adam Shoenfeld, who had been with Kenny from the early days of MuzikMafia and had continued with him as part of Big & Rich. The Mafia Nation's performance was a reunion of sorts for both luvjOi and Stroller, and their respective sets contained songs from pre-MuzikMafia days. For the audience, it was a chance to see Kenny perform as the rocker he once was: grabbing the microphone with both hands, leaning backward and forward over the audience at center stage, and yelling at the top of his lungs. For Kenny, "It was a blast." For Jon, the luvjOi and Stroller sets were the best parts of the show, but there were also other factors. "I thought that it was awesome, not that Kenny didn't play his Big & Rich songs, but that he did a luvjOi set. It was bitchin'. And then the Stroller set was awesome. The Seven Day Binge thing was fun, too. We had so many acts, but we didn't have any help. It's not like we had paid people. It was old school. We were hustling about [backstage] trying to get people ready to play."

For the MuzikMafia members who were present, the Mafia Nation show was like MuzikMafia had been at the Pub of Love, the Tin Roof, Two Doors Down, Dan McGuiness Pub, or even at the Mercy Lounge. Organization was almost nonexistent. Changes between artists and songs were awkward at times, adding to the impromptu flow of the evening. Artists like Damien and Shannon performed a whole array of songs; others, such as Buddy Jewel, who had won the first season of *Nashville Star*, sang only a single tune. Backstage Buddy told me that he was just happy to be there, playing with friends whom he had really only gotten to know at a gig the week prior. I estimated the number of artists backstage to equal that of the audience members out front. The Mafia Nation show was as important for the performers as the audience—just like MuzikMafia had been in 2001. After all, according to Jon, the Mafia Nation show was meant to "get back to the basics."

Also important was the fact that more than a handful of MuzikMafia fans attended the show. There were fans whom I had known since 2004 but had not seen in quite some time, a few from the Mafia Soldiers street team, and Chance, a former member who had been unofficially banned from MuzikMafia shows since 2006. I had not seen him in over a year, but I was aware of the events surrounding his departure from the MuzikMafia in late 2006 and Raybaw in 2007. His relationship with John Rich had deteriorated over time and eventually had almost come to a fist fight on John's tour bus after a MuzikMafia show at the Mercy Lounge. Chance left the MuzikMafia shortly thereafter. At the Mafia Nation show in January 2009, I could read Chance's face clearly; he was happy to be back among friends. Jon told Cory, Kenny, and me a few weeks later that he wanted to "give Chance another chance." Apparently, the first Mafia Nation show was a new beginning for a lot of people. Unfortunately, as of September 2009 there had been no repeat performances of Mafia Nation.

The commercial music industry is filled with artists who make it to the big time, but only a few stay there. A question that guided much of this study of the MuzikMafia has been, "How did a small group of dispossessed Nashville artists achieve such widespread popularity in an industry that had once marginalized them?" Perhaps a more important question should be, "What led to the MuzikMafia's eventual downfall?" Were they doomed from the start to be another brick in a long wall of Nashville outlaws? If so, how could they have affected so many people's lives in positive ways? How can other artists learn from the MuzikMafia's mistakes? Were MuzikMafia members simply absorbed by the industry, attracted to the money and power that came with fame, and consumed by their own greed for more? For some MuzikMafia artists, this may have been the case; for others, these and other questions remain unanswered.

The early tension between John and Kenny could have foreshadowed some of MuzikMafia's later difficulties, but that tension was not always a problem. According to Kenny in 2009:

[In the beginning] we were jamming and really having fun together, but it wasn't long before he [John Rich] started doing some things that were just embarrassing. He probably thought that I was doing the same thing. It was like putting two stallions in the same pen. We are really different people. But I still love him, and I'd do anything for him if he called me right now. But I didn't approve of all the stuff that he was doing and I didn't condone it. . . . so we'll come back around; everybody does. What was really great about it was all the wonderful songs . . . I hope and pray that John and I can sit in a room together and write and it be something meaningful and collective of where both of us come from.

Even in 2009 Kenny still had hope for a future for Big & Rich and the MuzikMafia, just as he had had in 2001. Yet the commercial side of the music business took hold of MuzikMafia and did not let go. Kenny was never fond of the corporate entity of MuzikMafia LLC but accepted it, as did most MuzikMafia members, as the logical next step toward expansion. When I queried Kenny in 2009 about the LLC, he responded:

I would say that it [MuzikMafia LLC] was definitely engineered to the point that they [MuzikMafia managers, record labels, promoters, etc.] wanted to use the organization to market; they wanted to turn it into a marketing entity, 'cause they knew that we had a hell of a database, and they wanted to use it. We never wanted to get into the marketing business. They wanted to use it as a machine, to advertise other artists on the website, or something . . . I don't know. I never paid any attention to that crap.

Although Jon agreed to some extent with Kenny, Jon did see the LLC as a valuable resource with some very specific flaws:

I think that initially the idea of it was good. They [the godfathers] had big ideas and I think that it could have worked. But then it started not working. John started having ideas. Charlie started living at John's place practically so they got to communicate a lot about stuff, so MuzikMafia LLC started going towards John's initiative, because he was the one that had the communication with Charlie.

In many ways the commercial aspect of the LLC was the anti-MuzikMafia, causing the organization to spiral downward almost from its inception.

However, MuzikMafia's problems were not just a question of marketing and branding. Another contributing factor was the fact that there were four godfathers who had equal control over the whole organization—like a family having four parents instead of two. As Bill Moore told me in a 2009 interview, "You can't have four chiefs in a tribe."

And each godfather had his own set of skills, strengths, and weaknesses. According to Max:

John Rich was the top of that pyramid, not necessarily as a percentage owner, but as an organizer and a ringmaster. It was a mistake for the three [other godfathers] to fill those shoes the way that he did. If you watch the tapes even from that Code Blue show, John is the center of the wheel. You can see how graciously he gets people on and off the stage. How fun that show was. How everyone's attention was focused on that stage. He got acts two songs on and then off. Then he leaves the stage, and it's a very different thing. The mistake people made was thinking that they were John's professional and intellectual equal and thinking that they could do that job as well as he did. As soon as they made that assumption and started putting things into practice, things started to fail.

However, the other godfathers saw things differently. Jon was eager to share his thoughts on the matter.

When you start to think that you're the only person who's doing anything for something and you should be the sole benefactor, that's when you run into problems. John's problem with this whole thing is that he doesn't see what's going on when he's not there. He doesn't realize that Mafia shows happen if he's not there. Like when he wanted to start things back up again [at Code Blue], he said that he wouldn't be able to be at every one of them . . . like he's the Johnny Carson of the MuzikMafia. I told him, "Dude, we've done hundreds of Mafias without you even there, don't you realize that?" It was a self-centered thing.

My own experiences with the MuzikMafia support Jon's viewpoint. For much of 2004, I thought that Jon Nicholson was the MuzikMafia's only godfather. After all, he was the emcee for most of the Tuesday night shows that summer. John and Kenny were off on tour—Gretchen, too—and Cory usually remained either backstage or out in the audience. Jon was the one on stage overseeing a majority of those shows in 2004.

Another underlying problem with the MuzikMafia's development was the stark changes that the community embraced alongside its growing popularity. The schedules of MuzikMafia artists went from sitting around, hanging out, and writing songs with one another in 2001 to a detailed itinerary of radio tours, marketing meetings, meet-and-greets, promotional appearances, tour dates, photo shoots, and call times for shows by 2004, all of which demanded responsibility and punctuality. Many MuzikMafia artists adapted to the new commercial environment, but others still acted as if they were back at the Pub of Love. As late as 2009, Kenny, Jon, and Cory still longed for what MuzikMafia was like in its infancy, as Kenny described to

me: "The Mafia was a joke for us in the beginning. It was just a few guys playing for each other . . . a freaking joke. And then it just got cool. It was cool for
people to get together and not give a shit, that they were getting together
to learn from each other. They wanted to help each other and expand from
each other. . . ." Jon added, "It's a joke that turned into an army"—an overt
reference to the musical "revolution" that later became a central theme in
the MuzikMafia's various advertising slogans in 2004 and 2005.

It is impossible to ignore the fact that money played an integral role in
the MuzikMafia's collapse. However, from 2001 through 2003, most MuzikMafia artists did not rely on the organization for money. According to
Max:

> I think that it started going badly when everybody started depend-
> ing on the Mafia entity for income. That was multiple times over the
> past two years [2006–8]. However, John Rich always made his money
> from John Rich, not MuzikMafia—Kenny, too. They didn't depend on
> Mafia for money, but Nicholson did. He didn't have a platform. Those
> guys were his platform, and that put him in a pretty awkward posi-
> tion. You can't be happy if you are dependent upon someone else for
> your livelihood.

Here Max raises an important point. In just a few short years, the MuzikMafia had gone from being an escape from the music industry—a place
where each Tuesday night friends could step out of their respective commercial images, play whatever they wanted to play, and do whatever they
wanted to do—to becoming a microcosm of the music industry itself driven
by profit, commercial image, and brand development. As MuzikMafia members gradually depended more on the organization for income, the more
destructively entangling the alliances became.

The MuzikMafia members who survived the community's downfall were
the ones for whom the organization played only a minor role in their lives,
financially speaking. John, for example, generated a substantial seven-fig-
ure annual salary beginning in 2004, only a portion of which came directly
from MuzikMafia gigs. Kenny, Gretchen, Troy, and Chance and later James,
Shannon, Shanna, and Damien also had careers that were independent of
MuzikMafia. Each artist began at various times to branch off, pursuing

their own interests and depending on the MuzikMafia for emotional rather than financial support.

Perhaps the grandest mistake was the illusion that millions of fans knew or cared what the MuzikMafia actually was. According to Max, some believed that "Just because there were 200–250 people in town [fans at Tuesday night shows] standing in front of them, that country music in general cared, and it didn't. Nobody gave a shit about MuzikMafia. Not that it wasn't an interesting piece of lore, because it was. [Unfortunately] there's only one top of the pyramid, and John was that top."

The 950 fans I surveyed at the CMA Music Fest in 2005 and 2006 confirmed Max's hypothesis. Most people identified themselves as either "Gretchen fans" or "Big & Rich fans." Very few people knew the names of the founding godfathers, their reason for creating the MuzikMafia, or what the organization was all about. When CMT declared in December 2004 that MuzikMafia had been the "Number One hit of the year," MuzikMafia artists believed, perhaps mistakenly so, that fans and the media knew what they were talking about. In actuality, the spotlight was focused on Big & Rich and Gretchen Wilson.

Aside from money issues a basic lack of communication fueled resentment among MuzikMafia members. Kenny realized this from the beginning:

> The biggest thing here that kept us [MuzikMafia] from being as great as it could be is the great demon of communication. People just need to get over it, clear the air, and get on. . . . I've learned it in the Caribbean [specifically, the Dominican Republic], where they always every afternoon when they finished up what they were doing for the day, they'd get together and have a beer. The next thing you know, one [guy] is blowing up at the other one for what he didn't do at work, and after fifteen minutes they're all laughing and drinking another beer. They clear it out and get over it.

Jon agreed; as he told me in 2009, "You can't hold on to that shit between your friends; it's just useless. And that's why we say that, if John would just sit down with us, we would be able to work it out. If he would agree to hang out, all the shit would work itself out."

The lack of communication among the four godfathers resulted in terrible surprises such as the Muscle Shoals gig in 2008, Jon's estrangement from Warner Bros., and the failed DVD project between John and Jon. The community's awkward development from 2004 through 2008 contributed to bitter feelings, considerable resentment, growing suspicions of others' success, and a common sentiment of "Where's my piece of the pie?" among many MuzikMafia members. The influx of negativity from within the MuzikMafia, along with industry demands for more music, soon became too much. By January 2009 the MuzikMafia was dead, with only a small glimmer of hope among its members for the future: the Mafia Nation.

From summer 2004 through spring 2009, I documented on a daily basis the MuzikMafia's birth, growth, and development in a scholarly attempt to explain the community within its Nashville commercial context; each member's historical and musical identity; and their social connections to each other as an artistic collective. I was moved by the MuzikMafia's music, its stylistic diversity, the strength of the members' songwriting abilities, and the high degree of talent that appeared on the MuzikMafia stage each week. I observed the highs and lows that affected so many of my MuzikMafia friends as if they were pawns, albeit ones with significant free will, within the chess game of the commercial music industry. As the "officiator, mediator, and communicator of the MuzikMafia"—a title Cory, Kenny, and Jon casually bestowed on me over a beer in January 2009—I would like to offer my own advice to the MuzikMafia, if there exists any genuine interest among the four godfathers to return the MuzikMafia to its original state.

First, the godfathers need to communicate with one another. I suggest a godfather meeting with John to take place on neutral ground in which they sit down and work through the problems that they have had in recent years with one another. A song, co-written by all four godfathers, that explains the good times and the bad would be a good next step—after all, it was music that brought them together but it was the music *business* that tore them apart. The godfathers should then arrange a free, Tuesday night show in Nashville—preferably at the Mercy Lounge, because of its creaky wooden interior, layout, and state-of-the-art sound equipment, and the fond memories from there in 2004. There should be no cover charge, no formal advertisement other than word of mouth or email, no set roster of performing artists, no schedule for the evening, no money for artists' appearances, no previous arrangements with the media, no guest list, no tour buses in the parking lot, and most importantly, no egos—just a group of artists wanting to get together to play great music, drink a few beers, and hang out with friends. After all, that is what MuzikMafia was in the beginning; that is what it was supposed to be all along.

BIBLIOGRAPHY

"Hideout." *Centerstage: Chicago: The Original City Guide*. [http://centerstage.net/music/clubs/hideout.html] accessed 24 February 2006.

"Lonestar: From There to Here, Greatest Hits – Bio." From *About Country Music.com* [http://countrymusic.about.com/library/bllonestar-bio.htm] accessed 5 April 2005.

ASCAP. 17 October 2005. "2005 Awards Show Celebrates ASCAP at the Ryman." Press Release. [http://www.ascap.com/press/2005/101705_ascapcma.html] accessed 28 May 2007.

Bangs, Wally. 31 January 2005. "Nashville Rock, Post 1978: Part I" [http://wallybangs.blogspot.com/2005_01_01_wallybangs_archive.html] accessed 17 May 2006.

Bostick, Alan. 2003. "Circus Maximus Throws Creativity into the Ring." In *The Tennessean* newspaper, Friday 21 November 2003, tennessean.com/entertainment/arts/archives/03/11/42800407.shtml] Accessed 6 February 2005.

Broome, Paul J., and Clay Tucker. 1990. *The Other Music City: The Dance Bands and Jazz Musicians of Nashville, 1920–1970*. Nashville: self-published.

Country Music Association. 5 January 2005. "Country Music Has a Strong Year in 2004 with Double Digit Sales Increase over 2003." Press Release. CMA website cmaworld.com/news_publications/pr_common/press_detail.asp?re=393&year=2005] accessed 11 March 2006.

———. 9 January 2006. "Country Music Wraps Up 2005 on a Strong Note." Press Release. [http://www.cmaworld.com/news_publications/pr_common/press_detail.asp?re=498&year=2006], accessed 28 March 2006.

Eck, Tara. 3 January 1998. "Exit/In Looks to Past Glory in Hopes It'll Fuel Future Growth," *Nashville Business Journal*. [http://www.bizjournals.com/nashville/stories/1998/01/26/story4.html] accessed 17 May 2006.

Ellison, Curtis. 1995. *Country Music Culture: From Hard Times to Heaven*. Jackson: University Press of Mississippi.

Getahn, Ward. 2006. "Projects Begin to Sketch Future for 'SoBro' District: Convention Center Tints Images of Neighborhood's Possibilities." In *The Tennessean*, "Business Section," Sunday 2 April, [http://www.tennessean.com/apps/pbcs.dll/article?AID=/20060402/BUSINESS01/604020378] accessed 22 April 2006.

Gilbert, Calvin. Thursday 27 May 2004. "Muzik Mafia Make Vegas an Offer It Couldn't Refuse." CMT official website, [http://posting.cmt.com/artists/news/1487969/05272004/otto_j ames.jhtml], accessed 10 March 2006.

Guier, Cindy Stooksbury. 2005 [1998]. *Insider's Guide to Nashville*, 5th ed. Guilford, CT: Globe Pequot Press.

Inskeep, Scott. 20 October 2005. "Gretchen Wilson: All Jacked Up." *Stylus*. stylusmagazine.com/review.php?ID=3477, accessed 27 March 2006.

Jensen, Joli. 1998. *The Nashville Sound: Authenticity, Commercialization, and Country Music*. Nashville: The Country Music Foundation Press and Vanderbilt University Press.

Jones, Jerry. 9 February 2001. "Teen's Song Sparks Music Row Interest." *The Reporter* (Vanderbilt University Medical Center).

"Katie Darnell." in *Wynonna: 20 Year Tapestry*. wynonna.com/katiedarnell.htm, accessed 9 April 2005.

Keel, Beverly. 2005. "Faith Hill: Soul Set Free." *Country Music Today* (Fall): 36.

Loy, Robert. 2004. "Kenny and John Make It Big, Strike It Rich." *Country Standard Time* (September). countrystandardtime.com/bigandrichFEATURE.html, accessed 5 April 2005.

Malone, Bill C. 2002 [1985]. *Country Music, U.S.A.*, 2nd rev. ed. Austin: University of Texas Press.

Mainsfield, Brian. 14 February 2001. "Musician Rescues Cancer Patient's Song." *USA Today*.

McCall, Michael. Online biography for Shannon Lawson. William Morris Agency website. wma.com/shannon_lawson/bio/Shannon_Lawson.pdf, accessed 14 February 2005.

Mercy Lounge. "History." mercylounge.com/history, accessed 28 July 2005.

Morris, Edward. 2005. "Faith Hill, John Rich Showered with Honors: ASCAP Party Raises the Roof for 'Mississippi Girl.'" cmt.com. cmt.com/artists/news/1510892/10042005/hill_faith.jhtml, accessed 28 March 2006.

Murray, Noel. 8 November 1999. "Hollywood Bound: Two Nashville-based Acts Emerge with Albums on Disney Imprint." *Nashville Scene*.

Naujeck, Jeanne Anne. 5 September 2004. "Executive Q&A: Paul Worley, Chief Creative Officer for Warner Bros. Nashville, Talks about Signing Big & Rich and What's Ahead for the Label." *The Tennessean*. vh10317.moc.gbahn.net/business/qanda/archives/05/03/56952072 .shtml?Element_ID=56952072, accessed 25 March 2006.

Night Train to Nashville: Music City Rhythm & Blues, 1945–1970. 2004. Nashville: Country Music Foundation Press.

Peterson, Richard A. 1976. "The Production of Culture: A Prolegomenon." *The Production of Culture*, Richard A. Peterson, ed. Beverly Hills, CA: Sage Publications.

———.1995. "The Dialectic of Hard-Core and Soft-Shell Country Music." *South Atlantic Quarterly* 94 (Winter): 273–300.

———. 1997. *Creating Country Music: Fabricating Authenticity*. Chicago: University of Chicago Press.

Princeton Songwriters. 2001. "Interview with BNA Recording Artist John Rich." *New Jersey Country Music Scene*, Jackie Hinczynski, ed. April issue. babswinn.com/Archives/Old/Articles/JohnRich4–01.htm, accessed 6 April 2005.

Raines, Patrick, and LaTanya Brown. 2006. "The Economic Impact of the Music Industry in the Nashville-Davidson-Murfreesboro MSA." Study prepared for Belmont University and the Nashville Chamber of Commerce. nashvillechamber.com/president/musicindustryimpactstudy.pdf, accessed 21 April 2006.

Sanneh, Kelefa. 8 November 2004. "Mixing Rednecks and Blue States." *New York Times* l website. nytimes.com/2004/11/08/arts/music/08coun.html?ex=1142312400&en=6f3335813f5942c1&ei=5070, accessed 12 March 2006.

Schmitt, Brad, and Peter Cooper. 16 November 2005. "Country Goes Urban." *The Tennessean*. tennessean.com/apps/pbcs.dll/article?AID=/20051116/ENTERTAINMENT0105/511160427, accessed 26 March 2006.

Trieschmann, Werner. 9 August 2005. "Big & Rich Outrides Brooks & Dunn." *Arkansas Democrat Gazette*. Northwest Arkansas edition. nwarktimes.com/story.php?paper=adg&section=Style&storyid=124493, accessed 24 March 2006.

Underwood, Ryan. 11 January 2006. "Study Defines Music's Economic Strength: Industry's Impact on City Comes to Tune of $6.38 Billion." *The Tennessean*. tennessean.com/apps/pbcs.dll/article?AID=/20060111/BUSINESS01/601110394, accessed 21 April 2006.

Wilkins, Jason Moon. 30 November 2005. "A Year in the Life of Nashville's Music Scene: The Sounds of the Season Past." *Nashville Rage*. nashvillerage.com/apps/pbcs.dll/article?AID=/20051103/RAGE02/511030334/1199/RAGE, accessed 15 May 2006.

VIDEOGRAPHY

"Jon Nicholson Electronic Press Kit (EPK)." 2005. Produced by Live Animals Productions. MuzikMafia website. muzikmafia.com/?action=artist&artist_id=12&PHPSESSID=62b8od 5f5555bba320a3e7012d5a9ba5, accessed 10 January 2005.

20 Biggest Hits of 2004. 2004. CMT. Produced by Terry Bumgarner. Directed by Bill Bradshaw. Narrated by Devon O'Day. First broadcast on 18 December 2004.

38th Annual Country Music Association Awards. 2004. CBS. Produced by Walter Miller. Directed by Paul Miller. First broadcast on 9 November 2004.

39th Annual Academy of Country Music Awards. 26 May 2004. CBS. Executive producer Dick Clark and R. A. Clark. Produced by Barry Adelman. Directed by Jeff Margolis.

47th Annual Grammy Awards. 13 February 2005. CBS. Directed by Walter Miller.

CMT Outlaws. 29 October 2004. CMT. Produced by Audrey Morrissey. Directed by Ivan Dudynsky.

Gun Shy. 1999. Written and directed by Eric Blakeney. Produced by Sandra Bullock, Hollywood Pictures.

MuzikMafia TV. 2005. CMT. Executive producer Audrey Morrissey. Produced by Ivan Dudynsky, Gary Chapman, and Marc Oswald. Directed by Ivan Dudynsky. Six episodes that premiered in January/February 2005.

The Godfather. 1972. Directed by Francis Ford Coppola. Paramount Pictures.

The Last Castle. 2001. Directed by Rod Lurie. Written by David Scarpa and Graham Yost. DreamWorks Pictures.

DISCOGRAPHY

Anderson, John. 2007. *Easy Money*. Produced by John Rich. Warner Bros/WEA 44438.

Big & Rich. 2004. *Horse of a Different Color*. Produced by John Rich and Paul Worley. Warner Bros. 48520–02.

———. 2004. *Big & Rich's Supergalactic Fan Pak*. Produced by Big Kenny, John Rich, and Paul Worley. Warner Bros. 48904–2(also on DVD).

———. 2005. *Comin' to Your City*. Produced by Big Kenny, John Rich, and Paul Worley. Warner Bros. 49470–2.

———. 2007. *Between Raising Hell and Amazing Grace*. Produced by Big Kenny and John Rich. Warner Bros. 43255–2.

Big Kenny. 2005 [1999]. *Live a Little*. Produced by Big Kenny and Gary Burnette. Hollywood Records 2061–62236–2.

Brown, Shannon. 2006. *Corn Fed*. Produced by John Rich. Warner Bros. 49323–6.

Cowboy Troy. 2001. *Hick-Hop Hysteria*. Produced by Cowboy Troy and Joe Beebe. Bull Rush Recordings (no catalog number).

———. 2002. *Beginner's Luck*. Produced by Cowboy Troy. Bull Rush Recordings (no catalog number).

———. 2005. *Loco Motive*. Produced by John Rich, Big Kenny, and Paul Worley. Warner Bros./Raybaw 49316–2.

Hall, Dean. 1994. *Shed My Skin*. Produced by Dean Hall. Dean Hall Music (no catalog number).

———. 1997. *The Ghost of James Bell*. Produced and arranged by Dean Hall. Python DH73197.

Hill, Faith. 2005. *Fireflies*. Produced by Byron Gallimore and Faith Hill. Warner Bros. 48794–2.

Lawson, Shannon. 2002. *Chase the Sun*. Produced by Mark Wright. MCA 088 170 233–2.

———. 2004. *The Acoustic Livingroom Session*. Produced by Shannon Lawson and Dan Friszell. Galoot Music (no catalog number).

McBride, Martina. 2003. *Martina*. Produced by Paul Worley. RCA 82876 54397 2.

Nicholson, Jon. 2005. *A Lil' Sump'm Sump'm*. Produced by Angelo and Jon Nicholson. Warner Bros. 48969–2.

Otto, James. 2004. *Days of Our Lives*. Produced by Mark Wright and Greg Droman. Mercury B0002110–02.

———. 2008. *Sunset Man*. Produced by John Rich, James Otto, and Jay DeMarcus. Warner Bros./Raybaw 49907–2.

Rich, John. 2006 [2000]. *Underneath the Same Moon*. Produced by John Rich and Sharon Vaughn. BNA/Legacy 07683 67917 2.

Stroller. 2003. *Six Inches Off the Ground*. Produced by Jon Nicholson. Compadre Records (no catalog number).

The Last Castle. 2001. Soundtrack produced by Jerry Goldsmith. Decca Records 440 016 193–2.

Wilson, Gretchen. 2004. *Here for the Party*. Produced by Mark Wright and Joe Scaife. Associate producer John Rich. Sony/Epic EK 90903.

———. 2005. *All Jacked Up*. Produced by Gretchen Wilson, John Rich, and Mark Wright. Sony/Epic EK 94169.

———. 2007. *One of the Boys*. Produced by Gretchen Wilson, John Rich, and Mark Wright. Sony/BMG 82876–89201–2.

Wynonna. 2003. *What the World Needs Now Is Love*. Produced by Wynonna and Dann Huff. Asylum/Curb 78811.

INDEX